Betting on Bernie

A Memoir of a Marriage

Martha Marks

Betting on Bernie, A Memoir of A Marriage

Copyright © 2023 by Martha Marks
All rights reserved.
First edition. Printed in the United States of America.

ISBN 978-0-9795193-6-9   paperback
ISBN 978-0-9795193-8-3   large print

The people, places, events, and subjects discussed in this book are or were real. The incidents happened as described. The medical facts, prices, products, and place descriptions are accurate. Included are the true names and images of the protagonists (Bernie and Martha), their close family members, and two of their long-time friends. Others' names are either changed or not mentioned, but nothing of substance has been invented about them or their actions.

No part of this book may be reproduced in any form or by any electrical, mechanical, or AI means, including by storage and retrieval systems, without the prior written permission of the author or her estate. The only exception is for brief quotations in a book review.

Editor: Alice Douthwaite
Cover designer: Vanessa Mendozzi
Layout designer and typesetter: Martha Marks

This book is dedicated with enduring love to
Bernard Louis Marks,
who made my life worth living and our story worth telling.

Bernie on a train in Holland, 1994

ALSO BY MARTHA MARKS

The Ruby-Viper Trilogy

A suspenseful first-century family saga

Rubies of the Viper

The Viper Amulet

The Ruby Ring (in progress)

College Spanish Textbooks

Coauthored as Martha Alford Marks

All are out of print now but available used online.

Destinos (McGraw-Hill)

Al corriente (Random House)

¿Qué tal? (3rd edition, Random House)

RELATED WEBSITES

bettingonbernie.com

bernardmarksfineart.com

marthamarks.com (historical fiction)

marthamarksphotography.com

CONTENTS

Introduction		9
PART I	**Betting on Bernie in Love and Life**	13
Chapter 1	The End and the Beginning	15
Chapter 2	Waffles at the Diner	25
Chapter 3	My First Grown-up Conversation	37
Chapter 4	The Telephone Gossip Game	47
Chapter 5	Ten Tense Days	55
Chapter 6	Three Questions, My Turn	63
Chapter 7	Three Questions, His Turn	75
Chapter 8	Mr. Marks Goes to Linden	87
Chapter 9	His Lawfully Wedded Wife	95
PART II	**Betting on Bernie in Work and Art**	107
Chapter 10	Uprooting and Transplanting	109
Chapter 11	Our Journey Continues	119
Chapter 12	The Proudest Days of Our Lives	131
Chapter 13	A Sharp Bend in the Road	147
Chapter 14	The Golden Goose of Gigs	159
Chapter 15	A Fateful Getaway	167
Chapter 16	The Villa on the Hill	177
Chapter 17	A Full-time Professional Fine Artist	187
Chapter 18	BluCon and the Calm Before the Storm	193
PART III	**Betting on Bernie in Sickness and Death**	203
Chapter 19	Unusual Activity in the Brain	205
Chapter 20	Do You Know Who I Am?	213
Chapter 21	The Most Awful Day and Night	227
Chapter 22	Beating the Odds in the Worst Possible Way	235
Chapter 23	Highest Angel. Praise Jesus. Coffee Pot.	245
Chapter 24	Living the Post-E life	255
Chapter 25	You Married a Lemon.	273
Conclusion		285
Acknowledgments		294
A personal request		295

**And thus does Fortune's wheel turn treacherously
And out of happiness bring men to sorrow.**

—Geoffrey Chaucer

"The Monk's Tale" in *The Canterbury Tales*

INTRODUCTION

Dear Reader,

As I write this, I'm 76 years old, so you won't be surprised to hear that I now realize things that weren't obvious to me when I was young. Wisdom, supposedly, is one of the few benefits of growing old.

And yet most seventy-somethings don't set out to write a book.

So why have I?

I've done it because my life with Bernie Marks was both magic and tragic. We were not predestined to find one another, much less to fall in love. Not guaranteed success in any endeavor we undertook at any point along our path. Not promised prosperity or an upbeat ending to our story.

Bernie and I came from radically different cultural, ethnic, and religious backgrounds. Our ambitions were polar opposites, yet we made our marriage work. Together, we were happy far more often than not.

But life isn't always pretty. Fate is fickle, striking first from one side, then from the other. Fortune is a crapshoot. Luck—both the good kind and the bad—sends you down metaphorical roads on bright, cheery days and dark, stormy nights. In my life, I've traveled all sorts of highways in all kinds of circumstances, so I do know what I'm talking about.

This book is not a how-to instruction manual for getting through the tough times without falling flat on your face. But perhaps, if you're bogged down a bit, it may inspire you to persist, to find your way without giving up, to accept what comes, and to live amicably with another person even as your dreams and ambitions tug you in opposite directions.

My primary goal here is to make this true story of my life with a fun, funny, smart, and talented guy named Bernie enjoyable for you to read, as well as interesting and informative on many levels.

My secondary goal, specific to Part III, is to introduce you to the fluky and devastating malady that befell Bernie later in his life. I'll delve into its impacts on us as individuals and as a couple while alerting you to certain brain conditions that, in my opinion, we all should know a lot more about than we probably do.

Throughout this book, I offer scenes that include dialogues that aim to sound real in a novelistic way. They are essential to telling my story, so I could not have left them out. All the facts and expressions of emotion presented in those dialogues are true, even if the specific words spoken are lost to time.

I've included images of Bernie's family and childhood and also of mine, and of our fun times together, too, because a good set of photos is worth many tens of thousands of words. In addition, I invite you to visit bettingonbernie.com to see in color these same shots and many more, plus anecdotes, backstories, personal newsletters, and other items that didn't make it into this book.

Please feel free to email your comments or questions to me at the address below. I enjoy corresponding with readers and will try always to respond as appropriate.

Martha Marks
martha@bettingonbernie.com

The author in Santa Fe, New Mexico, USA, 2023

PART I

BETTING ON BERNIE IN LOVE AND LIFE

Chapter 1

The End and the Beginning

Tuesday, December 8, 2020

A nurse entered the cool room, injected into Bernie's right arm something to ease this final journey of his life, and turned to me. "We're right outside if you need us," she whispered. She further lowered the already-dim lights and pulled the door shut, leaving a thin white rectangle shining through from the hallway.

My eyes soon adjusted to the dark.

Bernie continued breathing on his own without an oxygen mask. I held his hand, stroked his arm, repeated that I loved him. Over the next hour, his breath gradually slowed until it stopped.

My mind heard his old lilting call, "Is that you?"—pronounced with two syllables, *'S'at-CHOU?*—as if I'd been away and just walked into the house.

My mind answered with the same cheery cadence, "It's me!"— pronounced, *Itz-'SMEEE!*

That call and response was one of the many bonding rituals that we'd built up over fifty-two years and ten months of marriage. But since Bernie no longer possessed the ability either to call or to respond, I had to content myself with the echoes of his voice in my head.

Saturday, April 3, 1965

Just about nine a.m., Christine bounced into my dorm suite, trailing behind her an odd blend of "Puff the Magic Dragon" and Beethoven's Fifth that blared from competing AM and FM stations up and down the hall.

Her cheerful features glowed with the assurance of an accomplished matchmaker. "Martha, got a date tonight?"

It was hard to ignore the excitement in her Dallas twang, but I tried. "Four midterms this week. I'll be in the library till it closes."

"You can't study all weekend. Everyone needs a break, even you."

"I'll take a break next weekend."

"No, listen. John has a new neighbor we think you'd like. We helped him move his stuff into the studio apartment next door to John. Nice guy, just came up from N'awlins two days ago."

Normally, Christine wouldn't pronounce New Orleans like that. But after seven months at Centenary College of Louisiana, we both had fallen into the habit of saying things the local way, if only as an in-joke between us foreigners from Texas.

"The guy left N'awlins for Shreveport?" I asked. "What's wrong with him?"

"Nothin'. Came for a job. Didn't know a soul in town. He joined us for beers last night, and I promised to find him a date for tonight."

"Doubling with you and John?"

"Yep, and you'll be perfect."

"To see a movie? Go bowling?"

"Better." Christine's enthusiasm sparkled. "The head of a local civic group that John just joined this week is hosting a barbecue at his house. Great chance to meet more townies."

"I'm tired of townies. All they know to talk about is their work. I like guys who're interested in the wider world."

Still, Christine kept up her sales pitch. "My aunt's on a trip, and I've got the key to her house. It's ours for two nights if we want it."

Not something Mama and Daddy would approve of.

But then I thought again.

They did give written permission for me to check out overnight if I wanted to. In all these months, I've never done that.

Christine's well-tuned antennae picked up my ambivalence. "If you're not interested, I'll ask someone else, but you'll be missing out on something special."

It's been a tough year. Not a lotta fun.

On my way out the door, I rolled the dice, hurling over my shoulder an impulsive reply that would reroute the carefully planned trajectory of my life. "Sure, I'll go."

Christine was back in my dorm room that evening when the intercom buzzed and the voice of our house mother, Mrs. Lawson, came through with news that two gentlemen had arrived to pick us up.

Shreveport turns pleasantly warm by April, so I'd donned a short-sleeve linen dress

My photo of Centenary College of Louisiana in Shreveport, spring 1965

Betting on Bernie

with scooped neck, bell skirt, and what *Seventeen* magazine styled a self-belt, all in horizontal stripes of red, yellow, orange, and purple. And in case that didn't catch the eye well enough, I had punched it up even more with red flats and a matching clutch. Back then, I was slim enough to carry off such a girly look. Daddy even called me "Skinny Winny."

Christine and I each toted a blue Samsonite Silhouette "Hat Box," a round, hard-sided overnight bag with carry strap that was a popular '60s high-school graduation gift for girls. We stepped through the swinging doors into the lobby, where Christine's boyfriend John stood beside a slightly older-looking man.

Christine kissed John before introducing me to the one I already thought of as "N'awlins Guy." She must have provided our names, but I have no memory of that. Can't even recall if my date said anything to me before we left.

The one thing I do remember was his smile, so big and broad and bright that it almost kept me from noticing his dark, wavy hair and his too-blue-to-be-true eyes.

Almost.

Me with my family's red Ford Galaxie outside our carport in Linden, Texas, spring 1965

The front seat of John's car was a standard cloth bench, so Christine snuggled up to him as '60s girls often did.

Meanwhile, in the back seat, as prim and proper as my Mississippi mama would have wanted, I kept my distance from N'awlins Guy.

My favorable first impression of him vanished when we pulled out of the parking lot. Without warning, the handsome fellow with the toothy smile, wavy locks, and dazzling peepers turned into a smart aleck. A wise guy. A big mouth in more ways than one.

N'awlins Guy leaned forward and began asking John a series of questions so rude that they actually offended me, even though I wasn't the intended offendee.

"Couldn't you pick up a chick in something cooler than this old junker?" He released a deep belly-laugh, as if that were the wittiest wisecrack any late-night comedian ever uttered.

"Wouldn't you at least wanna buy a decent sofa before inviting friends over to your apartment?" More self-induced amusement.

"Shouldn't you shop for furniture somewhere other than the flea market?" Shoulder-shaking mirth.

"Didn't your ma teach you to stop before stop signs, not after 'em?" Chuckle, chuckle, chuckle.

Five minutes into the date, I was disgusted. He was trying too hard to be funny and sounded like a jerk instead.

How obnoxious can a guy get? What he's carping about isn't even true.

John's car was reasonably new and clean. And he hadn't run any stop signs. And after visiting his place several times, Christine hadn't mentioned ratty furniture. And to my knowledge, Shreveport didn't even have a flea market.

It struck me as a terrible way to treat your only friend in town, especially one whose girlfriend had scrounged up a date for you at the last minute.

And I hated the sloppy way he pronounced contractions.

He turned "Couldn't you…?" into *"C'n't you…?"*

And "Wouldn't you…?" into *"W'n't you…?"*

And "Shouldn't you…?" into *"Sh'n't you…?"*

And "Didn't you…?" into *"D'n't you…?"*

I'd never heard anyone talk like that.

We rode along through Shreveport's well-maintained neighborhoods, on rolling streets lined with sidewalks, bluegrass lawns, sturdy sweetgum and delicate redbud trees, pink-flowering azalea bushes, and brick ranch houses, many with bicycles in the driveways and basketball hoops over the carports.

The jerk was so busy tormenting John that he didn't say a word to me until we reached our destination on the outer fringe of a new suburban residential development.

But then, the instant John turned off the engine, N'awlins Guy leaped out. Scooted behind the car. Opened my door. Offered his hand. Helped me out. Flashed his flamboyant smile. Engaged me in light-hearted banter.

Such courtesies hinted at some potential for redemption, but not enough to diminish my need to be on guard. Mama had warned me about men, after all. I wasn't going to succumb to trickery.

I remained wary as we walked around the last house on a cul-de-sac to a wide, fragrant expanse of fresh-mowed grass, metal "tulip" chairs in yellow and green, charcoal grills already fired up and sizzling, wooden picnic tables and benches, a self-serve bar, a projection screen, and a crowd settling in for an enjoyable time.

Bottles of beer popped. Trays of appetizers landed on tables. Folks talked, laughed, drank, and slapped each other's backs. All was well until I realized one thing.

Christine and I were the only females present.

For another hour, as the light waned, the temperature dropped, and the aroma of roasting meats passed the stage of merely smelling good, John and N'awlins Guy, beers in hand, mingled with all the other men. Their exchanges consisted of head-shaking, self-conscious, embarrassed-sounding laughter.

"It's kinda creepy, isn't it?" I said to Christine at some point.

"Yeah, I dunno what's going on."

"Maybe we should leave."

"How?"

"Tell John we want to go."

"But he's having so much fun."

So we stayed, munching appetizers and sipping wine. At eighteen, we were barely legal to drink, but that was good enough.

No more girls showed up by the time the meal was served, so John, N'awlins Guy, and a few others joined us as we ate.

Two hours later, darkness enveloped us as our dates delivered Christine and me and our matching "Hat Boxes" to the unlit front door of her aunt's house. Christine and John promptly stepped inside to say goodnight in private.

As N'awlins Guy and I lingered on the porch, he dropped the off-putting tomfoolery. "I want to apologize for tonight," he said.

All I wanted was for him to disappear, but I answered politely, as Mama had taught me. "What for?"

I barely saw his face, but his voice reflected a degree of disbelief. "Didn't you think there was something odd about the party?"

"Well, yeah, it was strange that Christine and I were the only girls there."

"Have you figured out why?"

"Haven't spent a lotta time thinking about it, to be honest."

"But didn't you wonder?"

"Yes."

"Shall I tell you?"

I was looking for a way to escape into the house when a new sense of awareness emerged in his words.

"Everyone but us four," he said, "and I do mean everybody else, knew it was a stag party." He paused for my reaction, which didn't come, so he kept talking. "John didn't know that until we arrived, and since I'm new in town, just tagging along with him, I certainly didn't know."

"What didn't you know?" I asked.

"That it was meant to be a stag party."

"What's a stag party?"

It seemed to dawn on him that I wasn't playing games. "Our host," he said, "had a stack of eight-millimeter films."

I said nothing.

As before, he gave me time to respond but went on when I didn't. "He was planning to start showing them at sundown."

I was slow to catch on. "Eight-millimeter films?"

"Yes."

"You mean..." I must have hesitated a full minute. "You mean pornography?"

My eyes were adjusted well enough now to see the jerk's head bob. Clearly relieved, he waited for me to say more.

I didn't say more, however, because I had no idea what more to say.

So he went on. "Our host couldn't show porn movies with college freshmen girls in his back yard."

The full import of what he was saying sank in on me, but not the way he likely intended. "You're saying Christine and I spoiled the fun."

"Oh, no. It wouldn't count as spoiling if you didn't know you were doing it."

That attempt at an explanation didn't work for me. "I think your double negative means, 'Yes, you two girls *did* spoil everyone else's fun'."

Abruptly, he changed the subject. "Look, Martha, I like you. I'd appreciate the chance to start over with you. Can we do something together tomorrow?"

"No."

"How 'bout breakfast? Pretend tonight never happened."

He seemed less obnoxious now, but still.

"I've got four midterms next week," I said. "That's a lot to study for, and I hadn't planned to be out tonight."

"I'll pick you up at nine. Take you wherever you like."

I remained reluctant but also grew aware that he might be my best chance to get back to the dorm in time to study.

No telling when I'll hit the books again if I wait for John to show up.

"And you'll have me on campus by ten?"

"How 'bout eleven? We'll need time to talk, not just wolf down some food. You'll be back at the dorm by eleven." With his left hand, he made a squiggly gesture over his chest. "Cross my heart and hope to die."

Out of nowhere, I laughed. "Okay, but with one condition."

His face lit up with a smile so brilliant that it shone through, even on that dark porch. "Shoot," he said.

"You have to tell me your name."

"My name?"

"Yes, and I do mean right now, so I'll know who's picking me up tomorrow."

"You didn't catch it earlier?"

"No."

An amused tone entered his voice. "To all those men at the weird party tonight, I'm Bernard Marks. But you can call me Bernie."

Chapter 2
Waffles at the Diner

Sunday, April 4, 1965

Promptly at nine the next morning, Bernie showed up at Christine's aunt's house in a burgundy-colored Ford Mustang. It was America's latest rock-star car, which until then I'd only seen on TV and in magazines. He helped me in, stashed my bag in the trunk, and slipped behind a curiously open steering wheel. The bulky box that my high-school driving instructor had called a "three-on-the-tree" was missing.

"How about Murrell's?" He cranked the engine. "I hear they serve the best waffles in Shreveport."

"They do. Your car smells new."

"Two weeks old. Do you like the bucket seat?"

"Can't tell yet. First time sitting in one." I pointed to a T-shaped metal rod poking up from a narrow chrome strip on the floor between us. "What's that?"

"Shift for the Cruise-O-Matic three-speed automatic transmission. It's pretty smooth." He moved the stick and eased backwards toward the street. "My last car had buckets, too. Sweet little Austin-Healy convertible."

"Why'd you get rid of it?"

"A month ago, in New Orleans, some drunken moron raced through a red light, smashed into the passenger side of the convertible, and crumpled it around me."

"And you walked away?"

"Yeah. Cuts and bruises but no broken bones. My sister thought I should be mad, but I figured I was alive and the moron had insurance, so why get upset? He ended up with a ticket and a ride to jail to sober up. I ended up with a new car."

We arrived at Murrell's early, so many tables were still available. Bernie accepted a cup of black coffee, but since I hate the taste of coffee, even though I like its smell, I declined. After perusing the menu, we both ordered waffles with maple syrup, thick-sliced bacon, and fresh-squeezed orange juice. And then we settled in to get better acquainted.

"You don't sound southern, Bernie. Where're you from?"

"New York. Ever been there?"

That explains the strange contractions.

I shook my head. "Daddy hates big cities. We drive cross country every year, but he won't even let us stop to eat in one."

"Hard to avoid 'em, isn't it? Big cities do take up a lot of space."

"Yeah, but there's more to it than that. Take August of '55, when we left Newport, Rhode Island. I'd just turned nine, and we'd lived there a year while Daddy attended the Naval War College. So, now we were on our way to visit Mama's family in Mississippi and Daddy's in Louisiana before he reported to his next assignment at Fort Hood, Texas."

"August. And no air-conditioned cars in those days."

"Nope, so Daddy pushed straight through New York City and Philadelphia. He refused to stop anywhere until we reached Virginia."

Bernie laughed. "Where it was cooler?"

"No. Where it was two o'clock in the afternoon."

Bernie frowned in puzzlement but said nothing, so I went on.

"Daddy has what he calls 'a neat trick to beat the heat.' When we're on the road, he wakes Mama and me up at two a.m., hustles us to dress and get in the car, and finally stops for breakfast and gas around dawn. Then he drives as far and fast as possible, smoking the whole way with

Seven Alford brothers and three of their kids in Many, Louisiana, 1950 (Truman, the baby of his generation, stands second from left. I'm in the center.)

the windows down, so our hair's blowing and we get smoke and dust in our eyes. He stops at two p.m. for gas and lunch and looks for a motor-hotel with a bright neon sign flashing 'refrigerated air.' Then we get to rest and sleep until two a.m., when he wakes us up to do it all over again."

"Your dad sounds tough."

"He had to be tough growing up as the youngest of ten kids in a poor, backwoods-Louisiana family. They didn't have anything."

"What's his name?"

"Truman Alford."

"Spelled A-L-L-F-O-R-D?"

"No. It's pronounced that way, but it's spelled A-L-F-O-R-D."

"That's odd."

"No, it's just like *also* and *always*. Or, as Daddy cleverly says, 'There's no *Al* in Alford.'"

Bernie chortled. "I suspect a guy that clever could've found motor-hotels with refrigerated air in New York or Philly."

"Yeah, but he likes the South better. Always in a rush to get home."

As the tables around us filled up, the noise level rose and so did our voices. I prodded Bernie for more information, the way he had with me. "Tell me about your New York City childhood."

"Actually, I'm from Elmira, on the southern edge of New York State, just below the Finger Lakes. We left there for Atlanta before I started high school."

"Kinda odd path, isn't it?" I peered at him over the edge of my juice glass. "Elmira to Atlanta to New Orleans."

"I was in the Army when Mom, Dad, and my siblings left Atlanta to live near our Uncle Irv in New Orleans. He and Dad were very close."

"They *were*? Past tense?"

"Dad died of lung cancer last fall. Really a hard time for us."

I slid my hand across the table and rested it on Bernie's arm. "Tell me about your dad."

"He was a quiet man. A sweet, gentle soul who played the violin."

"Does your Uncle Irv play the violin, too?"

Bernie's Uncle Irv Marks later in life, around 1990

"No, he's a tough guy like your dad." Bernie smiled. "Picture a hard-hitting Jewish boxer who fought all over New York State in his youth but wound up marrying a girl from a Creole Catholic family that used to own a big antebellum plantation on the Mississippi River."

"That's a crazy story," I said, "but I guess my family's crazy, too."

"All families are in some ways." Bernie flipped the discussion back to me. "So now, before the waffles arrive, give me a thirty-second history of your crazy family."

"It'll take me longer than that to think it through."

"So, try anyway."

"Okay. As I've heard it, we started with two troublemaking English brothers named Alford who in the 1690s got themselves deported to a coastal colony called Carolina. Soon after, Ulster Protestants began arriving in America from northern Ireland. Long before the Civil War, those Alfords and 'Ulsters' had spread as far as Mississippi's cotton fields and Louisiana's bayous, marrying each other along the way."

"Sounds pretty WASPy."

"You mean White Anglo-Saxon Protestants? Oh yeah, one hundred percent. I doubt there ever was a Catholic, Jew, Hindu, Buddhist, or Muslim anywhere in my family. But still, lots of strange stories. For example, you may have an Uncle Irv, but I have an Uncle Brother and an Aunt Sister. Wanna try figuring out those relationships?"

Bernie laughed again. "Nooooo."

The waitress brought our waffles and bacon, so we drizzled maple syrup over everything and dug in. For a while, all I focused on was the sweet-and-salty flavors dancing around in my mouth.

At some point, Bernie returned to my question. "You gotta admit, Martha. Calling someone 'Uncle Brother' or 'Aunt Sister' is strange."

"Maybe, but the story behind those names is as sweet as maple syrup. Would you care to hear it?"

"I'd be crazy to." He crossed his eyes and lolled his tongue out of the corner of his mouth.

That loony expression made me laugh, as Bernie clearly intended.

"So," I said when we got serious again, "in 1898, my grandfather, Carter C. Parnell, finished his MD in St. Louis. He went back to Mississippi, married his hometown sweetheart, and set off with her to practice medicine in the remote border town of El Paso, Texas."

My maternal grandparents, Dr. Carter C. Parnell and Martha Sloan Parnell, in Sledge, Mississippi, 1951

"Must've been a rough trip. No air-conditioned cars back then."

"No cars at all, just a buckboard wagon. Later on, in El Paso, they had a son and a daughter before the wife died of cholera. Granddaddy took the kids home, set up a new practice in Sledge, and married his late wife's sister, Martha Sloan. She's the one I was named for." I ate some more, then went on. "My mother Margaret was their first child together. She grew up calling her older siblings 'Brother' and 'Sister.' Eventually, two younger ones, Frances and C.C., called them that, too."

"Is that a Deep South thing?"

"I guess. My grandparents would say things like, 'Margaret, go with Brother' or 'Sister, take care of Frances.' Later on, after Mama and Frances gave birth to me and my cousins, we naturally called the older ones in their generation Uncle Brother and Aunt Sister."

"Now I get it. Not as strange as it sounds."

"No. And by the way, my southern-girl double name is Martha Frances. And, Bernie, there are lots more kooky stories on that side of the family. Don't get me started on my nutty Uncle C.C. And also, you should know that Uncle Brother lives in Shreveport, so you might run into him someday."

"Would he introduce himself to me as 'Uncle Brother'?"

"Not unless I was with you." I smiled at him. "Tell me about New Orleans. Did you like it there?"

"Loved everything about it. The French Quarter. Mardi Gras. Cajun food. Jazz clubs. Water-skiing with friends on Lake Pontchartrain."

"Must've been hard to leave."

"It was, but... Shreveport called."

"Ah yes, the famous siren song of Shreveport."

"That's cute, but there must be something to it, because, starting tomorrow, I'm advertising manager at Hemenway Furniture."

"Oh, Hemenway's is a wonderful store. My desk at home came from there, and our mattresses, too." I kept eating and tried to think up interesting things to say. "It's hard to believe you left everyone you knew in a city you loved to take a job in a place where you didn't know anybody."

"Yeah, but now, three days later, I know John and Christine, and those guys from the stag party, and a young lady named Martha Frances."

A warm flush crept up from my neck to my cheeks, but if Bernie noted it, he didn't show it.

"I gotta say, Martha Frances, despite that southern-style double name, you don't sound southern either. Where'd you grow up?"

I pulled out my standard answer. "Everywhere and nowhere."

Bernie furrowed his brow but said nothing.

"Army brat," I added to help him along.

Bernie's brow relaxed. "I should've realized that when you said your dad's next assignment was at Fort Hood, Texas. So, Miss Army Brat, tell me everywhere you've lived."

"Sure you wanna know?" I sipped some juice.

"I asked, didn't I?"

"Not everyone who asks truly wants to know."

"Well, I do."

"Okay." I took a deep breath and let it out. "Mississippi—but only because I was born there—then Iowa, Georgia, Vermont, and Mississippi again while Daddy was in Germany for something called 'hardship duty.' Then all of us together in Germany and on to Rhode Island, Texas, the D.C. suburbs of northern Virginia, and back to Texas again. All before I entered high school. And now, I'm in Louisiana for college."

"That's amazing. Any siblings to move around with you?"

Fun in the snow with my Mississippi Mama in Northfield, Vermont, 1948

A downtown parade for Miss Linden contestants, Linden, Texas, 1964

"Nope. Just my folks."

"Where's home now?"

"Linden, Texas. Nice little town an hour west of here. About sixteen hundred people with an 1850s courthouse and square. Piggly Wiggly. Ben Franklin. Western Auto. An ice house that makes wonderful ice cream. Plus Benny's Dress Shop, where I buy most of my clothes."

"How'd you wind up there?"

"Daddy retired at the Pentagon in December of '59 after twenty-five years in the Army. He wanted to get back to Louisiana but took a job with the Texas Forest Service on the condition that they'd assign him to the far-eastern edge of the state, close to Barksdale and his family in Many. That turned out to be Linden."

The noise level at Murrell's kept increasing as the after-church crowd showed up. Couples called and waved to each other across the big room. Kids ran around yelling. Bernie and I had to raise our voices even more to hear one another.

"What's Barksdale?" Bernie half-shouted.

"That's the Air Force Base in Bossier City, just across the Red River. Daddy, Mama, and I are able to use its hospital, commissary, and PX."

Bernie nodded to indicate he understood. "Another advantage to Linden—and I'm just guessing here—is that it's close to Centenary."

"Yep. Ever since I was a little girl, Daddy always said I should go to Centenary."

"Did you have any other options?"

"Yeah, I did. My grades in high school earned me automatic admission to any state school in Texas, but I wanted to go to a liberal-arts college and had no desire to stay in Texas. Mama thought it would be nice if I attended one of the well-known girls' colleges in Virginia, but they cost lots more. And they're too far away. And my folks drive to Barksdale twice a month. And Centenary's pre-med program is highly regarded. And Uncle Brother lives in Shreveport. And—"

For the first time in our budding relationship, Bernie cut me off. "You're pre-med?" he asked.

"I have been all this year, but I'm about to change majors."

"Being a doctor is a fine ambition."

"Sure, except it was Daddy's ambition for me, not my own. Since he doesn't have a son, I've received all the aspirations that he would've piled onto a son. And he would've loved bragging that he raised 'a lady doctor,' as he calls it."

"At least he encouraged you to aim high. My father never did that."

"Well, Mama and Daddy are both college grads, so…" I shrugged.

"That's an unusual situation in itself."

"I know. Each of them, on their own, had the drive to graduate from college during the Depression. Daddy landed a four-year ROTC scholarship at LSU and later served six years as an officer in the brand-new Civilian Conservation Corps. Then, when the war broke out, he got full credit for those years and entered the regular Army as an officer."

"And your mother?" Bernie asked.

"She studied one year at Grenada College, which was an expensive private girls' school seventy miles from Sledge. It was her longtime dream to go there, but her family couldn't afford it, so after her freshman year she had to transfer to nearby Delta State Teachers College."

"A medical doctor couldn't afford the higher tuition?"

I shook my head. "Not in the Mississippi Delta in those days. Granddaddy's patients mostly paid him in things they raised, grew, or made themselves. Chickens, vegetables, baked goods, hand-knitted socks or sweaters. Stuff like that. Mama says they ate well and stayed warm but hardly ever had cash. Anyway, growing up, I knew I'd go to college, just as my parents had. The only questions were, 'What college will Martha Frances go to?' and 'What will she study?'"

Bernie looked surprised. "That seems mighty progressive for a southern family."

"Probably because we've lived all over. We're not a typical southern family. I'm lucky my folks are willing and able to pay my way through Centenary. They'd do the same for med school, too, if I ever got there. But Daddy insisted I load up freshman year with math and science courses. 'Show 'em how smart you are,' he said. 'Get a leg up for med school.'"

"That doesn't sound like a bad strategy."

"It's not, except I got stuck in calculus, and it did me in. Nothing in Linden ever prepared me for that level of math. There were kids in that class at Centenary who'd already taken pre-calc in the big high schools in Dallas, New Orleans, and Shreveport. They were so far ahead of me that it felt like any one of 'em could've taught the course. But to me, it was gibberish. When I went home for Christmas, I warned my folks that I was gonna flunk calculus."

"And did you?"

"Yep."

Bernie winced. "How were your other grades?"

"All As and Bs, but that Day-Glo orange F on my transcript squashed all chance of med school."

"Why do you say that?"

"Because each med school reserves two spots for girls per class. Just two, and no more get in. With so many smart girls competing for so few spots, there's no way I'd make that cut with an F in calculus."

"You don't strike me as a quitter, Martha."

"I'm not, but what if I keep majoring in biology and don't get into med school? Do I want to spend the rest of my life teaching high schoolers to dissect frogs? Definitely not. I like frogs too much for that. Better to major in something I'm good at and would enjoy teaching."

"Such as?"

"Anything dealing with words." I glanced at my watch but finished answering his question. "History. Journalism. Foreign languages. Creative writing. See, Bernie, I just really and truly love words, even the names of the bones of the hands and feet, which I have to get back to memorizing soon." With that, I pivoted to a new subject. "Speaking of bones in the hands, I see you're a southpaw."

"Most creative geniuses are southpaws."

"I didn't know that. Are you a creative genius?"

"I am, and I fully expect to be recognized as such one day."

"Care to give a demonstration?"

Bernie nodded and asked the waitress for a pencil and a fresh paper napkin. For a few moments, he inspected my face and head. Five minutes later, he handed over a remarkably good portrait.

"That's amazing," I said. "May I keep it?"

"Forever and a day."

Chapter 3

My First Grown-up Conversation

Sunday, April 4, 1965 *(continued)*

As promised, Bernie got me back to campus by eleven, but then we sat in the driveway with both doors of his Mustang open and just kept talking.

After a while, he shifted his position to lean against the door frame, facing me. "So, what was it like moving from the D.C. area to Linden?"

"Massive culture shock. I lived there—and went to school there—for four and a half years but never felt like I belonged there."

"I thought military kids were used to change."

"We are, but since the schools we attend are either on or near bases, they're usually loaded with kids just like us. Gunston Junior High in Arlington is full of diplomats' children, Army and Navy brats, and others whose civilian parents work at the Pentagon. It's a great school, but I only had three semesters there before we moved to Linden."

"Nothing like that in east Texas, I'm sure. Were your new classmates friendly?"

"Yes, they were, but… I couldn't believe that some eighth graders hadn't even been to Texarkana, much less Dallas. They'd ask, 'Where're ya'll from?' But then, when I told 'em, they'd clam up. That felt strange to me, because whenever we military brats meet somewhere, the first thing out of our mouths is, 'Where've you lived?' And since we've all lived all over—and traveled even farther—our experiences often overlap, so we have plenty of things to talk about. That wasn't true in Linden."

As Bernie and I sat there, groups of students passed by, laughing and chatting among themselves. A few saw me in the car and waved.

At some point, I spotted a familiar bird in a nearby magnolia and pointed to it. "Oh look, there's a Rusty Blackbird!"

Bernie acted like he'd never seen a blackbird before. "How'd you even notice that drab little thing, much less know what it was?"

"Daddy has taught me how to look for birds and then identify them. He owns a pair of Nazi submarine binoculars that he brought back from the war. They're too heavy for me to hold, so he always carries 'em and supports 'em for me while I look. This time of year, we find Rusty Blackbirds all over the wet woods around Many."

My father, Major Truman Alford, at age 34, still in Germany at the end of World War II, 1945, the year before I was born

"And you enjoy that?"

"Sure. It's something he and I can do without getting all tangled up emotionally."

Martha Marks

Bernie eyed me with curiosity. "I never thought of emotions as something to get tangled up in."

"You have to understand Daddy. He's a country boy—a '*Loosiana* boy,' as he likes to say—and a pretty good amateur naturalist. Wherever we happen to go, especially on long trips, he gets me out of the car and takes me hiking. Thanks to him, I've learned to identify different kinds of trees and birds, tracks and scat, frogs and toads. It's a fun thing we do together, just as long as I don't tell him how I feel about something."

"What do you mean?"

I shrugged. "Emotions drive him nuts. He can't deal with 'em. Jumps down my throat. Makes me shut up. Even now, I can rattle on and on about things I've read or seen or done, but I choke up when it comes to expressing my feelings."

"He sounds like a man trying to turn his daughter into the son he never had."

"Maybe. He also can't stand it if I express an opinion he disagrees with. I learned early on to keep my thoughts and feelings to myself."

"Can you talk to your mom?"

"Yeah, but she's judgmental, too. Like the time in high school when I told her I'd had my first kiss on a date. It was her tone more than her words. 'Why, Martha Frances.' She sounded so sad, like I'd disappointed her by letting myself get kissed. Become what she calls 'a hussy.' After that, I never asked or told her anything. My grandmother was a prim Victorian lady, so I doubt they ever discussed sex either."

"You and your mom never talk about sex?"

"No. She says, 'Don't get pregnant. It'll ruin your life.' But she never explains how I actually might get pregnant."

"Just kept you clueless?"

"Yep, and so far it's worked."

"How so?"

"In high school, I was so scared of getting pregnant that I repelled every teenage boy in Linden. You see, if a girl there gets pregnant, the authorities kick her out of school. Fortunately, I made it through, but not everyone was so lucky. And the really bad thing was, I reached college age without the slightest idea as to how one gets pregnant."

My mother, Margaret Parnell, as a glamorous freshman at Grenada College, 1932-1933

"But you do know that now, don't you?"

"I think I've figured it out."

"You *think*?"

I nodded, then lowered my voice. "Can I tell you something I never told Mama?"

"Of course."

"Last fall, two weeks after I got here, a fellow freshman invited me out to dinner and a movie. It was my first college date, and I was so excited about it. But after the movie, instead of driving straight back here to the dorm, he pulled into a dark parking lot in town. He pinned me against the seat, forced his tongue into my mouth, and kept poking it deeper and moving it around in there. It was disgusting. Nobody had ever kissed me that way before. I actually tried to vomit to get his tongue out, but that didn't work. All I could do was pound and push against his chest until he stopped. Never felt so helpless in my life."

My eyes were wet when I stopped talking.

"You sure that's all he did?" Bernie asked. "Nothing more?"

I nodded. "He finally drove me back, and we never dated again. But here's the thing, Bernie. I spent the whole next week scared to death that I was pregnant, because I was sure he'd raped me. All I knew was that sex involved a penetration of some sort, which he definitely had done to me."

"How'd you learn otherwise?"

"Confided in another freshman girl who said there was no way I'd get pregnant from a kiss. Not even a 'French kiss,' as she called it. And then she explained what one actually does have to do to get pregnant."

"Did she tell you everything?"

"I guess so. More than Mama ever did anyway."

Bernie shook his head a couple of times, then he steered me off to what he probably hoped would be a cheerier topic. "I'm sure your dad gave you lots of other fine qualities, too, besides his belief in the value of an education and his love of nature. Am I right?"

"Punctuality, if that counts. When I was ten, he bought me a wristwatch and made me start paying attention to time." With that unintended self-reminder, I looked at my watch again.

Really gotta hit the books soon.

But this conversation was just too good to cut short, so I kept talking. "That same year, Daddy also taught me to touch type, and from then on he made me put 'written and typed by Martha Frances Alford' at the bottom of every school paper I turned in." I grinned as another fine quality popped into my head. "Then there's the amazing 'Alford stomach.' Over four summers of riding the back roads in Mexico and Guatemala and eating in strange places, not even the spiciest foods ever upset us."

Bernie laughed at that. "Nobody in my family has an Alford stomach. If Mom looks crosswise at food, it 'bothers' her. So, what good things did your mom give you?"

"Her love of books and music. Every week, we went together to the library and to piano and violin lessons. She was a leader in my Brownie and Girl Scout troops, too, and also my Spanish teacher in high school."

"Sounds like she's done well at everything but sex education." Bernie looked straight at me. "Do she and your dad get along okay?"

"No, actually, they don't. He's as hard on her as he is on me. All she has to do is say something he doesn't like and he explodes. Gets loud and threatening. He once swore to her face that he'd take me off somewhere where she'd never see me again. At the time, I thought he was bluffing, but I later learned he had a legal right to do that. It scared me, too."

"What do you do when those arguments start?"

"Go to my room. Close the door. Read till it blows over. And, Bernie, there's something else I've never told anyone. Even as a little kid, I knew my folks loved me, but I never was sure they loved each other."

My parents, Truman and Margaret Alford, early in their marriage, 1939

Bernie made no reply, so I kept on. "They got married during the Great Depression and couldn't afford a baby. When he left for the war, she went back to Sledge and taught school. When he returned, she was thirty-one and ready for a baby. But then something happened. My aunt once told me that they got along fine before the war, but after I was born they never seemed to be the same. As if something bad had come between them. Since then, I've often wondered—"

As I choked up and stopped, Bernie reached over from his side of the car, took my left hand, and silently squeezed it.

"I've often wondered," I struggled on after a while, "if I was the 'something bad' that came between them after he returned from the war."

Bernie kept holding my hand, but for a while he said nothing, so I went on. "Actually, I'm pretty sure that I am the reason why they aren't happy together. Why else would she say that getting pregnant would ruin my life, unless getting pregnant with me was what ruined hers?"

As before, Bernie guided me to less-stressful topics. "I'm glad to know you enjoy reading," he said, "because I do, too."

I brightened up at that. "How about creative writing? That's really my favorite thing to do, even if nobody reads my stories but my folks."

"I'm more interested in the visual arts. Mostly, I sketch."

I slipped his napkin portrait of me out of my purse. "Like this?"

"I prefer a quality sketch pad and pen. And as much as I do welcome any opportunity to draw lovely young ladies in diners…" He paused and grinned. "I'm best at catching figures in action. People walking down the street, or playing with their kids and dogs, or riding horses and bicycles."

"Do you paint, too?"

"Not yet, but I will someday." Another pause. "You know, Martha, I took two psychology courses at Tulane. I realize you haven't studied psych yet, but you should, if only to know yourself better. There's something called 'emotional equilibrium.' It's how we cope with life's upheavals while keeping ourselves in balance. With a new home and school every year, plus a father who'd hoped for a boy and threatened to take you away from your mother, it must've been hard to maintain your emotional equilibrium."

"Most military brats seem to handle stuff like that well enough."

"Having siblings along for the ride would help though. My brother Murray and I leaned on each other a lot when we left Elmira for Atlanta. But you went through many more moves—and a whole lot more personal trauma than we did—and you did it all alone."

"Fortunately, I'm good at being alone. Never needed other kids around to entertain me. Never even had a real best friend. Each fall in a new school, I'd find another newcomer who didn't know anybody either, and we'd be pals. Next year, next school, I'd find someone else."

"Would you visit each others' families? Have sleepovers?"

"Only if our fathers held the same rank. It was too awkward otherwise."

"Have you kept up with any of them?"

"No. I hardly remember their last names."

Bernie looked straight into my eyes. "Most people would say that's a strange way to grow up."

I laughed. "Most people would be right. But except for my four years in Linden, that's all I've ever known. Feels normal to me." I decided to share another secret with Bernie before going in to study. "Would you believe me if I told you my first week in Linden was frightening?"

"Frightening?" He looked and sounded puzzled. "How?"

"On my very first day in school there, a boy said something that one of the teachers didn't like. She yanked him up, and bent him over her desk, and whacked him hard on the butt with a wooden paddle. Over and over and over. The second day she did the same to a girl, only she hit her on the backs of her legs, not her rear end."

"I never saw that in Elmira or Atlanta. Must be a Texas thing."

"It felt like I'd gone backwards in time from 1960 to 1860."

"Sounds like you could have used some counseling. Was anyone around to help you make that big adjustment?"

"No. I didn't even tell Mama how scared I was. But then, on the third day, that same teacher was reading a paragraph aloud when she came to the word 'peculiar.' She stopped, looked out over her glasses, and asked, 'Does anyone know what peculiar means?' Everyone sat on their hands."

"But you knew." Bernie's eyes twinkled. "And the reason why you knew was that for years you'd been reading a lot and learning new words and using them in all those short stories you wrote." He paused. "So, what happened on that third day?"

"Well, right at that moment—having seen her in action—I was afraid to say anything. But then I decided to be brave. Take a chance. Raise my hand. And when she called on me, I said, 'Peculiar means odd or queer.' Which I knew was absolutely correct."

"I hope she was impressed with the smart new kid in her class."

"Oh, no. She puffed up and blasted me in the harshest tone I'd ever heard from a teacher. '*Maaaaaarrrrrrtha. We* don't use words like *that* around *here.*' Then she dropped her eyes and went back to reading aloud."

"That was it?" Bernie asked.

"Hey, I was just thankful she didn't paddle me."

"Did you know which word she objected to?"

"Not then, no. I later learned it was 'queer.' But to me that was just a perfectly good synonym for odd and peculiar."

"It is, except nowadays some people use it in another context. I imagine she could have taken that opportunity to point out how words evolve over time, gaining new meanings in different contexts and cultures, and so on."

"Oh, that would've required a whole lot more teaching skill than she had. Her greatest talent was wielding the paddle."

Betting on Bernie

"So, Martha, on that particular day, as my psych prof would say, you went through a loss of emotional equilibrium."

As noon approached and we were still talking in Bernie's car, I became aware that this grown-up man was treating me like a grown-up woman.

I'd been grousing about my parents and a particular teacher whose "instructional techniques" I didn't appreciate, but Bernie hadn't made me feel like a whiny child. Already, I was comfortable telling him personal secrets that I'd never shared with anyone else.

As a teenager used to adults talking down to me, this was a new experience. And I liked it.

Chapter 4

The Telephone Gossip Game

Sunday, April 4, 1965 *(continued)*

Bernie retrieved my round bag from the trunk. Then, as we walked toward the dorm, I realized I had one more thing to say. "Can I quickly tell you something else that surprised me in Linden? Then I promise I'll shut up about it."

His big grin reappeared. "Shoot."

"So, in junior-year history, we studied the war in Europe from 1939 to 1945. And since I'd moved with my parents to Germany in '51, when many towns were still in ruins, I'd seen how bad it was. Also, back in '45, Daddy had been present at the liberation of the concentration camp at Dachau. Years later, for some reason, he took Mama and me to see it."

"That's amazing," Bernie said.

"I hated that place, because I knew what had happened there, but nothing else we saw made me sad. The Cathedral at Chartres never was bombed. Daddy told Mama and me that an American colonel refused to do that, so it was still standing, and we got to go inside. And I loved Pompeii, too, and Versailles, the Vatican, the Leaning Tower of Pisa, the Alhambra and gypsy caves in Spain, plus Tivoli Gardens amusement park and the Little Mermaid statue in Copenhagen, and so many other things. We even spent a few nights in Amsterdam with the family that Daddy had stayed with after the liberation. They still couldn't stop thanking him."

"Those are all such fabulous experiences," Bernie said. "Not many Americans have seen places like that even as adults, much less as kids."

Me on the day I visited Pompeii and told my parents that I'd been there before, April 1953

"I know, and the most unforgettable day I ever had was when we visited Pompeii. I told my parents that I'd been there before, because it was all familiar. I knew I'd walked those same streets in some earlier time. That was a powerful experience for me, but years later in Linden, when I tried to tell my history teacher and classmates about it—both the good and the bad, the way we Army brats always did in school—nobody was interested, and I couldn't understand why."

"I think I can." Bernie's voice grew softer. "I'm sure none of your friends in Linden were Army brats. They'd never been to places like Pompeii, so they couldn't relate to your experiences."

"You weren't an Army brat, so can *you* relate to my experiences?"

"To be honest with you, Martha. No, I can't relate to any of that. When I was a little kid and long after—around the time you were doing all that traveling and visiting so many wonderful places—my family spent two weeks each summer at the same cabin on the same lake, splashing in the same swimming hole, and picnicking under the same trees."

I laughed. "And I can't relate to that."

"Of course not, because your life wasn't like mine. And you should know this, too. Shreveport is the farthest west I've ever been. I've never set foot outside the USA. Truth is, I'm dying to travel to the kinds of places you've been to. So maybe, sometime or other, you'll be willing to tell me a lot more about them and all the other things you saw and did in Europe."

Bernie about age ten or eleven, 1948-1949

Bernie set my bag down near the swinging doors that marked the boundary between the dorm lobby and our girls-only residential wing. "Martha, let's go out for a proper dinner after your spring break."

"I'd be crazy to." I rolled my eyes and lolled my tongue just as he'd done earlier.

We both laughed at how I'd swiped his goofy line and expression.

"Great," he said, still chuckling. "I'll pick you up at seven the first Saturday evening after you're back. Deal?"

"Deal."

Back in my room, I recalled dates with a couple of other townies, plus a pilot-in-training lieutenant at Barksdale who had treated me to dinners at the officers' club and the gaudy "Bossier Strip," thereby adding Mai Tais and Singapore Slings to my inventory of worldly delights.

Going off campus was not a new thing for me.

But after waffles and a long conversation with Bernie that morning, I felt all grown up. It didn't hurt that, apparently overnight, the jerk had turned into Prince Charming on a prancing, burgundy-colored steel steed.

I was headed for the library to try focusing on Monday's biology test when my classmate Edna Mae stopped me. "How'd the blind date go?" she asked.

She didn't hear about that from me. Wonder who told her?

"I didn't care for him much last night," I said, "but my opinion changed this morning."

"Pleasant sleepover while the auntie was absent?"

She knows about that, too?

"Nice ride and conversation in his sexy sports car?"

Where's she going with this?

Edna Mae kept up her nosy questions. "What's his name?"

"Bernie."

"Good lookin'?"

I pointed to the library. "Gotta get going."

But Edna Mae stuck with me. "What'd ya'll talk about?"

I laughed. "Be easier to tell you what we didn't talk about."

"Gonna see him again?"

I nodded, hoping that would satisfy her, but it didn't.

"So, maybe there's somethin' to it?" she asked.

I tried outpacing her. "Maybe."

Still, she kept up with me. "How excitin'."

Increasingly eager to dump her, I speeded up. "You never know."

"You gotta know somethin' after that long talk."

"Yeah, I'm feeling kinda…" I let my voice trail off.

"Kinda, what?"

I reached for the library door handle. "Really shouldn't say."

Edna Mae pursued me to the elevator. "Shouldn't say what?"

"It's a brand-new idea for me. Not sure I even like it."

As she followed me into the elevator, I blurted out something that had not occurred to me even once during my three-hour talk with Bernie.

"I think I may have met the man I'm going to marry."

That evening, a little after the ten p.m. curfew, as I studied on in my room, the intercom buzzed and the voice of Mrs. Lawson, our dorm's house mother, boomed throughout the suite. "Martha, your father's on the phone, asking to speak with you. He called twice already."

Never before had either of my parents tried to reach me by phone at Centenary. Operator-assisted long-distance calls were expensive and thus, in our frugal family at least, to be avoided. So I panicked.

Something's happened to Mama.

I raced down the hall, through the swinging doors, across the lobby, and into Mrs. Lawson's apartment. She gestured toward the ominous-looking, square black phone with its corded handset lying across the desk.

An instant later, Daddy's commanding-officer voice filled my ear. "Martha Frances, where have you been?"

"In the library, studying for tomorrow's biology exam. Why?"

"We don't like what we're hearing."

In the background, Mama said something that I didn't understand. Soon, they were yelling over each other into their own handset.

At least she's all right.

But Daddy's bark drowned her out. "We want to know everything you've been up to."

"Preparing for four midterms."

Betting on Bernie

"That's not what I mean, Martha Frances, and you know it." His fury stirred up years of angst in me.

So, as usual, I choked up. "No idea. What you mean. Daddy."

"Your mama's upset and can't stop crying."

Seldom had I seen Mama cry, so that only added to my distress.

Through the earpiece came a volcanic expulsion of air, as if Daddy believed venting would improve the situation. He kept dominating the call as he did everything else in our lives. "For a while," he said, "I thought your mama was having a nervous breakdown."

My own nerves flopped like a hooked fish. "Daddy, tell me what you've heard. Maybe it's not so bad."

His long pause only increased the tension.

At last, Mama's voice came through. "We understand you're getting married," she said.

Daddy cut in again. "Jenny says you're leaving Centenary this week to get married."

I'd never been so astonished in my life and was still sorting out the situation when Mama seized the handset on the other end of the line. "Don't get pregnant, Martha Frances. It'll wreck your life."

"I'm not getting pregnant, Mama."

Mrs. Lawson's expression suggested that either I or my folks—or maybe all three of us—were cuckoo.

As I struggled to come up with a response, Mama and Daddy yammered on.

"Jenny says you checked out of the dorm overnight."

"And spent the night with a man you'd never met before."

"An older man."

"Named Barney."

"Who already has a wife and kids."

"And races around town in a sports car."

"And took you to a vacant house."

"And kissed you for hours in his car outside the dorm."

Now I get it.

Jenny was a mutual friend of my folks and Edna Mae's parents. She didn't live in Shreveport and had no knowledge of my social life. Clearly, a few rounds of telephone gossip had taken place between someone who did know of my blind date and the overnight stay… and Edna Mae… and her parents… and Jenny… and my folks… and now the whole thing had circled back to me.

There was a slight lull before the onslaught started up again.

"You might get killed, Martha Frances."

"Or pregnant."

"Ruin your future."

"Throw away everything you've worked for."

"Everything we've wanted for you."

I tried to reassure them. "Mama. Daddy. Relax."

From that point on, they said nothing, so I breathed a few times and tried to answer more calmly. "I did not spend the night with a man. I'm not getting pregnant. I'm not leaving Centenary. I'm not getting married."

I paused to give them time to reply, but they didn't, so I bumbled on. "I'm only planning to go home with you on Friday for spring break."

Silence.

"Assuming you want me to," I added.

Ponderous silence.

"Let's discuss it when I'm back in Linden."

Chapter 5
Ten Tense Days

Friday, April 9 to Monday, April 19, 1965

The discussion began somewhere west of Shreveport. Even before we crossed into Texas, Daddy was huffing behind the wheel of our Ford Galaxie. "We did not save up all our lives and send you to college to watch you get married in your freshman year."

He didn't hear a thing I said on the phone.

"Daddy, listen to me." From my usual spot in the back seat, I leaned over the front bench seat so both he and Mama could hear me. "All I did was double-date with friends on Saturday night."

"Dollars to doughnuts, Barney has a wife and kids already."

"His name is Bernie, not Barney, and I don't understand why you assume that about him. Hemenway Furniture hired him to be their advertising manager, so he must have a good reputation. And if he had a wife and kids, he'd have brought them to Shreveport and wouldn't have rented a little studio apartment just for himself."

Mama piped up. "Be careful he doesn't take advantage of you."

"He's got wonderful manners, Mama. Treats me with more courtesy and respect than anyone I've ever known. Why assume he's a monster preying on college girls?"

"Well." Daddy snickered. "I do know something about men. Dollars to doughnuts, you spent the whole night with him in that vacant house."

That was too much, even for Mama. "Truman, we raised Martha Frances to be a respectable and responsible girl, so we ought to trust her. You don't know anything about that man, so stop making stuff up. Let her finish telling us what actually did happen."

"Thanks, Mama. What actually happened was..." I collected my thoughts. "I checked myself out of the dorm so Christine and I could stay at her aunt's house. Her boyfriend John drove us to a party, and later on, to the house, which was nicely furnished, not vacant. And then, after that, John and Bernie left. They did not spend the night with us in the house."

All of that was true. I didn't lie to my parents.

I did, however, commit a slight sin of omission by leaving out two teeny-tiny tidbits of truth. First, that Christine and I had been the only females at a party whose primary purpose was pornographic. And second, that she and I had been by ourselves in the house all night. Either fact would have launched additional volleys of parental protestations.

Feeling no guilt, I went on. "Bernie picked me up Sunday morning and took me to Murrell's, which, as you know, serves the best waffles in town. Then he drove me back to campus in his brand-new Mustang. He's proud of it, not about to wreck it and kill me. We spent an hour chatting in the driveway of my dorm, with both car doors open. Everyone who passed by saw us talking. Not kissing. Not petting. Talking. And then I studied all afternoon and evening until you called."

Finally, that—which also happened to be the total truth—pacified my folks. Even Daddy quieted down as we left the Interstate for the white-flowering dogwood- and sweet gum-lined roads of the Piney Woods.

Soon, a burst of joy brimmed in Mama's voice. "We're so excited to have you with us for ten whole days."

I responded with somewhat less enthusiasm. "I'm looking forward to it, too. Brought three recently published books to read: *The Bell Jar*, *A Moveable Feast*, and *To Kill a Mockingbird*."

Daddy shook his head. "Never heard of 'em."

On Saturday morning, dressing for breakfast in my bedroom, I caught the familiar sound of repeated two-second rings from our wall-hung rotary phone in the kitchen. Someone was trying to reach us.

When I entered, Mama stood by the counter stirring up pancake batter in her trusty Sunbeam MixMaster. Her well-worn *Betty Crocker Cookbook* lay open beside the mixer. Sausages spattered and sizzled too loudly in a skillet, so she lowered the flame to keep them from burning.

I joined Daddy at the antique maple table that I'd grown up eating on. Two years earlier, Mama and I had recreated the Pennsylvania Dutch look featured in *Better Homes and Gardens* magazine. So now, the patterned fabric on all four chair cushions matched both the wallpaper and the window valance, which nicely framed up a crepe myrtle shrub outside. It wasn't blooming yet but, like several others carefully spaced along the perimeter of our modest, white-sided bungalow, it soon would be covered with masses of purple flowers.

Daddy never lifted his eyes from the *Shreveport Times*, which he read every day because it covered the whole Ark-La-Tex region from Linden to Shreveport to Many and beyond.

Mama addressed me as she worked. "Mary Smith called. Their grandson is starting law school this fall. He's in town this week and bored, so she wondered if maybe you'd show him around."

"Show him around... Linden?"

"Smart young fellow, Martha Frances. A good prospect."

"I'm not looking for prospects right now. After a whole week of tests, I just wanna relax and read my books in peace."

Daddy was driving us home from Palm Sunday service when Mama glanced back at me. "Who'd you say introduced you to Bernie?"

"My classmate Christine and her townie boyfriend John."

"How'd they meet him?"

"Bernie moved into John's apartment building, so John invited him over for a beer."

"And then to a party?"

"Yes, and when Bernie accepted, Christine offered to find him a date."

"But she'd only met him that day, right? When did she invite you?"

"The next morning. A week ago yesterday."

"And when was the party and the sleepover at her aunt's house?"

"That same evening. A week ago last night."

"Seems a mighty short time to know a stranger in town before you arrange a date for him with an innocent young girl."

"Would you feel better, Mama, if John and Christine had known Bernie for a whole month?"

"Not really."

Monday's *CBS Evening News with Walter Cronkite* led with black-and-white photos of a Palm Sunday tornado outbreak. Forty twisters had struck the Midwest, killing hundreds and injuring thousands. As was the case in most houses in America, our "rabbit ears" antennae were perched atop a small Zenith TV set in our den, where we always gathered for half an hour in the evening to hear "Uncle Walter" tell us "that's the way it is."

Daddy, sitting on the sofa next to me, said during a commercial break, "He's Jewish, isn't he?"

I glanced up from *A Moveable Feast* and yanked my attention back from Paris to Linden. "Who, Daddy?"

"That older man you're dating. He's Jewish, isn't he?"

"We haven't talked about religion. Why do you think that?"

"Because I've known several Bernards or Barneys or Bernies in my life, and every one of 'em was Jewish."

"I dunno. I did watch him eat bacon at Murrell's." I cackled aloud at what seemed a stupendously stupid statement on my part. "But he also described his Uncle Irv as 'a hard-hitting Jewish boxer who fought all over New York State in his youth before marrying a girl from a Creole Catholic family that once owned a big antebellum plantation on the Mississippi River.' So, Daddy, you can draw your own conclusion."

Mama's face conveyed deep skepticism. "Pretty hard to believe any part of that tale."

"Yeah, I called it crazy, too, when Bernie told me."

Daddy's mood hadn't improved over the weekend. "Peddling cock-and-bull stories like that adds zero credibility to whatever else he tries to make you believe."

"To me," I said, "the fact that it sounds so odd probably means it's true. Who'd even think to make up such a farfetched story?"

Cronkite returned with the latest from Vietnam—Task Force Alpha of the second Marine battalion had secured Phu Bai airfield south of Hué—from which news I escaped once again into Hemingway's nostalgic portrait of Paris in the 1920s.

Before long, Daddy came up with another penetrating question that urgently, desperately needed a response from me. "What's Irv short for?"

Once more, I hauled my focus back to real life. "Irving or Irvin, I guess. Bernie's father's name was Sid."

Mama nodded. "Yep, they're Jewish, and that's okay. My daddy had several Jewish patients back home in the Delta. They were shopkeepers in neighboring towns and the only ones who ever paid him in cash, which we badly needed. I knew a few Jewish families on Army posts, too. They all were nice, as I recall."

Daddy harrumphed. "Margaret, did we send Martha Frances to a Methodist college in Louisiana so she could latch onto some Jewish fellow from New York?"

Betting on Bernie

I sighed and closed my book. "I haven't latched onto anyone, Daddy. Just went on a double date with friends."

Mama turned to me en route to our Tuesday choir practice. "Where'd Bernie go to college?"

"Tulane."

"What was his major?"

"I don't know. We didn't discuss it."

"When did he graduate?"

"No idea, Mama. Why?"

"Well, see, I've been thinking. Let's assume he finished college on a normal schedule and served two years in the Army, then got enough work experience to be hired at Hemenway's. That means…" She calculated on her fingers. "He must be at least thirty by now."

For a while, neither of us said anything more, but once in the church parking lot she started up again. "I don't mind that he's Jewish, but I'd be happier if you were still seeing that lieutenant at Barksdale. You know, the Cornell grad from Boston. He was smart and a lot closer to your age."

"Except, after he finished pilot's training two months ago, they shipped him off to 'Nam."

"What a shame. He seemed like the perfect prospect."

On Wednesday evening, back at the kitchen table, we all eagerly devoured the two deep-fried foods that Cajun-chef Daddy had perfected years ago—catfish and the tastiest homemade hush puppies anyone ever ate—always served with Jim Beam bourbon and Coke over ice.

He finished his drink and went for another. "So, how old is Bernie?"

I washed down the hush puppy I was eating with my bourbon and Coke. "I don't know."

Mama chimed in. "I figured it out. At least thirty."

"That can't be right," I said. "He doesn't look or act that old."

Daddy ignored me. "Way too old for you, Martha Frances."

I ignored him back. "Last night, I finished *A Moveable Feast* and started *The Bell Jar*."

On Thursday, I read all day, returned to church with Mama for the choir's final rehearsal of our Easter cantata, and finished *The Bell Jar* before bidding my folks goodnight. "Tomorrow, I'm on to *To Kill a Mockingbird*," I said.

Again, Daddy shook his head. "Strange title."

Friday morning, Mama was fixing pancakes and sausages again and Daddy was buried in his paper again when I proposed a brand-new idea that had just occurred to me overnight.

"If it's okay with you two," I said, "I'd like to take a couple of summer courses at Centenary."

Mama frowned. "We'd rather have you home with us."

"Yeah, that'd be fine, too, except… studying with a professor and other students is lots more intellectually stimulating than reading alone."

Daddy looked up. "What courses would you take?"

"Intro to Psychology and a repeat of calculus to prove to myself that I can do it."

"Does this change of plans have anything to do with *him*?"

"No, Daddy, my desire to go back for the summer session has nothing to do with Bernie." For the most part, that was true.

I kept reading *Mockingbird* on Saturday and accepted a last-minute invitation for dinner and a movie with a former high-school classmate.

That would be my last date with anyone not named Bernie.

On Easter Sunday, Mama and I sang in the choir while Daddy goofed around, as usual, with his buddies in the back row of the church.

That afternoon, I finished *Mockingbird*. My cultural markers—those shared characteristics and beliefs that people exhibit when they have a sense of belonging to a certain group—had been evolving steadily during my first year in college. Now, Harper Lee's controversial, groundbreaking novel had pushed them forward quite a bit.

The conversation was subdued as Daddy drove Mama and me back to Shreveport on Monday. At some point, he looked at me in the mirror. "Dollars to doughnuts, you're gonna find out he's got a wife and kids."

That strained spring break cast a sour spell over my second semester. The telephone gossip game had been an unfortunate way for my folks to learn of Bernie. I'd rather have gotten to know him better myself before deciding if I wanted to introduce him to them at all.

Back when I was still in high school, I'd developed an intense dislike of rumor-mongering. This episode only reinforced that.

From the moment Mama and Daddy had picked me up at Centenary, I knew I was dreading those ten days at home. By the time they drove me back, the thought of spending entire months in that environment made my decision to attend summer school easy and appealing.

Clearly, my world was changing, and the people, activities, and issues of greatest interest to me now were not to be found in Linden.

Chapter 6

Three Questions, My Turn

Saturday, April 24, 1965

For my first planned dinner date with Bernie, I dressed like a grown-up woman in a sleek rose-and-black sheath that complemented my dark hair and blush-prone complexion. The week before, with this special evening in mind, I'd snapped it up on sale at Benny's Dress Shop in Linden.

Bernie met me up in the lobby of my dorm, wearing a sport coat, a tie, and the sparkliest smile I'd ever seen in my life.

It wasn't lost on me that he was all eyes for me.

"What say we walk to Brocato's," he said, "for some fresh-made spaghetti."

"I'd love to. Whenever Daddy drives us past that corner, Mama and I ask him to stop so we can try it. But he claims it's too slow and expensive, so he speeds off for fast 15¢ burgers and 5¢ fountain Cokes."

Bernie laughed at that. "My new colleagues at Hemenway's praise Joe Brocato's 'Fish in a Bag' and 'Wop Salad.'"

I glanced up, genuinely surprised at his use of "wop," which I understood was an old and highly derogatory term for Italian. "Mama taught me never to use that word."

"Well, Joe's Sicilian, and they say he lists it that way on his menu."

"So, it's okay to say that word in his restaurant?"

Bernie's eyes twinkled as he pressed a finger to his lips. "Only when ordering his special salad."

The spindly posts supporting Brocato's half-circle portico contrasted with the stout glass blocks set horizontally into its external brick walls. A wiggly finger of yellow light from a dangling chandelier beckoned us toward the door. And then, beyond the foyer, dozens of white candles shimmered above black-and-white tablecloths and matching checkerboard floor tiles. It was the loveliest dining space I'd ever seen.

Once seated, we pored over the red-covered menu book. The $1.25 red snapper, cooked in parchment paper with a lemon-butter sauce, was what Bernie's culinary advisors had termed Fish in a Bag. We both ordered that with sides of fresh-cut spaghetti and Parmesan.

Served à la carte for 75¢, the Wop Salad carried a printed notice on the menu: "We have copyrighted trade mark." Intrigued, we ordered two of those, too.

Minutes later, two Wop Salads—each a mound of fresh greens topped with celery, capers, oregano, anchovies, black and green olives, and a hard-boiled egg—landed on our table with small cruets of olive oil and vinegar. Along with them came a loaf of crusty Italian bread and a serrated knife on a wooden board, plus a chilled bottle of Soave Classico that Bernie had requested. Eagerly, we dug into the salads and our next round of conversation.

"Bernie, you said you served in the Army."

"Yep. Drafted not long before the Cuban missile crisis. But then, after basic training, while everyone else was sweating out nuclear war with the Soviets, I sweated out a tough tour of duty in the engraving shop."

"How'd you manage that?"

"Some colonel discovered my artistic genius, and from then on my assignment was to create fancy trophies for the Army sports teams and personalized cigarette lighters for the top brass."

"Did you do that kind of engraving work later in New Orleans?"

"No, I landed a job drawing happy-looking people eating at dining tables or lounging on sofas and chairs."

I needed a moment to take that in. "Why?"

"Furniture store newspaper ads. Somebody has to make all those illustrations they use."

"How'd you get into that? Was your dad a commercial artist?"

Bernie shook his head. "He owned butcher shops. Made the best sausage anybody ever ate and brought home a fresh batch every week. I miss him and that sausage more than words can tell."

"You said his name was Sid. What's your mom's name?"

"Minnie. She's the lippy one who keeps us all laughing."

"Which one of them are you most like?"

"I inherited Dad's calm nature, but I can hold my own in a jest-fest with Mom."

"Like when you needled John in the car? Is that what you got from her?"

Minnie and Sid Marks with Bernie (left) and Murray in Elmira, New York, about 1947

"Yeah, we play games like that all the time at home."

"You should know, it really turned me off."

"Sorry. I assumed we were all having fun and John just didn't know how to give it back to me."

"Maybe he didn't grow up with people who consider insulting each other a form of entertainment. For sure, I didn't."

"With Mom, it's never one-way joking. All three of us kids got her smart mouth, but she taught us to take it as well as dish it out."

"Are your siblings older or younger than you?"

"Murray's eighteen months younger. He's twenty-four now. Rozanne arrived ten years after me, so she's sweet sixteen."

With that data, I made a quick-and-easy calculation.

Bernie's twenty-six. Eight years older than me, but nowhere close to thirty. I knew Mama was wrong about that.

After we polished off our fish, pasta, bread, and two glasses of wine apiece, an impish expression crossed Bernie's face. "Martha, what say we play an amusing little game of Three Questions. Are you gamy for that?"

"Gamy?" Already well impacted by the wine, I giggled. "Yeah, I'm gamy for a game."

His eyes glinted in the candlelight. "So, you start by asking me three questions. Anything you want to know about me, I promise I'll answer truthfully. When you're done, I'll ask you the same three questions. In between, we'll get follow-ups as needed. It'll be fun, I promise."

"Will they let us stay here if we're just talking?"

"As long as we're lingering over desert and coffee, we can stick around as long as we like."

So he ordered two servings of something I'd never heard of before, which the menu identified as *cannoli siciliani*, that came packed with ricotta, pistachios, and chocolate chips. Plus, of course, black coffee for himself.

Meanwhile, as a confirmed non-coffee drinker, I allowed the waiter to top off my glass with what remained of the Soave.

And then, digging into the cannoli gave me some much-needed time to think as the dark dining room seemed to quiet down around me.

"Okay, Bernie, here's my first question: **What's the one thing you most want to accomplish in your life?**"

"Aw, Kid, that's almost too easy."

"But you didn't say they had to be genius-level questions."

"True." His nod conceded my point. "So, let's start with a bit of background. Over the past two years, I've made hundreds of drawings of furniture and appliances for newspaper ads. How does that sound to you?"

"Boring."

"Yep, it is. *Was.* And I say *was* because that's not my job anymore. Part of my deal with Hemenway's was that they'd bring in another artist to do that kind of thing. I hired the guy last week, so now I can focus on my main project, which is—" He paused to make an appropriate noise and drumming gesture. "*Drum roll!!!* Developing a full and complete, long-term marketing plan for the company."

"That sounds impressive. Have you ever done it before?"

"No. The owners are making a big bet on me, but only because my two previous bosses vouched for my ability to create more than line drawings. This job is a nice step up for me, and I intend to knock it out of the famous Shreveport Baseball League's ballpark."

"Is there a Shreveport Baseball League?"

"No," he repeated, but with a grin this time. "However, even if there were, moving up from drawing newspaper ads to developing a complete, long-term marketing plan for a company that sorely needs it is *not* the one thing I most want to accomplish in my life."

That statement confused me. "So, what is?"

"I most want to become a full-time professional fine artist."

That wasn't the answer I expected. There never had been an artist in my family—not that I knew of anyway—much less a fine artist. I didn't even understand what the term meant, much less see it as a career track.

Having no clue as to what to say next, I tossed back what remained of my wine and remained silent.

Fortunately, Bernie kept talking. "Please understand, Martha. I don't mean any plain ol' garden-variety fine artist. My dream is to become a superfine fine artist."

"Aren't all fine artists superfine artists?"

"No. Some who call themselves fine artists are mediocre. I intend to be the kind of superfine artist whose superfine art earns a superfine living by selling in superfine galleries in superfine cities with superfine reputations for selling superfine art."

I laughed at his ridiculous rush of redundancies. "As opposed to the kind who sketches girls' faces on napkins in diners?"

"Hey, Picasso's sketches on napkins are worth millions." He sipped his coffee. "So, be sure to hang on to that one."

"I'll never let it out of my sight." I laughed again. "But I have to ask, how are you working toward that goal? Did you attend art school?"

"No, I created trophies and lighters for the Army, remember? After that, I drew furniture by day and took art classes at Tulane by night."

"Didn't your parents want you to go to college? To aim higher?"

"They made sure I finished high school, which was more than they had done. After that, I had to work to support myself and the family."

"That sounds very Old World."

"It is. My Russian-born grandparents brought all their Old-World values with them when they came to America, so Mom and Dad grew up with those values and did their best to pass them on to us."

At that, my wine-woozy brain blurted out the first thing it dredged up. "I never met a Russian before."

Newborn Bernie Marks with Minnie, his American-born mother, and her Russian-born father in Elmira, New York, November 1938

"And you still haven't, because I'm not a Russian." Bernie's eyes locked onto mine. "I'm a second-generation American-born Jew with a genetic and family history unlike that of any ethnic Russian. All four of my grandparents arrived at Ellis Island around 1900, thanks to American charities that paid their way and helped them get established here."

"Did they speak English?"

"Not at all when they got here, and not well even after I arrived."

"Was Russian their native language?"

"No. Yiddish."

"Is *Marks* a Yiddish name or a Russian name?"

"Neither, because it wasn't their real name. Someone on Ellis Island told them to make their marks on the register and it stuck. We don't know anything about Dad's family. We do know that Mom's father was literate

Betting on Bernie

in Russian, served in the Czar's army, and met his wife in America. They came from Minsk and Kiev in what's now the USSR. Their families had lived there for centuries, but they were lucky to escape when they did."

"Why?"

"The *pogroms*."

"*Pogroms?*"

Bernie's smile had vanished after we talked about art. Now a tighter version of it returned. "So, the girl who traveled all over Europe hasn't heard of the *pogroms*?"

I bristled at that unexpected joke at my expense. "We traveled in Western Europe, Bernie. Never went behind the Iron Curtain."

At that, he relented. "And since your parents aren't Jewish, or even eastern-Europeans, they wouldn't know about *pogroms* either. *Pogrom* is the Russian word for what the Nazis later did to the Jews."

"Holocaust?"

"Yes, except the Russian *pogroms* lasted a hundred years. They began in the early 1800s with anti-Semitic riots in Minsk and Kiev. Thousands died in each wave. My *bubbie* told me all about it, how so many of her family members were murdered and how the *pogroms* continued long after she escaped to America with nothing but her life."

"Your *bubbie*?"

"That's the Yiddish word for grandmother. So, given that background, it's no surprise that my grandparents' highest aspiration was to raise American kids who could speak, read, and write English well enough to help support the family. That's why our parents made sure we graduated from high school. Beyond that, we were on our own."

As my mind grappled with all that new information, it ricocheted from shock at Bernie's traumatic family history… to amazement that a mid 20th-century American could be raised with 19th-century Eastern European values… to astonishment at how different his background was from mine… to surprise that the mismatch came not only from religion and ethnicity but also from our parents' levels of education and aspirations for their children... and then on to acceptance that Bernie was simply unlike anyone I'd ever known before. And that was okay with me, because I found him delightful to be with.

Except for his intentionally silly sayings, needling humor, and oddball contractions, Bernie was well-spoken. His demeanor, manners, intellectual curiosity, general knowledge, and easygoing temperament put my own college-grad, career-officer father to shame.

Unsettled by the contradictions, I fumbled my next followup question. "I'm guessing that you've never— You didn't actually— I mean — You never *really* went to college."

He produced another tight-lipped smile, so unlike his regular one, as if aware he'd revealed too many potential problems to me too fast. From that point on, he didn't volunteer so much.

But now I was curious, so I pushed on, even as the waiter lay the bill on our table. "You said you studied art and psych at Tulane."

"Yes, and other subjects that interested me, like classical Greek drama. I audited all those courses."

Still, I struggled to understand. "You audited them? Because you couldn't pay full tuition? Because you had to help the family?"

"Because I could barely afford even that lesser fee." Bernie looked at the bill and reached into his pocket for his wallet.

To me, auditing courses was every bit as foreign a concept as fleeing *pogroms* or choosing to limit one's education to help the family get by. Confused, I stumbled on a while longer. "So, you sat in on the lectures?"

"Yes, but I also studied all the course material, did all the outside reading, and learned a lot, which was the most important thing to me."

"Did you write term papers?"

"No, and I never took exams either." His tight smile reappeared. "I have no college credits, Martha. Never gave a thought to earning a degree."

Even as I wondered if this game was turning out to be as much fun as he expected, I moved on to my bound-to-be-too-easy Question #2.

"So, Bernie, what's the one thing you absolutely don't want in your life?"

His answer came right back. "I don't ever want to fret over paying the bills. I'll own a company someday and achieve financial success."

"But the world is changing, and without a college degree—"

For the second time, Bernie interrupted me. "As I told you, Martha, I'm loaded with talent. I'm a hard worker. I keep my promises. I go over and above what everyone expects of me. Whatever I do, I make a point of doing it well. People seem to like me and want to help me. I'm confident I will succeed in life." Given the unexpected emotional weight of this topic, I was relieved to see Bernie's big smile emerge again. "Guess it's because I'm so charming and good looking," he said.

"That's it." I nodded. "So, why not start earning a degree now?"

"I'm not interested. Don't think I'll ever need it."

"With your new job, you'll have the money."

"Not sure how I'd find the time."

"I suspect you could find both time and money."

He said nothing. Clearly didn't want to talk of this.

"Why not take an evening course at Centenary this summer?"

"I'll be working on my marketing plan."

"But only in the daytime, right?"

"Hard to say so far out."

I let the subject rest as I finished my *cannoli*, and then returned to it. "Bernie, over the break I told my folks I wanted to take classes at Centenary this summer, and they agreed."

He made no reply, so I kept on. "I've been looking at the schedule. Lots of good offerings both days and evenings. Why not pick a night course that interests you and take it for credit? Start small. Just as long as it counts toward a degree."

"Ask me your Question #3," he said.

In my earlier question-concocting moments, I hadn't gotten that far along, so now I scrambled to think faster than my mind was in the mood to do. Finally, something that seemed like a good third question popped out on its own.

"Do you have a deep, dark secret that nobody else in Shreveport knows, but you're willing to tell me?"

"A deep, dark secret." Bernie bobbed his head. "Yeah, I do."

I experienced a fleeting moment of regret for the question.

Hope he doesn't reveal the existence of a hidden-away wife and flock of kids.

But his sweet smile reassured me. "By now, you know I'm Jewish, but are you ready to learn my really deep, really dark secret about that?"

I borrowed one of his favorite words. "Shoot."

He smiled, leaned forward, and whispered, "I'm not properly and formally Jewish."

"Sorry, but I don't understand."

"That's because you're not Jewish. If you were, you would."

I'm sure I looked puzzled at that.

So Bernie went on. "My proud Jewish heritage goes all the way back to King David and King Solomon and King Whoever Else."

Now I chuckled. "You're descended from royalty?"

"A long, long way back. All my ancestors were Jewish. All my genes are Jewish. I identify as a Jew because, ethnically, I am Jewish. So my deep, dark secret is this: I'm what's known as a 'secular' Jew."

"What's that?"

"It means I'm nonreligious. Not a practicing Jew."

"You have to practice to be a Jew? I assumed it came naturally."

"For some, it does. For me, it didn't. As a little Jewish kid in Elmira, I was supposed to do all the usual little-Jewish-kid things. Go to Hebrew School. Learn to read Hebrew. Study the Torah. Obey the laws. Follow the rituals. And I did." He held up an index finger. "For one day. One class."

"That was it?"

"When I got home, I told Mom I now knew all the Hebrew I would ever need in my life and wasn't going back."

"And did you?"

"Nope. I never got beyond page one of the Torah."

"Sounds like me and the calculus book."

We both laughed at that.

"So," I said, "you flunked out of Hebrew School?"

"I prefer to think I opted out. Mom and Dad didn't care. They let me do it."

"Why would it matter if you went to Hebrew School or not? Weren't you already attending a public school and speaking English?"

"It mattered, because if I didn't go to Hebrew School and learn Hebrew well enough to satisfy the requirements for my bar mitzvah, I never could be a full participant in the Jewish faith community."

I must've looked confused, because Bernie shook his head. "It doesn't matter, Martha. You don't need to understand any of that."

He settled up with the waiter, and then we walked out into the soft, northern-Louisiana night.

"Your game worked," I said. "I learned a lot about you."

"Probably more than you wanted to learn." He smiled at me. "But if you're willing, I'd like to continue the game next Saturday. I'll ask you the same questions you've asked me and learn a lot about you, too."

"I'd be crazy to," I said, giving him his own goofy line back once more.

Of course, he grinned at that. "So, listen up, Kid. A couple nights ago, I ate Cajun deviled crab at Don's Seafood and Steakhouse. Maybe the best I ever had, even in New Orleans. Would you be gamy for that?"

My inexperienced and inebriated self had no idea how to respond, so for a few moments I said nothing.

"I'm gamy for anything" was what I finally came up with.

Chapter 7
Three Questions, His Turn

Saturday, May 1, 1965

The hostess at Don's Seafood and Steak House led us through an arched brick opening into a large, dark space where recessed wine racks alternated with brick walls. A single wide, stubby candle in a green hurricane-style glass holder flickered on each of the dozens of tables. Room dividers with exotic-looking sea creatures etched into backlit green glass echoed the pale-green dress that I'd chosen for my second dinner date with Bernie.

How cool that I picked this one to wear tonight.

As the tables filled up around us, I read the menu by the light of our candle and marveled at the variety of seafood on offer and the intriguing ways it was served.

Bernie and I each ordered the deviled crab with fries and a side salad. Our waiter recommended a Riesling, so Bernie ordered that, too.

But I, recalling the previous week, was cautious. "Don't let me drink three glasses of wine tonight," I told Bernie.

"Hey, Kid, I'll do my best, but you're the one who insisted on finishing off that Soave. So, now, are you ready for my three tough questions for you?"

"I am very well prepared, so…" I smiled at him. "Shoot."

The same impish expression that I'd seen the previous week danced across his face as he reacted to my latest appropriation of one of his favorite words. And then he relaunched our game.

"Okay, Martha. Question #1: **What's the one thing you most want to accomplish in your life?**"

I had decided to turn my first answer into a guessing game, so "a teaching career" was all I said.

"What grade?" Bernie asked.

"No grade at all."

At first, he seemed confused by that, but then he appeared to catch on. "You mean not grade school but high school. What subject?"

"Something related to mastering words but not dissecting frogs."

"That certainly does narrow it down." He eyed me sideways. "Why not just go ahead and tell me?"

"Okay." I nodded. "Earlier this spring—once I realized I wasn't going to med school and probably would wind up teaching—I asked myself two questions: What would I most like to teach? and Where would I most like to teach it?"

"Good questions. Did you come up with equally good answers?"

"Sure did. I'd most like to teach a foreign language at the college level."

"Oh." He paused for several seconds. "Sounds interesting."

"Yeah. I love languages, and I love Centenary. Can't think of any better way to spend my life than as a professor of German or Spanish at a college like Centenary."

Bernie's eyes narrowed. "But you know, it is kinda weird."

"Why is it weird?"

"Because last Saturday you said you'd never known anyone other than me who aspired to be a fine artist. Now I can say, I've never known anyone other than you who aspired to be a college professor." He looked straight into my eyes. "That's an ambitious goal."

"I enjoy challenges, except for calculus."

"Wouldn't high-school students challenge you, too? Couldn't you enjoy teaching at that level?"

"Maybe, but no younger. Little kids give me the willies. And I remember how even I—who up to then had been a hard-working, well-behaved student—became a blithering idiot in junior high."

And with that, having made it through Question #1, we both began ravaging our newly arrived crabs.

Meanwhile, I awaited his Question #2 for me.

"So, Martha, what's the one thing you absolutely don't want in your life?"

"My mother's life."

Bernie cocked his head. "You'd be a teacher like her, but otherwise, nothing?"

"Certainly not the military-wife life. Packing. Unpacking. Repacking. Re-unpacking. Moving in and out of 'homes' you never get to choose or spend much time in. Living with a man who believes God Almighty ordained him to be your commanding officer."

"Is your dad really that domineering?"

"Yes, he is. There's a clear pecking order in our family. He tells her what to do and what not to do. They both tell me what to do and not do, and if there's ever any disagreement between them, his order tops hers. And since I have no younger siblings, the pecking order stops with me."

"That'll change once you marry and have kids."

I munched a few fries, then a few more.

What happens if I tell Bernie I don't want children and won't marry at all unless I find someone very different from Daddy?

Eventually, I mustered up half the courage. "I don't believe I'll ever have children."

It was too dark for me to see if his expression changed, but I did notice that he set down his fork. "I've never heard a girl say that before," he said.

"Neither have I, to be honest."

"So, why'd you say it?"

Betting on Bernie

"Because it's true. I'm not comfortable with babies. Didn't grow up around any." I waited for him to respond, but when he didn't, I went on. "I'm almost nineteen, Bernie, and I've never even held a baby."

His silence spoke more eloquently than words, so I looked away and kept munching.

This'll probably be our last date.

But then he relaunched the topic. "How will you avoid getting pregnant if you're married?"

"Take the Pill. It shouldn't be hard to get, because this summer the Supreme Court is expected to guarantee married couples a Constitutional right to birth control. I'm rooting hard for that, because if it doesn't get approved, I probably won't marry anyone at all."

Bernie polished off what remained of his fries before looking back at me. "Seems there might be some other reason why you feel so strongly about not having kids. It can't just be a lack of experience with babies. Am I right?"

Oh, that's perceptive.

My fifth birthday, at my grandparents' home in Sledge, Mississippi, July 1951

"Yes, you are. You're absolutely right. The main reason is that I have a congenital heart murmur that could put my life at risk if I got pregnant."

Bernie said nothing, so I went on.

"Remember how I told you my grandfather was a doctor? So, back in '51, the year I turned five, Mama and I stayed in Sledge with him and my grandmother before flying over to join Daddy in Germany. One day, the adults were talking in the dining room when they thought I was playing outside, but actually I was in the kitchen. I overheard Granddaddy tell Mama and Grandmother that I'd been born with a heart defect. He said he'd been listening to it through his stethoscope my whole life. And, he said, the physical stress of pregnancy and giving birth could kill me."

"Did that scare you?"

"It sure did. So much that I decided right then and there that I'd never get pregnant. Never have a baby."

"Have you and your mother discussed this with other doctors?"

"Yes, and they've all confirmed Granddaddy's diagnosis. I have what one doc called a 'notably noisy murmur.' My heart valves don't open and close right. They leak a lot of blood back and forth, but as long as I don't get pregnant, it's not much of a threat to me."

At that point, I went back to eating my yummy spicy crab. And while I was aware of lots of activity and voices around me, I paid little attention to anything or anyone but Bernie.

He watched my face for a while without saying anything. But then, he broke his silence. "You seem to know your own mind, Martha. I've even picked up traces of a stubborn streak in you, and that's not all bad. You do have to look out for yourself in life."

"Daddy once described me as pigheaded." I chuckled and sipped some wine. "Personally, I prefer to think of myself as determined and resolute. It helps me get around his dictatorial tendencies. Wanna hear an example of Little Martha's Rebellion?"

Bernie uttered our favorite newly shared word. "Shoot."

"So," I began, "every teacher at our American School in Heidelberg came from the States, but they'd bring in a local *Fräulein* named Frida to teach us the German alphabet, numbers, basic words and phrases, popular songs and Christmas carols. But the important part of my story is this. From my toddler days on, Daddy tried to make me sound like a proper, well-bred Louisiana girl. Yes, sir. No, ma'am. No, sir. Yes, ma'am. And so on."

"Every kid in New Orleans sounds just like that."

"I'm sure, but you never said those things, did you, Bernie?"

"No, ma'am." He chuckled then, too. "I'm a Yankee, remember?"

"Pretty hard to forget that." I pursed my lips. "But I didn't say those things either, and that's my point. I refused to say 'sir' or 'ma'am,' which always blew Daddy's gasket. And then in the first grade, thanks to *Fräulein* Frida, I found a better approach. Call it the *Fräulein* Frida Fix."

"Or better…" Bernie's eyes twinkled. "The *Fräulein* Frida *Frix*."

"*Frix?*" I repeated, somewhat incredulously.

Bernie laughed so long that it was hard for me to finish my story.

"Hey, Bernie," I said, "settle down and listen up."

"Yes, ma'am," he said as he struggled to stifle his laughter.

"So, from first grade on, whenever Daddy told me to do something, I'd say '*ja*' as politely as could be. He'd get mad every time."

"He assumed you were being rude, saying 'yeah.'"

"Of course, but even as a first grader I was prepared and waiting for him. 'I'm not saying yeah, Daddy. I'm saying *ja*. I'm practicing my German. You know, *ja* is short for *jawohl*, which means, 'Yes, sir.''" I broke down laughing then, too. "Poor Daddy never figured out any response to that."

"Do you still say '*ja*' to him?"

"*Ja*. And if I'm annoyed, I lay it on thick. '*Jawohl, mein Herr.*'"

Bernie got into the spirit. "Do you ever say '*Jawohl, Herr Führer*' with a crisp Nazi salute?"

"Oh no. He spent four years fighting the Nazis in awful conditions. He despised them then and still does. We never joke about that."

"Does your mom manipulate him, too?"

"Oh yeah. Whenever they argue, she quotes her younger brother C.C. to support her position, which only makes Daddy madder. He goes berserk at the mention of C.C.'s name, so naturally Mama talks about C.C. all the time."

"Is C.C. her favorite brother?"

"I dunno. She just always stands up for him and takes his side. But Daddy and C.C. have hated each other my whole life. A long time ago, Mama took a picture of them together with a big catfish that they'd caught in a local river. I appear in the picture, too—as a topless toddler—but I sure don't remember it. My aunt says that's the last day those two ever got along. Something or somebody stirred up a feud."

Uncle C.C., a giant catfish, Daddy, and me in Sledge, Mississippi, 1948

Betting on Bernie

"And you really don't know how the feud started or why your mom pushes that button to upset your dad?" Bernie's lips twitched. "Maybe it's the Curse of the Catfish."

We shared a long chortle, and then I went on. "I only know that the many hundreds of parental fights that I've lived through always seemed to have something to do with C.C. Wanna hear an example?"

"Sure, if it's something you want to tell me."

"Why not?" I looked at him. "You already know so many strange things about me."

"And every strange thing I learn about you is even more fascinating than all the other strange things I already knew about you. So, shoot!"

I produced another grin, even though the story I was about to tell him wasn't funny to me at all.

I described how, two years earlier, Daddy was driving Mama and me out to the high school for the Miss Linden pageant. It was my first time as a contestant, so Mama and I had picked out a pretty pink dress that we both thought was perfect.

Me wearing my fringed pink dress—but not my uncle's gift necklace—at the Miss Linden Pageant, 1963

82   Martha Marks

But Daddy said the two rows of little fringes around the top edge of its bodice made me look fat and cheap. He told us to return it.

Mama had chosen to ignore his order, but Daddy didn't know that until we were in the car.

So then—as my new, fringed, pink "ball gown" hung beside me in the back seat—a nasty fight erupted up front.

Mama told Daddy that C.C. had sent me a pink necklace, which was why we had looked for a pink dress in the first place.

Daddy exploded and demanded that I give him the necklace, which I did. He crammed it into his pocket, but then he and Mama kept arguing on and on about C.C.

I told Bernie how I'd sobbed the whole way to the school. And how it took scrubbing with baby oil—which someone at the pageant just happened to have on hand—to get the black mascara smudges off my cheeks and eyelids. And how I then had to remove all my makeup and put on someone else's, which didn't match my skin tone. And how, whenever I went out on stage in that dress, even to play my violin in the talent competition, the words *fat* and *cheap* rang like a bell in my brain.

When I finished my story, Bernie shook his head. "It's hard to imagine anything like that happening in my family."

"Be glad," I said. "I wish it didn't happen in mine. Why it does is the greatest mystery of my life. I don't believe I'll ever understand it."

The waiter stopped by to remove our used plates and silverware and ask if we needed anything more.

Bernie ordered two portions of Don's special bread pudding with plum sauce before giving me his usual sweet smile. "Well," he said, "that certainly was informative. Dare we venture on to Question #3?"

"I'd be more'n happy to." That was my first time to try out on Bernie a goofy line of my own creation. I liked it because nobody could tell if I was saying "more than happy" or "more unhappy," which my adolescent mind considered clever enough to match his "gamy" joke.

"So, Martha, is there a deep, dark secret that nobody else in Shreveport knows but you're more'n happy to tell me?"

I got an immense kick out of his variation on my original question. Our emerging pattern of swiping each other's silly sayings seemed to do a lot to ease difficult moments.

"Yes," I said, "there is. My deepest, darkest secret is, I don't believe there's an old man with a long white beard hiding out behind pearly gates as choirs of angels flap around, playing harps in the sky. I also don't believe there's any sort of divine spirit lurking 'up there,' eavesdropping on our conversations, and taking time out of his busy day to meddle in the lives of us mere mortals 'down here' on Earth."

Bernie didn't interrupt, so I went on. "Also, I seriously doubt there's any kind of red, lizard-like demon with horns and a pitchfork who roams the earth in search of men and women dumb enough to sell him their souls so he can toss 'em into some fiery hot-spot deep underground."

As the bread pudding arrived, Bernie jumped into the middle of my blasphemous diatribe, obviously intending to play devil's advocate. "But, Martha—as a good Southern girl, a good east-Texas girl—aren't you supposed to believe in God and Satan and angels and demons and heaven and hell and fire and brimstone?"

"Maybe I *am* supposed to, but I *don't*. I enjoy singing traditional hymns and gospel songs in the church choir, but that's the extent of my interest in organized religion. There are a few reasons I could mention, but one particular incident in Linden stands out. Mind if I tell you?"

"Not at all," Bernie said. "Please do."

"Two years ago, 1963 again, lots of unmarried teenage girls were getting pregnant, mostly because there weren't enough things to do. So, the pastor and elders of our church decided to offer us young Methodists what they called 'folk games' in our church basement on Saturday nights. We kids soon found out that chaperoned square dancing was a fun way to stay out of trouble… just as long as we didn't use the 'd' word."

"What's the 'd' word?"

"Dancing."

"Of course." Bernie laughed. "Can't have any of that sinful dancing stuff in Linden."

"Yep, 'sinful' was what some people called it. And so, on the Sunday morning after the second Saturday-night round of 'folk games' in our church basement, the pastor of the main Baptist church stood up in his pulpit and used his hour-long sermon to blast the 'liberal Methodists' who were 'promoting dancing' to their own children in their own church."

Me in 1963, the year Linden's Methodist elders offered "folk games" to keep teenage girls like me from getting pregnant (I'm holding two Purple Martin fledglings that had fallen out of a nest box in our yard, keeping them safe from neighborhood cats while Daddy went for a ladder to put them back.)

"Clearly," Bernie said, "the Devil was afoot in Linden."

I nodded. "Clearly. So, guess what happened? In the face of furious Baptist opposition to our harmless Saturday-night fun, the Methodist leaders folded. No more folk games for us."

"And no more courage for them either."

"Nope, and can you guess what lesson I learned from that episode?"

Betting on Bernie 85

"What?"

"I learned that the super-religious people would rather see a naive, unmarried teenager like me get pregnant and kicked out of school than enjoy chaperoned, healthy square dancing in the basement of my own church with my parents' permission." I snickered. "That did it for me. Totally turned me off organized religion."

"It would have turned me off, too. Personally, I consider myself a 'chicken agnostic'."

"What's that?"

"A joke, Martha." Bernie laughed at his own joke about a joke. "But the truth is, I'm happily nonreligious."

"'Nonreligious' describes me pretty well, too. I see wild birds and wild creatures and wild places as the best evidence that God exists. Man-made churches only prove that men exist. I feel more spiritual out in nature, and you know, that's something I'm really glad I got from Daddy."

"Are you two Gaia worshippers, like the ancient Greeks?"

"No, I don't think either one of us worships nature. I see Earth as God's best creation, which means that the most important thing any of us can do is protect it. Take care of all its living plants and animals, including people. We humans are a part of creation, but we're not the whole thing. Not all-important, the way we think we are."

Bernie and I finished our desserts. He paid the bill. Then we returned to my dorm, where other couples stood by themselves, saying goodnight under its wide, tall-columned, Old South-style portico.

For the first time ever, Bernie draped his arm around my shoulders and pulled me close as his eyes filled with their usual twinkle and tease.

"If I were to kiss you tonight, would you tell your mother?"

A warm flush crept up my neck. "Probably not."

"How 'bout your father?"

"Definitely not."

And so he did.

Chapter 8

Mr. Marks Goes to Linden

June to October 1965

I turned nineteen that summer, rejoicing in my escape from Linden and the promise of three intellectually stimulating years to come at Centenary College.

Adding to my satisfaction was the fact that, in June, the Supreme Court approved married couples' access to contraception, including the long-anticipated Pill. On that day, women like me became the first fortunate generation in history with both the legal right and the medical power to control our own bodies and lives. Later on, I took full advantage of that freedom.

Along with millions of other young women, I read Betty Friedan's *The Feminine Mystique*, which reverberated with first-year Baby Boomers who knew we wanted more out of life than what our mothers had been allowed to achieve. Friedan inspired our journey from the fuddy-duddy '50s to the previously unimaginable world of personal, educational, and professional opportunities of the '70s, '80s, '90s, and beyond.

Throughout the summer—as I relished my liberation from mom-and-pop oversight, adolescent-male gropings, small-town gossip, and pre-med pressures—I hardly contained my zeal to explore Centenary's wealth of offerings in the liberal arts.

The last thing on my mind was "hunting a husband," as some girls called the top goal of their lives. Dinner dates with an attractive, amusing, non-authoritarian, and secular Jewish guy were quite fine with me.

After May 1st —when we hadn't yet dated for even a full month but somehow managed to discuss the Pill—Bernie seemed to accept my desire to remain, as I called it, "child-free."

And that had the benefit of boosting him high up the scale of my desire to avoid any man who displayed even the slightest tendency to become my commanding officer. By continuing to invite me out that summer, Bernie eliminated both of those concerns for me.

Also during those months, he showed a further willingness to please me by taking—*for credit!*—a Centenary course that met two evenings a week. So, after Dutch-treat suppers at nearby Strawn's Eat Shop, topped off with oozy-good slices of strawberry "iced box" pie, he'd go to class and I'd head for the library. Later, he'd come to find me there and walk me back to the dorm, where a good-night kiss was now part of our routine.

By summer's end, he had earned his first three college credits with an A. Great excuse to go for spaghetti and baggy fish at Brocato's.

I aced the psych course, too, and passed Calculus with a C, which—while not erasing that Day-Glo orange F on my transcript—did boost my confidence. When fall came, I leaped with joy into my new double major in German and Spanish. My grade-obsessed parents' happiness levels skyrocketed from the end of that semester on, when my name appeared on the dean's list of high-achieving students and stayed there until I graduated.

One thing always impressed me. Bernie wasn't trying to date me on the cheap. He liked good food and nice places, and we didn't just eat spaghetti, fish from a bag, or deviled crabs either.

At our favorite riverfront joint, Beachcomber, we feasted on exotic-to-us Polynesian food and slow danced in the romantically dark lounge.

Bernie re-introduced me to pizza at the delightfully fragrant Piccadilly Italian Restaurant. I recalled enjoying pizzas in 1953, during my memorable childhood trip to Italy, but hadn't had one since.

On warm summer evenings, we'd ride out of town to Smith's Cross Lake Inn, where mossy threads dripped from cypress trees, a stuffed-and-mounted 'gator greeted us with a grin even more gargantuan than Bernie's, and superlative sunsets flared across the lake in time for dessert.

For barbecue, we'd cross the Red River to a hole-in-the-wall Bossier City lean-to smoke pit. I've forgotten its name but not the aroma that permeated its family-style dining area or the charismatic owner who exhorted his customers to "pick up them ribs with your fingers."

For my birthday and other celebrations, Bernie would splurge and treat me to sublime marinated crab claws at Ernest's Orleans Restaurant and Cocktail Lounge.

That said, the foodie lessons didn't only go one way.

Before we met, Bernie never had tasted authentic Mexican food. Maybe he'd chowed down a Tex-Mex taco somewhere, but certainly not hard-to-find-at-that-time, prepared-to-your-taste-at-the-table *guacamole* with house-made, fresh-cut, and hand-salted *tostaditas* served hot from the fryer.

Or every Mexican café owner's homemade special *sopa de pollo*, always presented with fresh-baked *bolillos* and home-churned *mantequilla*.

Or grilled *carnitas* drizzled with tantalizing *mole* or *tomatillo* sauces.

Or caramel-coated *flan*, cinnamon-and-sugar *churros*, and *tres leches* cakes.

I'd learned to love them all during summertime trips south of the border with my folks after we moved to Linden.

Eventually, I came to realize that Bernie wasn't alone. In those days, few Americans had experienced real Mexican food. No restaurant in Shreveport offered it. But after we discovered several of what I called "True-Mex" eateries in east Texas, as opposed to "Tex-Mex," we went out of our way to patronize them.

Those meals—with food that could be quite delicate, not overloaded with spices, as Bernie had feared—whetted his appetite for more of the same in Spanish American countries.

Bernie and me getting the Mustang ready for his first visit to my folks, fall 1965

By the fall of 1965, my folks had heard more of Bernie than they cared to but still hadn't met him. At some point, we all agreed, it was time.

I, of course, desperately wanted that first visit to go well. Bernie was charming and motivated enough to pull it off, but I knew that one issue had the potential to ruin the day. That issue was *education*.

So, on a glowing Saturday morning in October, as Bernie pointed the Mustang west on the recently completed I-20, I told him my folks' personal histories, with emphasis on how each of them had gotten where they were through an intense desire to attend and graduate from college.

En route through the Piney Woods, I also made sure that Bernie knew we were not the kind of snobby, old-money WASPs that his parents or grandparents might have encountered in New York State. We boasted no VIPs in our known family history. No antebellum mansions. No prep schools. No Ivy League colleges. No generation-skipping trust funds. Nothing on either side but rural poverty gradually overcome by hard work, grit, and, again, education.

I assured him that my parents were good-hearted people whose personal and professional successes had carried them far beyond whatever prejudices they might have inherited by the circumstances of their births. And that the most-important thing to them was their only child's happiness and wellbeing. And that I felt sure they would overlook any perceived "differences" in a man their daughter loved if that was what it took to keep her close to them.

And then, as we neared Linden, I fervently hoped my folks would live up to that fond image that I had painted of them.

They met us in the driveway.

Daddy opened the passenger-side door of Bernie's Mustang, and after I stepped out, he leaned down for a hug. Then he and Bernie shook hands and exchanged the blandest of comments on the weather and traffic.

Mama also shook Bernie's hand, but her tense eyes suggested a recent argument with Daddy. I knew her too well not to read her body language.

But still, she and Daddy made an effort, and the squeaky-clean Mustang turned out to be an ice breaker. As Mama settled into the passenger's side to see how that newfangled bucket seat felt to her, Bernie encouraged Daddy to wedge his long legs under the curiously open steering wheel and wrap his fingers around the T-shaped "stick."

Inside the house, we engaged in more small talk about their collection of hand-crafted 18th- and 19th-century furniture and how they had found all the pieces while living in Vermont and Rhode Island when I was young.

We leafed through photo albums from those years, too. Each thick black sheet was covered with black-and-white images pasted down with silver-paper corners and labeled in white ink with Mama's precise schoolteacher printing.

Mama had set the dining table in her special-day-lunch style: a hand-embroidered white tablecloth and matching napkins, fresh flowers in a crystal vase, the sterling flatware that her not-rich-at-all Mississippi kinfolk had pooled their resources to buy for her Depression-era wedding gift, and the Rosenthal china that she and Daddy had purchased in Heidelberg.

Bernie made a special show of savoring the blended fragrances of Mama's masterfully fried chicken, her tangy Dijon green-bean casserole, her just-out-of-the-oven cornbread, her cut-fresh-that-morning coleslaw, and her homemade bread-and-butter pickles.

She filled the top plate on the stack in front of her with a plump half-breast of chicken and a scoop of beans and set it on the tablecloth in front of Bernie. "It's good to have you with us, Bernie," she said. "Martha's told us so much about you."

Bernie inhaled once more, extra luxuriously, looked up, and gave her his sweetest smile. "She's told me lots of good things about you, too."

As Mama served the remaining plates, Daddy passed a napkin-lined basket of cornbread with his usual urging to "butter your bread while it's hot."

We all had individual bowls of slaw and bread plates with curled pats of cold butter and tiny sterling butter knives that clinked against the plates as we put them to use.

Ice rattled when Daddy scooped sugar into his tall glass of tea and stirred it with a long-handled sterling spoon.

And then we all dug in.

Polite chatter focused on the burning issues of the day.

"What's been going on in Linden lately?" I asked my folks.

"How're your classes this fall?" my folks asked me.

"Tell us about your job at Hemenway's," they asked Bernie.

And so on and on.

But the inevitable moment arrived when Daddy hauled out his sternest top-dog voice and launched into the topic that I had been expecting and dreading since before we left Shreveport. "Margaret and I have been wondering what degree you hold and from what college."

Bernie responded quickly, smoothly, and in the worst way I ever could have imagined. "Oh, I've knocked around a bit in night school."

I was horrified. Couldn't even look at him.

That's exactly the kind of thing I tried to warn him not to say. Did he mean to say it in that frivolous way? Or was it just his mom's smart-mouth training coming out?

Silence fell like midnight in January in a New England graveyard, with all the warmth of owls lurking with eager ears and waiting wings and trenchant talons, alert for the sounds of small, hapless rodents scurrying under the snow.

As the silence lingered, I jumped in, trying to help. "Bernie served two years in the Army instead of going to college."

But that didn't help, of course, because—like those ravenous raptors—Daddy had no intention of relenting. "What rank?" he demanded.

"Buck private," Bernie said.

Silence.

"He's taking courses for credit at Centenary now, Daddy."

Silence.

After a while, Mama piped up with some fill-the-void facts that didn't help either. "Truman's been curious, Bernie, because last winter Martha dated an Air Force lieutenant, a pilot-in-training at Barksdale."

"I didn't know that." Bernie turned his head in my direction.

But I still couldn't look at him. "The lieutenant and I only dated for a few weeks, Mama. It's not worth bringing that up now."

She didn't take the hint. "But he had an Ivy League degree and a promising military future. There must be plenty more like him still around Barksdale."

My hackles rose at that, since another commanding officer was the last person I wanted in my life.

Throughout this awkward exchange, I recognized Daddy's game: to intimidate Bernie and chase him off, as he'd done so well with two of my high-school boyfriends whom he disapproved of.

Likewise, I recognized Mama's game: to make sure no male human ever came close enough to get me pregnant and ruin my life.

In the past, their games had worked, but now I was older, bolder, and savvier. I would pick my own path and partner going forward.

Chapter 9
His Lawfully Wedded Wife

January 1966 to January 1968

Hard as it may be to believe, my folks slowly accepted the reality that I loved Bernie and intended to marry him. But still, right up to our engagement, they pushed back. Daddy, in particular, often spoke of his disappointment.

"We hoped you'd bring home a smart pre-med student."

"That lieutenant would've given you such a good life."

"Oh, Bernie's smooth, for sure, but..." always followed by a shrug.

Nevertheless, we persisted.

One Saturday a month, Bernie and I drove to Linden and treated my folks to lunch at the bustling restaurant near Highway 59.

Afterward, back at their house, we did chores. Washed the windows. Waxed the furniture. Polished the silver. Mowed the grass. Pruned the crepe myrtles. We even got excited over Daddy's new hobby, a colony of bees in the hives that he'd built into the old garage beside our carport.

Later, as we relaxed over ice-cold bourbons and Coke and Daddy's luscious homemade hush puppies, we encouraged him to tell us of marching in his heavy wool uniform on the ROTC parade ground at LSU, through four scorching-hot Augusts in Baton Rouge in the '30s.

Or of his subsequent role as what was known then as a "Tree Soldier," a young officer leading a crew from President Franklin Roosevelt's Civilian Conservation Corps as they built new state parks in Louisiana's buggy swamps and Mississippi's hot-and-humid forests.

Or of wangling an invitation for Sunday dinner at the home of a cigar-chomping dignitary in the town of Clarksdale, Mississippi, where he wound up smitten with the man's college-grad niece, a beautiful girl named Margaret, whom he wooed for a year before finally marrying her.

Or of being delayed en route to their 1937 wedding because a tire went flat on some muddy road and he lacked a way to let Margaret know that, not only would he arrive late, but that he'd be filthy from changing the tire in the muck and greatly in need of a bath before tying the knot.

Or of serving in France, Holland, Belgium, and Germany as part of a deadly-to-the-Nazis tank-destroyer unit.

Likewise, we encouraged Mama to tell us of her own recently deceased parents, and also of growing up in Sledge with Brother, Sister, Frances, and C.C. as the children of that area's revered only doctor.

Or of her one precious year at Grenada College, before she had to leave for a cheaper state teachers college.

The first posed photo of Bernie and me together, in my parents' home in Linden, Texas, spring 1966

Or of those seemingly endless cross-country car trips that she and Daddy had made on two-lane roads in steamy summers and whiteout winters, many of them with a nursing baby or toddler Martha and stinky cloth diapers that had to be washed by hand in a bucket each night.

Gradually, the walls of parental opposition crumbled.

Mama even took the first posed picture of Bernie and me, all dressed up for a friend's wedding in Linden.

During World War II, as a young officer in that deadly-to-the-Nazis tank-destroyer unit, Daddy had seen terrible things. His presence at the 1945 liberation of the concentration camp at Dachau seared him forever.

So it's no surprise that, in those three postwar years when we drove all over Western Europe, he and Mama taught me that history matters, because its impact on the future never ends. They told me how Fascist, Nazi, and Communist dictators had murdered millions of innocent Jews, Gypsies, "intellectuals," and others. They insisted that one should defend such people when their lives are put at risk by forces beyond their control.

But even as I absorbed those lessons on hatred and cruelty in recent European history, there were ongoing issues back home in America that my parents could have enlightened me about but didn't. Specifically, that we and all previous generations of our extended families in Mississippi and Louisiana had been born into a white-supremacist culture that accepted and benefited from slavery, Jim Crow laws, and segregation.

As late as 1951, Mama's brother-in-law owned a sharecropping plantation with his brothers. I have memories from that year when I was five of visiting the shanties occupied by their Black tenant farmers. I was puzzled by the layers of old newspapers pasted inside the walls of their homes. Now I understand that was an effort to block the winter wind and insulate the occupants from the summer heat, but as a child I didn't know. Not until the '60s media attention focused on President Johnson's "War on Poverty" did I finally realize what I'd seen in those sad little shacks.

Despite my parents' fervent opposition to Fascism in Europe, they never supported the American civil rights movement. I suppose it just hit too close to home for them.

Something else that my folks failed to mention was the presence in America of radical racists and anti-Semites, including Mama's younger brother C.C., who from the late '50s on was a dues-paying member of the radically right-wing John Birch Society.

On June 9, 1966, a press photographer covering a civil rights march twenty miles from Mama's hometown of Sledge shot a closeup of C.C. haranguing the Rev. Dr. Martin Luther King, Jr., about theology, of all things. The caption identifies him as Carter Parnell, because he was named for his father, my grandfather. But this is my Uncle C.C.

Used with permission. Original caption:

Carter Parnell of Sledge, Mississippi in pith helmet, suggests to Dr. Martin Luther King that he should read the theological writings of Martin Luther in an encounter at the close of the day's Memphis-to-Jackson march near Como, Mississippi on June 9, 1966. Parnell proposed Christianity as a basis for understanding between African Americans and whites. (AP Photo)

Learning of that helped me solve the greatest mystery of my young life. It had to be C.C.'s sympathies for the Fascists and Nazis—which, apparently, he often expressed after the war—that caused the post-catfish feud between him and Daddy, the Nazi fighter.

Daddy hated the Nazis, whom C.C. never failed to praise. Mama loved her younger brother and tried to defend him, which drove a wedge between her and Daddy. By the time I was old enough to know what was going on, Mama was in the habit of throwing C.C.'s name up to Daddy whenever they had an argument… as if that would hurt him.

So finally, thanks to that AP photographer, six weeks before I turned twenty, I learned the identity of the "something bad" that had come between my parents when I was little. No question about it.

It wasn't the Curse of the Catfish, and it wasn't me. It was C.C.

One Friday afternoon in that same spring of 1966, Bernie and I drove to the New Orleans suburb of Kenner for my first meeting with his family. A power outage had shut off the lights and air conditioning, but still, in her dark apartment, Minnie Marks graciously welcomed me with a flashlight and settled me into her guest bedroom. Bernie's sister Rozanne was a decade younger than Bernie, but just two years behind me, so we easily became friends.

The next day, Bernie and I joined his brother Murray for lunch in the French Quarter. They were close in age and had a warm relationship.

Even though I was officially a double-major, German was my main interest, due to those formative years in Heidelberg. For me, Spanish was just something I'd studied in high school and learned to speak reasonably well on family trips to Mexico and Guatemala.

I had signed up for a junior-year-abroad program in Germany, but as the fall of 1966 approached, my love for Bernie led me to cancel it, because I feared I'd lose him if I left for ten months.

Cancelling that trip was my first big bet on Bernie, with impacts that seemed minor then but gained significance over time. For one thing, it set a precedent of my sacrificing for him something that would have meant a lot to me. For another, it kept me from completely mastering German, thereby depriving me of the full range of benefits of that major. "But," as Yeats had written a century earlier, "I was young and foolish."

In December 1966, on our second trip together to New Orleans, over dinner at Commander's Palace—which Bernie called his "favorite restaurant in the whole wide world," as if he actually had seen the whole wide world—he proposed to me with a one-carat diamond, unset, so I could choose my own rings. Five seconds later, I said yes.

The next weekend, we drove to Linden so Bernie could formally ask Daddy for my hand in marriage. Five minutes later, Daddy—who later told us he greatly appreciated what he called Bernie's "proper, traditional approach, as opposed to eloping"—also said yes.

In January 1967, based on Hemenway's retail sales growth, a furniture manufacturer awarded the company a two-week junket for two people to Austria and Switzerland. Bernie's bosses gave him the trip, as their way of acknowledging the impact of his remarkably good marketing plan.

Bernie in Lucerne, Switzerland, 1967

If we had been married, I could have skipped classes and gone with him, but no '60s girl who valued her reputation would travel abroad with a man she was not related to.

Instead, I spent two months teaching Bernie conversational German to help him enjoy his first European travel experience, only to kiss him goodbye that spring as he left to enjoy it in the company of strangers from other companies while I stayed on campus. Oh, the irony.

Not once in the nearly three years that Bernie and I dated did he try to pressure me into sex. Unlike some guys in high school or during my first year in college, he never groped under my skirt or drove me to dark parking lots or pinned me down in his car. He was willing to wait for marriage, he said, and we did, even though that meant he ultimately had to teach his bride a lot.

Such mores were starting to feel old-fashioned even then, given that our dating years coincided with some of the greatest social upheavals of the twentieth century. But for a girl raised by a prim-and-proper Mississippi mama, it was the right approach.

Throughout our dating years and the first year of our marriage, Bernie took me to Shreveport Symphony concerts and visiting opera productions. I reciprocated with tickets to well-done student productions at Centenary's Marjorie Lyons Playhouse and recitals by its world-touring choir.

We also went to movies in the kind of big, free-standing, single-feature theaters that made every new release feel significant. Dressing for dinner and a show was the way to go.

Fabulous films from those years included *The Sound of Music* ('65), *A Man for All Seasons* ('66), *The Graduate* ('67), and *2001: A Space Odyssey* ('68). We saw and loved those shows and many more that were every bit as good.

Thanks to the three summers' worth of courses that I'd taken at Centenary, I completed my degree requirements and student teaching in December 1967 and then could focus on planning our wedding.

Without complaint, Bernie accompanied me to two counseling sessions with the pastor of our church, which seemed appropriate given that we were asking him to administer our vows, bless our union, and sign our certificate of marriage. I knew my dear fiancé considered it just one more hoop to jump through, but his willingness to do so improved Mama's opinion of him, and mine, too.

I appreciated the gracious way our pastor welcomed Bernie and his family to the Linden Methodist Church, and how he celebrated our love and only in the gentlest way warned us of potential problems that might lurk in even a nominally interfaith, interethnic marriage.

Likewise, I learned even more than I cared to about my Uncle C.C. when he refused to come to our wedding. Knowing by then what I did about him, I was glad he didn't attend.

As I had told Bernie early on, my parents were WASPs to the core. Their ancestors were WASPs. Their extended families were WASPs. Their closest friends were WASPs. Those friends' kids, with whom I'd spent much of my childhood, were WASPs. Even my yearly "classroom pals" were WASPs. Our destiny was to graduate from WASPy colleges, find WASPy spouses, produce WASPy kids, build WASPy careers, and keep living WASPy lives until we died. That's what was expected of us.

By marrying the Jewish man I loved, I would make a radical break with centuries of my family's traditions, culture, and religion.

Previously, I had promised myself that I would never get pregnant or marry a commanding-officer type of guy.

Now, mere days before my wedding, I made three more important promises to myself.

First, that I would do everything in my power to make sure that Bernie and I never fell into the pattern of fighting that had afflicted my parents' marriage for as long as I could remember.

Second, that nobody would ever hear me complain about Bernie as Mama and Daddy had complained about each other to me.

Third, that if any Nazi, Fascist, or Communist ever came to power in America, I would protect Bernie. I would use my very WASPiness to defend my Jewish husband from any murderous dictator who might set up a death camp like Dachau.

I never forgot those promises and consciously made an effort to keep the first and second ones throughout our marriage.

During the 1967 Christmas season and beyond, the planned arrival in Linden of a Jewish family for a wedding at the Methodist Church caused the local hot-pot of gossip to boil over. It's safe to say that both our families approached the day with trepidation.

To be sure, Minnie Marks would have preferred that her first-born son marry a nice Jewish girl in a New Orleans synagogue with all their family and friends in attendance. But she did tell Bernie how sad she was that his father Sid wasn't still alive and able to attend his son's wedding.

I never learned what Minnie's talks were like with Bernie and Rozanne, both of whom already had met my folks. I do suspect that their discussions resembled those taking place in our home, where Daddy would ask me variations of a single question: "What's she like?" And by "she," of course, he meant Minnie.

Even though I knew how horrified Daddy had been at the Nazis' brutality to European Jews, and even though I'd never heard him utter an anti-Semitic slur, I also suspected that he harbored old stereotypes. He would want to be able to enjoy the company of all the members of our extended family and may have been influenced by unflattering portrayals of Jewish people from New York.

Each time he asked "What's she like?," I gave him the same answer. "Minnie is delightful. I like her a lot, and you will, too."

On a balmy east-Texas Friday afternoon in January, an unlikely mix of people gathered to rehearse in our church sanctuary.

The pastor coached those of us with speaking parts.

For some reason, Bernie seemed determined to insert the western-movie cliché word "lawfully" into his vow to take me as his wedded wife. He kept stumbling over the line, saying "my *lawfully* wedded wife" despite snickers and giggles from the rest of us.

Finally, after Bernie seemed to have that line down right, the pastor walked three more participants through their roles and responsibilities: Daddy to escort me down the aisle and give me away; Best Man Murray to safeguard our rings; and my dear final roommate at Centenary, whose job as my maid of honor was to keep me from tripping over my train.

That evening, Mama and Daddy finally met Minnie at the Excelsior House Hotel, known as the "Oldest Hotel in Texas," which had operated non-stop since 1858 in the Jay Gould-era railroad town of Jefferson, Texas. Members of both our families were staying there.

Daddy turned on the country-boy charm for which he was known everywhere except in the bosom of his immediate family and beamed as I introduced him to my soft-spoken, well dressed, and congenial mother-in-law-to-be. "Hello, Minnie! Margaret and I are glad to meet you at last."

Minnie accepted his handshake and beamed back. "Truman, I think you're the tallest man I've ever known."

Then, naturally, she and Mama exchanged warm hugs.

After that, Bernie and I enjoyed dinner with our parents, siblings, aunts, uncles, cousins, and friends who had come from Sledge, Many, New Orleans, and Shreveport to celebrate our union. Champagne would have been *de rigueur* almost anywhere outside east Texas, but we toasted with the locally preferred beverage. Sweet tea.

Back at home after the rehearsal dinner, on my last night as an unmarried woman, Daddy gave me an enormous smile.

"She's charming," he said.

"I told you so," I said.

During our wedding in the Linden Methodist Church's sun-bright, blossom-filled, and jam-packed sanctuary, Bernie swore to take me as his *lawfully* wedded wife, at which point those of us who had been at the rehearsal, including the pastor, exchanged subdued glances and silent, secret smiles.

And so, on January 27, 1968, I made the biggest and best bet of my life by marrying Bernard Louis Marks. In doing that, I gained not only a husband, a lover, and a soulmate but also the one thing I had missed most throughout my childhood.

A best friend.

Truman and Margaret Alford; Martha and Bernie Marks; Minnie, Murray, and Rozanne Marks in the Linden Methodist Church, 1968

PART II

BETTING ON BERNIE IN WORK AND ART

Chapter 10
Uprooting and Transplanting

1968–1969

We honeymooned at the Bourbon Orleans Hotel in the French Quarter of New Orleans, which wasn't new to Bernie but still felt exotic and fun for me. The hotel was gorgeous and two years new, despite being built into the walls of a structure that predated the War of 1812 and once was destroyed by fire.

After that, as we settled into a brand-new, one-bedroom, one-bath apartment in Shreveport, with the wildly popular wall-to-wall shag carpet in the '60s top color, avocado green, I began learning to cook in my own way. Determined to make a healthier variety of meals—less fried, more fresh—and perhaps as a show of independence from Mama, I turned to printed materials. Bernie cheerfully played the role of guinea pig, eating my experiments with recipes gleaned from wedding-gift cookbooks and store-bought food magazines.

Sometime that year, also with Bernie's approval, I set out to "fix" his pronunciation of contractions. We began by exaggerating the number of syllables, then pulling back. Deliberately, we turned *D'n't you?* into a super-stuttery *Didididn't you?* and then into *Dididn't you?* and finally into *Didn't you?* We turned *W'n't you?* into *Wouldidididn't you?* and then into *Wouldidn't you?* and finally into *Wouldn't you?* And so on.

Soon, Bernie became a standard speaker of American English, and the wannabe language teacher in me was pleased.

Bernie and me with Daddy on the day I graduated from Centenary College, June 1968

Throughout 1968, in contrast to the domestic tranquility in the new Marks household in Shreveport, civil disorder was spreading elsewhere.

Two months after our marriage, the April 4 murder of Dr. Martin Luther King Jr. provoked conflagrations in cities across the country.

The June 6 murder of presidential candidate Bobby Kennedy led to similar protests and even more political chaos.

In August, following the Los Angeles police's brutal beating of a Black man, that city erupted in what became known as the Watts Race Riot. Similar events occurred in Chicago and Detroit. Also in August, the Chicago cops' skull-smashing assault on anti-war protestors at the Democratic National Convention further damaged the image of that city.

In September, on the Atlantic City boardwalk, activists from the Women's Liberation Movement held a noisy march during the Miss America pageant. They offered a "freedom trash can" into which the "libbers" dumped their no-longer-wanted wigs, curlers, false eyelashes, bras, girdles, and issues of magazines such as *Cosmopolitan*, *Ladies' Home Journal*, *Family Circle*, and the like.

College students engaged in "sit ins" to protest the Vietnam War.

The counterculture was in full swing, but I was too busy learning to be a wife to get involved in it.

I turned twenty-two that summer—smack in the middle of the greatest social and political turmoil since the Civil War—and registered to vote. My parents and Bernie were Republicans, so what else could I be?

And that's how I lucked into the opportunity to cast my first-ever presidential ballot for the astoundingly awful ticket of Richard Nixon and Spiro Agnew. While both were later shown to be total crooks, at the time they offered themselves as moderate, fiscally responsible, law-and-order candidates matching the center-right philosophy that I'd grown up with.

Throughout 1968, I was happier than ever before, and Bernie seemed to be, too. Otherwise, it was one helluva year to start out.

That December, I surreptitiously bought a small tree stand, a single string of multicolored lights, a set of cheap plastic Santa ornaments, a six-pack of bright glass balls, a box of little metal hangers, and a package of long, silvery "icicles." I picked up store-made cookies and a quart of refrigerated eggnog in which not a single drop of alcohol swam. Shreveport was part of the Bible Belt, after all. (But still, I knew we'd enjoy a delicious homemade version with good Kentucky bourbon when we visited my folks on Christmas Day.)

Then, on the Saturday before Christmas, I coaxed Bernie into going tree shopping with me. We brought home a fragrant little pine, and once it stood upright in our apartment, I showed him how to decorate it.

At first, he went along just to humor me, but then he found himself enjoying the novel experience. We laughed a lot. Clowned around. Had loads of fun. Wound up with something that brightened our living room to the end of the year. (And with that, we launched our own non-religious, nearly lifelong holiday tradition of choosing and decorating a tree as we sipped nicely spiked eggnog and ate homemade cookies.)

Early in 1969, Bernie and I began to contemplate the possibility of life beyond Shreveport. With all the wisdom of our youth, we put two cities, New York and Chicago, on our too-big, too-cold, too-dangerous, we-won't-ever-move-there blacklist.

It's not hard to imagine what happened next.

Bernie spotted an ad in the *Wall Street Journal*. The Bloomberg Furniture Company—a century-old, family-owned chain of stores located throughout Illinois and Wisconsin, with its corporate headquarters in the lakefront town of Waukegan, Illinois—was seeking an experienced advertising and marketing manager.

Four successful years at Hemenway's qualified Bernie for the position, so he sent his application and secured an interview. A week later, he flew to Chicago's O'Hare International Airport, drove north to Waukegan, and hit it off well with the people he met there. That night, on an expensive operator-assisted, long-distance phone call, we discussed the situation and agreed he should take the job.

The next morning, he accepted Bloomberg's offer.

A week later, we flew together into O'Hare, suffered sticker shock while searching for an affordable place to live, and ended up renting a minuscule apartment in the far-northern suburb of Northbrook.

One day in April, after the movers had picked up our stuff in Shreveport, we went to Linden for lunch. My parents had no standing to object to our departure, since they'd done the same to their own parents decades earlier. But still, it had to be hard to watch their only child move so far away. After teary good-byes and urgings to take care and write often, Bernie and I headed north through Texarkana and into Arkansas.

Bernie drove his burgundy-colored Mustang, and I drove the white Plymouth Satellite that my folks had given me in the fall of 1967, when I started student teaching. (At the time, Bernie and I had laughed at the slogan used to market that car: "For the midsize coupe driver with the heart of a devil." We wondered if there was some reason why my folks had chosen that particular model for me.)

So there we went, a woman of twenty-two and her thirty-year-old husband on a two-car, four-day, thousand-mile journey. Credit cards were rare then, but we each carried cash and traveler's checks. Both cars had air conditioning, bucket seats, power steering, power brakes, and AM radios but lacked seat belts. We cranked the windows open by hand.

Former President Eisenhower's Interstate Highway System was far from finished, so we mostly took roads that forced us to a crawl as we passed through the heart—and before the eyes of the deputy sheriff—of every tiny town on the way. Speed traps were common, time-consuming, and expensive.

Our sole navigational tool was a folded paper map that I had marked our route on in red pencil. As we crossed Arkansas and Missouri on our way to southern Illinois—with me navigating in front and Bernie following—we succeeded in maintaining visual contact.

Only in St. Louis traffic did we get separated. Thanks to a previous just-in-case agreement, we met up at a park near the newly built Gateway Arch. After that, the Mustang never disappeared from my rear-view mirror, and the big Bernie grin that I loved flashed every time he pulled close enough to wave at me.

Chain lodgings were scarce and reservations hard to make, so late each afternoon, if I spotted a promising-looking motor-hotel—a term fast turning into "motel"—I pulled over, and we both went in for a look-see.

Gas stations charged 30¢ a gallon while providing full windshield-washing, headlight-cleaning, and oil-checking service by a cordial, uniformed attendant who accepted cash and mentally calculated the change at the pump. The stations also provided free maps, navigational guidance, clean restrooms, vending machines, and repair shops. Mileage in both our cars was terrible and the gas was leaded, so we unwittingly polluted the air all the way to Northbrook, where our tiny new home awaited.

In that sweet spring of 1969, settling into a fast-growing village filled with other young couples, kids, dogs, cats, and Schwinn bicycles (which we soon bought, too), we began creating a new life for ourselves.

Somehow, Bernie managed to make room in our kitchen for a small drawing table and a stool. Others might have real tables and chairs in their kitchens. Not us. But it was a good tradeoff, since that was where he began honing his natural artistic talent.

Each weekday, he drove half an hour north from our apartment to the large, multistory Bloomberg Building, located near the Lake Michigan waterfront in Waukegan. Like Hemenway's owners in Shreveport in 1965, Bloomberg's owners in 1969 were making their own bet on a young man they'd never heard of until he responded to their ad. Unbeknownst to him at the time, they were starting to be battered by financial storms and may have counted a bit too much on their new advertising-and-marketing guru to calm the turbulent waters.

We liked living in Northbrook—near the Edens Expressway and almost perfectly in the middle between Waukegan and Chicago—because it was an easy drive to both cities in about the same amount of time.

Our appetite for unusual foods lured us to Chicago's famous ethnic neighborhoods, where generations of newcomers from the American South, Italy, Mexico, Greece, China, Russia, Poland, Ethiopia, Pakistan, India, Peru, Chile, and elsewhere had arrived, lived, worked, and died.

We also dove into cultural treasures like the Art Institute of Chicago, Shedd Aquarium, Field Museum of Natural History, Museum of Science and Industry, and Chicago Symphony. When my folks came for their first visit that summer, we gave them a good tour.

We became regulars at a '50s-vintage bar in Northbrook, which over time became our go-to place to celebrate and mourn. Charlie Beinlich's Tavern—whose sign on the door proclaimed, "Food served for the convenience of our drinking customers"—wasn't one to coddle its clientele. No waiting room. No reservations. No printed menu. No listed

Daddy's photo of Bernie, Mama, and me—with the year-old John Hancock Tower, the second tallest in the world at that time, appearing to grow out of my head—on my folks' first visit to Chicago, summer 1969

prices. No credit. No coffee. No dessert. Just the best shrimp cocktails and cheeseburgers on Earth.

Every Saturday night, alone or with friends, we'd queue up outside in the cold or heat, waiting for a table or seats at the bar where Charlie's bartender/son-in-law kept a friendly eye on things.

We always ordered the same items. Two beers for Bernie. Two whiskey sours for me. Two large shrimp cocktails with a tangy horseradish sauce. Two cheeseburgers deluxe with grilled onions, fries, and creamy slaw. Before departing, Bernie would leave a $20 bill in full payment for all that fabulous food and drink, including tax and tip.

Not long after we arrived in Chicagoland—a common local term that includes the city, Cook County, and its five collar counties—we adopted a black-and-white tuxedo kitten whom we named José Gato and soon taught to lift his right paw for a handshake. One of our neighbors quipped that it was like living next door to a friendly used-car salesman.

José Gato turned out to be a superb icebreaker, because almost all our new friends loved shaking hands with him.

On weekends that summer, after Bernie assembled a watercolor kit, we started exploring still-rural Lake County, just north of Northbrook, and even-more-bucolic Wisconsin

José Gato ("Joe Cat")

just a bit farther on. As he learned to paint marshes, lakes, streams, hills, barns and farms with flocks or herds of animals, I'd hike the new-to-me natural habitats—oak-hickory woodlands and the rivers and streams that ran through them—trying to ID birds, trees, tracks, and scat as Daddy had taught me.

Despite all those different ways we found to have fun, the spring and summer of 1969 were not a pure delight for me. I spent frustrating weeks on end seeking a public high-school teaching position in German or Spanish. At the time, I possessed a BA from a college that most

Illinois school personnel hadn't heard of, plus a license to teach in Louisiana. What I didn't have was any real teaching experience, a license for Illinois, or an advanced degree.

Focusing my search on the northern suburbs, where each city, large town, or group of villages ran its own school district, I made the rounds, asking for interviews. All I got was advice: "Come back when you have a master's degree or three years of teaching experience. Even better, come with both."

Grad school was out of the question. I couldn't afford it. Needed to earn money. Gain experience. Build a résumé. So I turned to the classified job postings in the *Chicago Tribune*.

Toward the end of May, a large international corporation on Chicago's North Shore ran an ad for a bilingual English-Spanish secretary. I had zero secretarial training. Zero ability to take dictation. Zero knowledge of world trade. But I did have a degree in Spanish and—thanks to Daddy—was an accurate typist, so I applied and got both an interview and the job, starting June first.

Bernie and I celebrated that evening at Charlie Beinlich's.

Southpaw Bernie learning to paint in watercolors in Wisconsin, fall 1969

Unfortunately, it became clear that I wasn't cut out for the life of a secretary, bilingual or otherwise. Confinement in a gray-walled cubicle for long, tedious hours at a stretch wasn't my thing. But still, I was earning money, gaining experience, and building a résumé, so I stuck with it.

Early in August, a woman who taught Spanish at nearby Notre Dame High School for Boys (NDHS) arrived as a temp worker, filling in for someone on vacation. We soon became friends.

"I want out of this job," I confided on her last day there. "Do you know of any opening, anywhere, for a teacher of German or Spanish?"

She shook her head. "Schools are all fully staffed by now."

Which, of course, I already knew.

And then she left.

The next Monday, she phoned me. "Our dean of men died suddenly a few days ago. One of the Spanish teachers will take his place, so we have an unexpected opening. Classes start in one week. I told our chairman about you. He'd like to interview you at seven tomorrow evening."

I took a few moments to ponder the multiple fickle fingers of fate that for some reason or other had chosen to beckon in my direction, leading to an amazing turn of events.

And then I grabbed that fortuitous, out-of-the-blue, heaven-sent, windfall opportunity with both hands. "I'll be there," I said.

Chapter 11

Our Journey Continues

1969–1974

Bernie drove me to Notre Dame High School for Boys and waited in the Mustang. An hour later, I popped back in, squealing with joy. "Got the job, starting Monday!"

He said nothing. Didn't even congratulate me.

So I went on. "You'll never believe where this priest grew up."

"Where?"

"Jefferson, Texas. His home church is blocks from the hotel where we had our rehearsal dinner. And he knows all about Centenary. Said he'd be honored to have a Centenary grad join his department faculty."

Bernie remained silent, not sharing my enthusiasm, as I kept on. "He teaches French, so he couldn't interview me in Spanish, but he said if my Spanish is good enough for a big, international company, it's good enough for him. Which means, my miserable summer wasn't a waste at all."

"Is an all-boy Catholic school a good fit for you?"

"As good as anything I see right now. I'll get paid. Gain experience."

"Does this guy—"

"This priest."

"Does he know you've never taught a day of class all by yourself?"

"He's desperate. Needs a Spanish teacher by Monday."

"Does he know you're not Catholic?"

"Yep, and he doesn't care."

"What if he tries to convert you?"

Betting on Bernie   119

I cackled. "Good luck with that."

The priest emerged and headed to his car. He spotted me and waved. I waved back, but Bernie didn't.

Instead, he exhaled noisily. "How many classes?"

"Three first years, one second, plus a study hall."

"Four teaching classes a day? How many kids?"

"About forty each."

Bernie's jaw dropped. "That's a whole lotta testosterone."

"I want this job, Babe."

"Why not sleep on it? Call him tomorrow with your final answer."

"I already accepted. Can't weasel out now." Bernie's concerns were valid, and I knew it, but fear of typing in a gray-walled cubicle until my hair turned a matching shade was a powerful incentive to make the change. "I'll aim for three years, then look elsewhere."

"A more likely scenario is, you'll run screaming out that door long before the last day of class next spring. Either that or they'll boot you out at midterm and turn those boys over to an experienced Catholic teacher."

Bernie assumed I would fail miserably. I set out to prove him wrong.

On Wednesday morning, I gave a too-short, two-day notice at work.

On Friday morning, as one of the new teachers at an orientation session at NDHS, I barely contained my excitement.

On Saturday evening, Bernie and I attended a faculty party at the school. It was the first for either of us in a Roman Catholic setting, but the priests and lay teachers welcomed us warmly, even though—or, more likely, because—they knew we were "different." Wine flowed. A young priest played old favorites by ear on a piano as the rest of us sang along. I even interjected a bit of Methodist church-choir harmony.

Everyone asked where I'd gone to college.

"Centenary," I told everyone.

"Oh, St. Mary," everyone said. "That's such a good school."

On Sunday, I pored over the two Spanish-language textbooks that I would begin using for my lessons the next morning.

On Monday morning—less than a month after my twenty-third birthday—I arrived early, eager for my first day as an actual teacher.

On Monday evening—one hundred and sixty students and forty study-hall attendees later—Bernie hauled me off to Charlie Beinlich's for a serious de-stressing session.

My take-home pay for the 1969-70 school year was $500 a month, $6,000 a year. It was a rookie-female teacher's salary at a parochial school, less than I'd have earned typing in my cubicle, but I didn't care. It opened the door to the career I craved.

Thanks to my parents' generosity and lifelong lessons in frugality, I had no college debt, the Plymouth Satellite was mine free and clear, and my personal needs were few. But still, to save a bit, I bought a sewing machine and began making my own clothes. Yearbook photos from NDHS show me in homemade dresses. Fortunately, I was young enough to look good in anything.

The only boys I'd known growing up were reasonably well-behaved cousins, classmates, boyfriends, neighbors, and my parents' friends' sons. I knew them all as individuals, too, not as masses with a herd mentality.

At NDHS, that changed fast.

Likewise, few of my students had experience with anyone like me. Most came from Catholic grade schools where, in their telling anyway, every teacher was a ruler-rapping, black-habited harridan. They didn't see brightly dressed, early-twenties, non-nun females as authority figures.

Complicating things was the fact that 1969 was only the second year that women served on the NDHS faculty. There were five of us that fall, up from three the year before. Needless to say, we were objects of great curiosity and amusement.

Betting on Bernie

The new dean of men—the same disciplinarian whose classes I had inherited—was a stern fellow who always had taken on the school's "known troublemakers," voluntarily accepting them into his freshman and sophomore classes. They were afraid of him, but not of me.

One of my classrooms, designed for typing courses, was wider than it was deep and equipped with long tables instead of desks. Doors on the two ends offered students an easy exit whenever I turned in the opposite direction. Not a day passed when the dean of men didn't haul in three, four, or more escapees. "These appear to be yours," he'd say in a tone that suggested I needed to be a whole lot more fearsome.

Once, in a different classroom, a door at the back opened and a tire rolled in, apparently of its own volition. When questioned, none of the hall monitors reported seeing anyone carrying a tire through the school.

That evening, when I told Bernie about the curious little episode, he grinned, raised his hands, and exclaimed, "It's a miracle!"

Then there was the delicate matter of bathroom logistics.

When NDHS was built, nobody had imagined a day when women would teach there. So if I needed to "go" at the end of a class, I had five minutes after the bell rang to grab my personal items, extricate myself from my classroom, sprint down hormone-heavy hallways, zip around corners, traverse the lobby, and scoot upstairs to one of the two stalls provided for female office staff... only to retrace my steps in hopes of arriving before the next bell, because if I didn't I would encounter chaos in the classroom.

Alternatively, I might beat a path to the gym, where the thoughtful architect had provided a restroom for women attending basketball games.

Both routes presented an obstacle course for a young female plowing through packed passageways as kissing sounds, romantic suggestions, and crude catcalls like "Hope you didn't forget to wipe!" rose from anonymous masses of male mouths.

Usually, if I arrived late from that five-minute trot to the bathroom, I'd find a roomful of rambunctious rapscallions sailing paper airplanes, banging chalk-covered felt blackboard erasers on the heads of the smallest kids, and yelling out the windows at passersby on the sidewalk.

But on one particular day, I stepped into a still room. Every boy was seated and silent. Not a single aircraft or eraser flew through the air.

My antennae began twitching.

And then, as I walked between the rows toward the front, a faint whisper rose to my ear. "Don't sit down."

The words were barely there, and I didn't reply, but I did catch them. So I set my purse on the desk and pulled out the chair, where lay a grungy, dead mouse. At that moment, for sure, someone—or more than one someone—was hoping that I'd sit on it and scream and faint.

But I had been warned, and I was ready.

I reached down, lifted the pathetic creature by its tail, and turned toward forty freshmen faces. Smiling and dangling it before their wide eyes, I slowly walked back down the aisle and into the hallway, where I hailed a passing custodian to dispose of it.

Word spread that I was tougher than I looked, and nothing like that ever happened to me again.

Students in all first- and second-year language classes were required to pass the first semester before going on to the second semester. So early in December, the academic dean requested the names of students whom I did not expect to pass.

I went to his office with a list of thirty, most of them from my first-year freshman classes. That large number boggled even my own mind. I couldn't imagine what the dean would say about it. And then I sat there, expecting to be fired on the spot, as he scanned my list. After what seemed eternity, he looked up and said, "No new teacher should have been stuck with all those troublemakers. I'll find other courses for them next semester."

Betting on Bernie

As students returned to classes in January 1970 and observed all those empty seats, my time of sharing comedian Rodney Dangerfield's famous lament—"I don't get no respect"—was over. Even the hordes in the hallways behaved better when I moved through.

Higher-ups noted the improvement, too. Toward the end of the second semester, they renewed my contract and gave me a raise. Bernie proclaimed it another miracle and took me to dinner at Charlie's.

Also in 1970, with a job in hand, I decided to pursue a master's in Spanish. I applied to the Department of Spanish and Portuguese at Northwestern University (NU) and was accepted into a two-year, part-time program designed for teachers, which I would finish in June 1972.

This time, I proudly paid my own way through.

Bernie decided to take a year of Spanish at Northwestern, too. I was delighted, since two Spanish speakers would be better than one on the trips we planned to make in coming years. He signed up for beginning

Bernie and me in the kitchen of our tiny apartment in Northbrook, hosting our first-ever party, New Year's Eve, 1970

Spanish, for credit. The class met on the same Tuesday and Thursday evenings as mine did, so over the next three quarters we'd eat supper at home, then practice our Spanish driving all the way to the NU campus in Evanston and back. By June 1971, he'd earned nine credits on top of the six from Centenary.

Bernie and me sharing a comically oversized chair at a furniture show, 1971

After my summer 1971 courses ended at NU and before my NDHS classes began, we left José Gato in the care of a cat-loving neighbor and flew to Mexico to put our Spanish to use on our memorable first foreign trip together. Bernie wowed me with how fluent he'd become.

We spent a few nights in a hotel on Mexico City's main square, the Zócalo, and explored on foot the historic Chapultepec park, castle, and anthropological museum. Bernie painted picnicking families and balloon sellers, producing watercolors that he would sell the next summer at North Shore art festivals. A public bus took us to Teotihuacán, the famous archeological site, where we walked the long Avenue of the Dead and climbed both the Pyramid of the Moon and the Pyramid of the Sun. That was hot and tiring, but we had the youthful energy to do it.

The best memory of our stay in Mexico City was dinner in a restaurant named *Blanco y Negro* ("Black and White"), where we were the only gringos. After the jolly crowd of tequila-sipping patrons discovered that we spoke Spanish, they competed to recommend their favorite dishes and chatted nonstop with us as we ate. When we finished and rose to leave, our waiter shook Bernie's hand and said in unexpectedly good English, "You two are young and charming. We all hope you have fun in *México*."

And we did have fun as Bernie drove a rented car to colonial towns like Guanajuato and Taxco, where groups gathered in the streets to watch him sketch, thereby stimulating conversations that we benefited from and enjoyed.

Me in Taxco, Mexico, 1971

One clear night, under a couple million stars at a rooftop eatery on the still-unspoiled coast north of Acapulco, we ordered *paella*, which was newly popular at home but traditional there. Served "for two," the dish consisted of four huge prawns with their eye stalks and antennae still attached, lounging atop a steaming bed of *bomba* rice and chicken in a round pan. I suppressed my natural urge to squeal *"ew"* as all eight eyes of our dinner gazed up at us… and instead set about savoring their succulent, spicy flavor, nicely enhanced by gentle breezes off the sea.

And then, before heading back home to Chicagoland, we briefly air-hopped to Guatemala City and spent two nights at an inn in historic Antigua, the centuries-old original Spanish provincial capital. Getting there involved creatively painted "chicken buses," whose local passengers

Bernie in Acapulco, Mexico, 1971

either carried onboard cages of fancy-feathered fowl or stashed them in the roof rack. We laughed and swapped witticisms with people and poultry alike.

On repeated visits to Mexico and Guatemala—with my parents in the '60s and with Bernie in the '70s—I felt no threat or hostility. Driving country roads and riding local buses seemed safe. Locals like those we met at *Blanco y Negro* and on the lively chicken buses appreciated that we spoke Spanish and left us with happy memories. They welcomed our money but didn't steal it. Nobody threatened us with guns or anything else. Truly, those were the good ol' days.

In the spring of 1972, at the end of my third year at NDHS and the completion of my MA, the priest who had hired me retired. The administration promoted me to be department chair, making me both the first woman and the first non-Catholic in such a position there. With a reduced teaching load and control of class assignments, I passed my freshmen on to someone else and happily taught the upper-level courses.

Best of all, Bernie had to admit that I had succeeded far beyond his expectations.

Meanwhile, he was taking full advantage of the many growth opportunities that a chain of stores offered, maturing in the related fields of advertising and marketing, building a superb reputation, and making good friends and valuable contacts. Around the same time, after his mother, brother, and sister moved north to live and work near us, we began hosting very-cozy holiday meals with them and my parents.

The first Thanksgiving dinner I ever made, 1972
(Clockwise from left: Daddy, Minnie, Murray, Bernie, Mama, and Rozanne)

In 1973, Bernie and I took our first European trip together, visiting Rome, Venice, and Dubrovnik, the medieval "Pearl of the Adriatic" in what was then communist-ruled Yugoslavia.

For that final stop, we stayed in Cavtat, a town near Dubrovnik on the lovely Dalmatian Coast. Every evening, we'd walk to seaside bars to try their local wines and the catch of the day and chat with fellow barflies. Few spoke English and none Spanish, so we muddled along in German.

My photo of Cavtat, Yugoslavia, 1973

As 1974 drew near, I found myself antsy, at a crossroads, and running out of time to change course. After five years at NDHS, I probably could stay until retirement: earning a decent salary, running the department, educating endless waves of teenage boys, teaching the college-bound kids in the upper-level classes, and tumbling into tedium.

Or I could gamble on my longtime dream of teaching college. Leaving NDHS for doctoral studies would reduce our income for years to come, which was especially risky given Bernie's employer's unstable financial situation and a serious national stagflation recession.

I would be risking more than money, too. Job security was a concern. Tenure-track college positions were difficult to get and keep. Non-tenure track jobs were commonplace, insecure, and notoriously low-paying. PhDs in all fields—a dime a dozen, according to the media—were forced to trot from one spot to another without an office anywhere. And even if one managed to secure a tenure-track position, waiting six years for the yes/no retention decision made it hard to put down roots. Few got a second bite of that apple either, since not achieving tenure could leave you branded as "too old" or "a failure" or both.

Then there was the already-significant educational gap between Bernie and me. How would he react if I chose to widen it?

But still, I had been to the academic mountain and taken a few steps up its steep slope. I'd glimpsed what lay at the top and knew that was the career I wanted.

Bernie and José Gato, 1974

For weeks, Bernie and I discussed the idea. We didn't argue, so those conversations were amiable. In the end, he gave me his blessing to trust my gut and follow my heart. "If that's what you want, Kid," he said, "go for it. We'll make it work."

So in March 1974, once accepted into Northwestern's doctoral program, I gave NDHS plenty of advance notice of my departure.

Full-time studies starting that fall would, in theory at least, lead me to a PhD in the spring of 1978, at the age of 31. And so, beginning in September 1974, I earned my tuition and a small stipend as a teaching assistant.

Chapter 12

The Proudest Days of Our Lives

1975–1981

From childhood on, Bernie's path forward was unclear. He was artistically talented and academically lazy. His parents lacked the knowledge, resources, and motivation to help him reach his potential, so they let him drift. He didn't know or care about that until he saw all the ways that my parents had boosted me.

Once we married, he set aside his dream of becoming a fine artist and got serious about earning a living. High on his wish list was owning a business, but he had no idea what it might be.

By the mid '70s, he'd only worked at old-style furniture stores. He knew that academic training and credentials would help him step up into more-modern companies and, for the first time, he admitted that his lack of a degree might hold him back. But he was in his late thirties, needed to work, and couldn't take years off to go to college full-time.

So, while I was on track to finish my doctorate, Bernie still had no prospect of earning his bachelor's degree. During our dating years, my parents had been the only ones concerned with our educational gap. But as I kept climbing the academic ladder, that gap became the elephant in our living room.

One spring day in 1975, the *Chicago Tribune* ran an article on the Executive Program, or XP, at the University of Chicago's top-rated Booth School of Business. It was a two-year course meant for mid-career professionals seeking to earn an MBA. What made it special was that students didn't have to quit work to attend. Classes met on alternate Saturdays, and students teamed up in study groups on evenings and weekends in between to master the material together.

According to the article, the typical XP participant already had a bachelor's degree or higher and was successful at some level of business, including legal and medical practices. Bernie didn't fit the degree part of that description, but one sentence suggested an alternative route. Individuals with qualifying work experience who lacked a degree might still be admitted to the XP if they scored well enough on the Graduate Management Admissions Test (GMAT) to meet Booth's high standard of excellence.

After reading that twice, I folded the paper to focus on the article and handed it to Bernie. He glanced at it, set it aside, and said nothing.

I let the subject rest, but not for long. The running argument that followed was one of the few serious disagreements we ever had in our entire marriage. Over the next week, I launched several conversations that collectively added up to something like this:

"You're smart, Babe. You could do it."

"I'm not prepared for grad school at the U of C."

"You don't know that."

"I can't push myself that hard."

"When it comes to academics, you've never pushed yourself. Why not at least talk with the admissions office?"

"And miss a day of work?"

"Not a whole day, just a few hours. Your boss is a U of C grad. Tell him what you're thinking. He'll be proud of you. Maybe even write a letter of recommendation for you."

"The Booth guys won't be interested in me."

"You don't know that either."

"And even if I did get in, it'd be too expensive."

"That's what our savings are for."

"We'll need that money to live on if the company goes down."

"So, you'd throw up your hands without even trying?"

"I'd rather finish my BA before going for an MBA. You of all people should understand that."

I laughed. Too loudly. Not nice of me. "You're pushing forty, Babe, with fifteen college credits. You haven't taken a course in three years. You'll never earn a BA that way. Why not check this program out?"

"I'd rather study things I enjoy, okay?"

"Oh, yeah, I get it. I'm the one who wanted to major in languages, not biology, remember?"

"Yes, I do, so stop bugging me about it."

"But you keep saying you want to start your own business. Wouldn't it help to learn how to do that and make a success of it?"

"Sure, but why there? Other schools have MBA programs, too."

"Because only the U of C lets you earn an MBA while working full time and not already having a BA." I sighed. "That's why."

"I'm just not interested, okay?"

At some point, I pulled out my super-nasty, if-all-else-fails argument. "You're afraid you won't pass the GMAT."

Of course, he took offense at that. "That's not it."

"I think it is, Babe. I think you're scared."

"I'm not scared. Just cautious."

"Either you're afraid you won't get into the XP program at all or you're afraid it'll be a disaster if you do."

He shot me an angry look and left the room. And with that, the subject died.

Several weeks later, when I arrived home late from a program at Northwestern, Bernie called from the kitchen. "Is that you?" It was our long-standing greeting, which we always pronounced as two syllables, *'S'at-CHOU?*

I responded, "It's me!"... pronounced, *Itz-'SMEEE!*

He wrapped his arms around me and kissed me. "Can you drive me downtown Saturday morning?"

"Sure. Why?"

"Got an appointment at the Booth admissions office." His eyes offered up their familiar teasing twinkle. "They interview for the XP on Saturdays, so if you'll drive me in and drop me off, I won't have to mess with parking. When it's over, I'll catch a cab and meet you for lunch in Greektown. Deal?"

I kissed him back. "Deal."

Wearing the megawatt smile that I loved, Bernie strode into our favorite Greek restaurant, The Parthenon, which was famous for having introduced Americans to *gyros* (meat cooked on a vertical skewer) and *saganaki* (flaming cheese) when it opened in 1968. As we waited, we accepted the bartender's complimentary shots of anise-flavored ouzo.

Bernie raised his glass for a toast. "Guess what, Martha."

"They'll take you. I knew they would."

"I still have to pass the GMAT."

"You can do that."

"Yep, I believe I can."

Unbeknownst to Bernie until that day—but not to me, because I'd instigated it—his boss, the U of C graduate, had sent the XP admissions team an enthusiastic letter of recommendation.

I was home alone when the GMAT envelope arrived, addressed to Bernie. I opened it anyway.

Reading the letter and its report, my head nearly exploded. Not only had he passed all four tests, but his scores on three were well above the requirement. Based on what the XP team had told him, with such good results his admission to the MBA program was almost guaranteed.

That fall of 1975, Bernie began his two-year course of study. He got along well with his classmates, most of whom never knew of his unusual route into the program. His study group of five in Chicago's northern suburbs included the only woman in the entire class, reflecting the reality that few women were present at any level of corporate management in the '70s.

His biggest hurdle came when a professor assigned the class its first term paper. He had almost no experience writing such things. His two courses at Centenary were a decade back, and the Spanish-language classes that he'd taken at Northwestern didn't require them.

I asked if he wanted any tips about how to go about it.

Naturally, he took umbrage. "I know how to write. Been writing ad copy for ten years."

"There's a difference between ad copy and graduate-level papers."

"Leave me alone. Let me do it."

So I left him alone to do it.

Every evening for weeks, he wrote in longhand on legal pads. Scribbling. Scratching. Revising. Rewriting. Finally, he pounded it all out on our portable Smith-Corona electric typewriter.

He finished on a Saturday, one week before the paper was due, and asked if I would proof it for typos. The word "flabbergasted" doesn't come close to my reaction as I surveyed five pages of numbered sentences, each followed by extensive bullet points with words and phrases.

I wondered if it was possible that the professor only wanted a rough outline that students later would turn into fully fleshed-out papers. That's how my freshman-comp prof had trained us at Centenary, but it made no sense for a graduate-level course.

So that afternoon, as Bernie and José Gato watched a Chicago Bears football game on TV, I closed our bedroom door and quietly called the woman in his study group. After swearing her to secrecy, I asked my question. Her answer was as I expected. The paper should be complete, polished, and ready to turn in the next Saturday.

After the game ended, I broached the subject without mentioning to Bernie that I had consulted his classmate.

"Babe," I said gently, "what you've written is an outline for a term paper. It's not the final paper. You can't turn it in this way."

We discussed what was expected of a graduate-level academic paper on which his grade for the course depended, and maybe even his ability to continue in the XP at all.

"It's good that you've organized the content so well," I went on. "Now, write an introduction. Two or three good paragraphs. Next, turn each numbered point into its own section. Flesh out all the bullet points as paragraphs. Link them together in a smooth, logical way, and finish with a conclusion that ties it all together."

I knew Bernie was embarrassed, but he accepted my advice without argument. On Sunday, he drafted an introduction and let me read it. Based on my comments, he reworked it. With more feedback, he made it shine. On Monday, he called his office to say he would be taking the week off. He then wrote the paper in longhand. Typed it up into a twenty-plus page draft. Asked for my input. Reworked it based on what I told him. Asked me to review. Tweaked it into a final form, which I proofed for typos.

The next Saturday morning, right on time, he turned in an excellent paper. That night, we feasted at Charlie Beinlich's.

Except for my trusted female confidante, nobody in the XP ever knew what had gone on behind the scenes. Bernie's paper earned a B+, as I recall, and he progressed to the next semester. Best of all, he now knew how to write a graduate-level academic paper at a top-tier university.

He never made that mistake again.

Throughout the mid-'70s recession, we had a tough time financially.

The XP tuition deflated our savings. Bloomberg Furniture's collapse wiped out almost all our income. My small stipend from Northwestern didn't pay the bills. America was in the grip of stagflation caused by an inflation rate over 12% and unemployment at 9%. President Gerald Ford's "Whip Inflation Now" (WIN) campaign became a national joke.

Normally, Bernie might have looked nationwide for a new job, but we both had to stay in the Chicago area to finish our degrees.

We loved Chicagoland, too, and had family and friends there. We didn't want to leave.

So, to get us through, starting in late 1975 and extending to August of 1977, Bernie managed and solo-staffed a small, stand-alone furniture store on the northern edge of Chicago. His advertising and marketing savvy was worthless. All that was needed was his physical presence six days and five evenings a week. Since he still had full-day XP classes two Saturdays a month, taking those days off work was a requirement for him. Fortunately, the store owner was willing to cover them.

During that time, his only work-related excitement came from two street gangs that competed to control the neighborhood. Groups of men would show up for no reason, perhaps hunting rival gang members. So we developed signals. A "just wanted to say hi" call filled with too-cheery chatter meant "alert the police if I don't call back in fifteen minutes." And each evening, he let me know before he left the store. If he wasn't home in an hour, I was to notify the cops.

Those weren't the best years of our lives, but we survived them.

As for me, my one true graduate-level distinction came toward the end of my studies, in December 1976, when Northwestern awarded me a Dissertation Year Fellowship (DYF) that I hadn't even applied for. It was a feather in the Spanish and Portuguese Department's cap, too, so it turned out that our chairman had nominated me.

Having a DYF meant that I would receive the same stipend for researching and writing my dissertation, without having to teach. It also included perks usually reserved for faculty: a private, lockable study in the high-rise library tower with a view east over Lake Michigan; privileged access to the library's entire collection of books and manuscripts; expert library-staff assistance; and parking in lots closest to the buildings.

Best of all, the DYF would underwrite a trip to Spain so I could meet for in-depth conversations with the novelist Elena Quiroga, who was to be the subject of my dissertation, and then explore the northern provinces where she had grown up and set her novels.

"Martha got the plum" was how our chairman announced it at the department's 1976 Christmas party.

Bernie and I were not standing together when we heard that new-to-us news, but our eyes met across the room. My dear spouse flashed his big grin my way, then cupped his hands to his mouth and shouted loudly enough for all to hear, "That's my Martha!"

Before finalizing my dissertation topic, I had read all the published novels by *doña* Elena, who had broken through the rigid gender barriers of early 20th-century Spain to earn her country's top literary prize for depicting social injustice from a woman's perspective in the years leading up to the Spanish Civil War. She was the second woman admitted to the Royal Academy of the Spanish Language, which was an important distinction in itself.

In June 1977, I flew to Madrid to spend two days talking with her. Northwestern's DYF required that I go purposefully to Spain, not just take a vacation, so Bernie stayed home.

In August 1977, Bernie's brave bet on himself—and the equally gutsy chance that the Booth School's admissions team had taken on him —paid off when he received his MBA in the University of Chicago's majestic Rockefeller Chapel.

I've never been prouder in my life than on that day, much more than when I received my own degrees. Especially given where Bernie had started and how much courage, intelligence, and hard work lay behind his achievement, it was far greater than my own.

His former boss at Bloomberg Furniture, who had written a letter of recommendation for him, attended the ceremony and took this photo.

Bernie and me on the day he received his MBA at the University of Chicago, August 1977

Minnie lived near us but wasn't physically able to be there, so the next day we took her out to lunch to celebrate. She kept saying, "I always knew my Bernie was smart." Which was true, of course, but I don't believe she ever grasped the full extent of his accomplishment.

Meanwhile, back in Linden, my parents definitely understood what a remarkable thing Bernie had done. Ironically, if anyone was as proud of him as I was, it was Daddy. He bragged to friends how Bernie had "received his MBA from the world's best business school—or at least the

Betting on Bernie

one tied with Harvard for #1—without ever coming close to earning a bachelor's degree first."

Mama later told Bernie and me that when a man in Linden all but called Daddy a liar, saying such a thing was impossible, Daddy had his answer ready. "Martha told us that Bernie was headed for success. We weren't convinced, but it looks like she was right and we were wrong."

From that point on, it was clear that the chance I had taken on Bernie in 1968 would have a big payoff in all kinds of ways.

He received his MBA nine months ahead of my PhD, thereby catching up with me. The gloomy elephant vanished from our living room, never to return.

Our financial situation improved, too, after Bernie's graduation. He secured an important position with a prestigious marketing firm in the Loop, which is Chicago's central business district, and began replenishing our savings, building a national network of connections, and using his commuting time to plan his future self-employment.

While working downtown, he loved spending his lunch hours at the Art Institute. It's no cliché to say he was in heaven there.

Several times a month, I'd leave my car parked at Northwestern and take the "L" (elevated train) from Evanston into the city. Bernie and I would enjoy the evening, either alone or with friends, before riding the "L" back to Evanston and driving home in my car.

With weekends free again, we resumed our painting and skiing jaunts to Wisconsin and northern Michigan. That winter, we even ventured to the Rockies for the first time.

Like other institutions in the late '70s, academia was changing in ways previously unknown. The push was on to diversify faculties by hiring more White women and Black and Hispanic men and women. In theory, it was a worthy goal that I supported.

But the effects depended on who one was or was not.

Newly minted White male PhDs in many fields found their usual glide path to an academic career blocked. They resented the competition.

Newly minted non-Hispanic, non-native-speaking PhDs in Spanish, like me, began hitting walls as Spanish departments—but not mathematics, chemistry, physics, English, French, etc.—focused on hiring native-speaking Hispanic profs. What better way for a college or university to comply with the new federal rules and regs?

That felt grossly unfair to those of us who had worked harder to earn the same degree in a tongue we had not learned as small children.

My doctoral graduation day at Northwestern University in Evanston, Illinois, June 1978

I wisecracked that it was like the old Astaire-Rogers movies. Fred got to lead while gliding forward in flat shoes and form-fitting pants as Ginger followed backward in spindly heels and a billowy skirt.

For me, it was just plain ol' lousy, unlucky timing.

Before my graduation, Northwestern's Department of Spanish and Portuguese offered me the position of Lecturer and Language Coordinator. I saw it as my professors throwing me a lifeline. They knew I needed to stay put in a metropolis where many native-speaking Hispanic PhDs would be fighting it out for the few professorial job openings in Spanish. After weighing the pluses and minuses, I accepted.

People in the department called it "Martha's second plum," and for sure it felt that way to me at the time.

The next month, Bernie and I bought a two-bedroom, three-story townhouse in nearby Glenview. After renting a tiny apartment for nine years, we were thrilled now to own a much-larger place.

A few weeks later, Bernie and I flew together to Madrid.

The highlight of that trip came when I hand-delivered a bound copy of my dissertation to *doña* Elena, who with her husband, the director of the Royal Academy of History, hosted Bernie and me for afternoon tea in their apartment in the Academy's building, built in 1737.

Bernie's photo of Elena Quiroga, her husband, and me in their home in Madrid, summer 1978

After three delightful days in Madrid, we set off by car to explore northern Spain's great medieval cities and fascinating Basque Country.

In fall 1978, with my larger salary locked in at Northwestern, Bernie's focus turned to starting his own business.

Ultimately, he decided to develop a monthly trade publication to showcase his extensive advertising and marketing expertise and—*Yes!*—his academic credentials. His twofold goal was to help home-furnishings retailers across the country improve their own capabilities while also increasing his potential for an even-more-lucrative role as a consultant.

Over many weekends at the public library, he researched retail advertising executives around the country. Writing on printed sheets that he'd already laid out with essential fields, he built a list of two thousand prospects.

On January 1, 1980, his commute shortened from the Loop to our basement, where he began designing letterhead and other items needed to launch *AD PIX*.

From the start, *AD PIX* was a joint endeavor.

Bernie was the front-facing business guru, creative genius, and star of the show. Using his new grad-level skills, he wrote and designed each issue with sharp, timely articles on the latest retail-marketing trends. Included were photos of successful ad campaigns across a variety of specialized fields and suggestions for customizing them to suit a client's specific needs.

He networked with previous associates, cultivated relationships with experts in various fields, featured many of them as guest writers, and developed mutually beneficial projects.

He spoke repeatedly at major retail-oriented conferences, raising his name recognition while attracting thousands of subscribers, many of whom became his (and in some cases, our) personal friends.

By 1980, I had settled into my Northwestern faculty position well enough to teach two classes and run the language program while handling *AD PIX* business on weekends. Essentially, I managed the "back end," keeping paperwork updated, organized, and filed in our basement office. I sent out renewals, special promotions, and regular monthly mailings; proofed every issue and promo letter before it went to print; and did whatever else needed doing.

As the owners of a start-up operation with no track record or credit rating, Bernie and I had to pay upfront and out of pocket for everything, including a twelve-page printed promotional issue of *AD PIX*. We also hired a commercial mailing house to enter by hand into a room-size IBM computer the two-thousand-name database built from Bernie's prospect list. Every month we paid them to update that database.

We bought two thousand first-class stamps, which I stuck onto the self-addressed return envelopes. Then, working together in the basement, we hand-assembled and shipped the first introductory packets.

Subscription checks began coming in even before the last packets were in the mail. In April 1980, the first full sixteen-page *AD PIX* went out to 400-plus paid-up subscribers. We celebrated that milestone at Charlie Beinlich's and went back even more often as that number steadily increased.

Each month, Bernie created a new issue, delivered layout boards to the printer, and hauled the final printed issues downstairs.

Then, in a unique two-person-one-cat assembly line, often while watching Chicago Bears' games on TV, we'd stuff, seal, and load envelopes of issues into trays for Bernie to carry upstairs and on to the post office.

José Gato always kept us company as we worked, causing me to joke that *AD PIX* subscribers must wonder why they sneezed every time a new issue arrived.

Bernie and his able assistant, José Gato, working in the basement, 1980

By January 1981, Bernie felt secure enough to draw a modest salary. Later that year, *AD PIX* revenues were growing so fast that we invested in—or maybe took a wild chance on—one of the newfangled desktop computers that would let us produce what we needed in-house. Literally.

We bought an Apple III "business machine."

The computer itself—with all of 512 KB of RAM—cost $4,000.

To go with that, the salesman said, we needed a "huge 5 MB" external ProFile hard drive to store our database and the page layouts. Although that cost another $3,500, the guy assured us that its vast capacity—"measured in megabytes," he bragged—was all the digital storage we'd ever need. He promised. He really did.

The third part of our essential package, a bi-directional inkjet printer with its own stand, cost another $2,500. It was clunky and noisy, but it produced beautifully formatted documents with black-and-white photos, charts, and graphics perfectly aligned on long sheets of folded paper.

To use and store all that gear, plus paper, ink, filing cabinets, etc, we turned our guest room into an "upstairs office."

At some point, we calculated that the two-year cash outlay to launch *AD PIX* was about $25,000 in '80s dollars, not including Bernie's unearned salary for over a year and my unpaid labor for several years.

That expensive, all-in gamble on the business turned out to be our third mutual big bet on Bernie, following the move to Chicagoland and the decision for him to aim for a master's degree. Fortunately, all those risky moves we made paid off.

Bernie in the upstairs office with the Apple III, the ProFile (under the monitor), and the bi-directional printer (behind him), 1981

Chapter 13

A Sharp Bend in the Road

1981–1985

Northwestern University was a happy place for me as the calendar flipped to the '80s. I enjoyed my students, my classes, my responsibility for the Spanish and Portuguese language program, and the prestige of being a faculty member.

Several notable things happened in my work life in 1981 and 1982.

First, scholarly journals began publishing papers that I'd pulled from my dissertation, which is how most new professors dip their toes into the publish-or-perish waters in which they'll swim going forward.

Second, by 1981, I had created and was enthusiastically teaching a two-years-in-one Intensive Spanish course. Ambitious students liked the option to satisfy their language requirement fast while learning to speak Spanish well.

Third, that same year, I received one of four annual faculty awards from Northwestern's College of Arts and Sciences (CAS), which were based solely on teaching ability. Undergrad students nominated their teachers and championed them through a highly competitive process. That award came with a cash bonus and recognition via an article about me in a newsletter that was mailed out to all CAS students and their parents. The best part was its proof that my students valued my work.

"Martha's third plum!" was how the department chairman cheered it.

"That's our Martha!" was how Bernie reacted when I told him, Mama, and Daddy about it on a Saturday-afternoon long-distance call.

Fourth, also in 1981, the US Department of Education invited me, as Northwestern's Spanish and Portuguese language coordinator, to spend a week in Houston learning an evaluation concept and testing technique called the Oral Proficiency Interview, or OPI. Selected participants would receive additional training to qualify to administer the test professionally.

I ended up being invited for both, and I accepted.

During World War II, the Army and the CIA had developed the original OPI as a spoken exam to train and test American spies and to catch foreign ones. By the '80s, modified for academia, the OPI emphasized the value to students of learning to speak a language, not just memorize words, conjugate verbs, and take written tests.

In 1982, having earned certification as an OPI *tester*, I was among a smaller group who received "invitational orders" to become *trainers* at the Defense Language Institute in Monterey, California. I spent three weeks there that summer, earning advanced certification to teach others how to administer the OPI.

Daddy, the retired Army officer, got a huge kick out of my "invitational orders," because (he said) he only ever had received orders, with nothing invitational about them.

Ultimately, the OPI would transform teachers, courses, departments, textbooks, and even the basic philosophy and process of teaching languages. Students enjoyed it. Its national impact was huge. My OPI activities brought major recognition to Northwestern University.

Ironically, around the end of 1982, fifteen months after receiving my teaching award, I decided to leave NU. Several factors led to my departure.

One was the sense of being stuck and slighted.

My position as a lecturer on a yearly contract meant that—no matter how hard I worked, how well I did my job, how many new courses I created or scholarly articles I published, how much internal and external recognition I received—I never could progress beyond the lowly position where I'd started in 1978. I chafed at having no job security, eligibility for tenure, or opportunity to teach undergrad lit courses.

Increasingly, it irked me when senior faculty members refused to treat me as a full-fledged member of that body. Even after I'd held my position for nearly five years, my former professors would introduce me to visitors as "Martha, the language coordinator" while identifying a brand-new assistant professor—an Hispanic man of my same degree and age—as "our colleague, Dr. So-and-So."

As I told friends at the time, it was like forever living at home with my parents, who never would see me as a grown-up adult.

But there was more to my discontent than casual slights.

Traditionally in higher education, sexual discrimination ran rampant, and Northwestern was no exception. By 1982, there had never been a tenured female in our department. None on tenure track stayed longer than two or three years, not even an Hispanic *doctora* whom they'd hired during the high-pressure period of the late '70s. Across campus, most female PhDs held lower-status, lesser-paid roles as lecturers, while most male PhDs flourished as professors with higher status, salary, and job security.

And yet, I knew of several non-Hispanic *doctoras* like me who had found tenure-track positions elsewhere. I wondered if maybe I should try, too, while I still was young enough to compete.

Even given those realities, which I could have ignored, the real kicker was the sexual aggression that, for me, began in 1982.

Throughout history, "women who worked outside the home" were expected to tolerate offensive remarks, unwelcome kissing and groping, even rape. That continued in academia into the '80s, with little notice except by the women involved.

Our department included several Hispanic men, among whom a sense of *machismo* reigned supreme. My aggressor was one of them.

I'm sure it never occurred to him that verbally offending or even directly hitting on a subordinate female might not be okay. But when you happen to be the subordinate female in question, it negatively impacts your job satisfaction. The specifics of what happened forty years ago no longer matter, but the truth remains. A guy who couldn't keep his hands and his mouth to himself changed the course of my life.

One snowy Saturday evening in December 1982, as a fire blazed in our living-room hearth and Bernie and I relaxed on the sofa after dinner, I dropped the news like a concussion grenade.

"I need to find another job, Babe."

He looked around, clearly surprised. "Why?"

I knew he'd been so immersed in AD PIX over the previous year that he hadn't noticed my changing mood. So I detailed my gripes, all but the last straw that actually had provoked my decision.

"There's lots of good schools around Chicagoland," he said when I finished, with the nonchalance of one who had no clue how competitive tenure-track jobs in such places would be.

"True, but it depends on the openings. I'm afraid the best spot for me might be located somewhere else."

"How will you know?"

"Toss my hat into the Modern Language Association circus ring, I guess. See if anyone around here picks it up."

"Maybe some other kind of work would appeal to you."

"Like what?"

"International businesses, using your Spanish skills."

"I tried that the first year we were here, remember?"

"So, maybe one of the suburban high schools would welcome you. You've got plenty of credentials now."

"Too many credentials. I'm way overqualified for a job like that. Besides, you know how much I love teaching college kids."

"High schoolers aren't the same?"

I ignored that. "Look, Babe, I worked hard to qualify to teach college, and my students say I'm good at it. So, I should be able to find a satisfying job teaching college."

A rare extended silence fell between us.

After a while, Bernie reached over and took my hand. "I want my kid to be happy." His eyes were warm as he smiled at me. It wasn't his usual big grin, but sweeter and more intimate. "If you can find a better job somewhere else, we'll make it work."

That was almost the same thing he'd told me in 1973-1974, when I considered leaving NDHS and going to Northwestern for my PhD.

We have made it work until now, but how much longer can we?

I knew I wanted nothing more to do with a big university.

Topping my list would be a nondenominational, four-year liberal-arts college. Also good would be one like Centenary, affiliated with a mainstream Protestant denomination. Farther down but still okay, given my positive experience at NDHS, would be one run by the Catholic Church. At the bottom, anything evangelical or fundamentalist.

Several Chicagoland colleges fit the bill, but none I knew of had tenure-track openings in Spanish. A few listings from around the country appealed to me, and I ended up going for on-campus interviews to two of them. I received offers from both and accepted the one that most closely matched my ideal and worked best logistically for Bernie and me.

Kalamazoo College—aka "K College" or "K'zoo" or just "K"—in southwest Michigan was founded in 1833 by a Baptist preacher but has no religious affiliation. Its innovative K-Plan sends almost all its students, not just language majors, for their junior year abroad.

As one of only two Spanish professors, I could teach the full range of courses from 101 to advanced conversation, literature, culture, history, and linguistics. It would be my dream job. No question about that.

Early in May 1983, I drove to K and spent two nights on campus. Several professors interviewed me, as did the Spanish majors as a group.

The academic dean also interviewed me before surprising me with the news that he knew one of my intensive-Spanish students at NU, who had recommended me to him after learning that I'd applied to teach at K.

I even gave a talk in English to the community at large on a Spanish playwright about whom I'd recently published an article.

I appreciated the warm vibes at K and was delighted when, soon after I got home, the chairman called to invite me to join their faculty.

Kalamazoo was a four-hour drive from Glenview, by I-94 all the way, which meant that Bernie and I could spend weekends together in either place. We bought a small condo minutes by car from the K campus. José Gato would live there with me and travel back and forth to Glenview since, even on the road, he was a cool cat.

Once classes began, I enjoyed the job as much as I'd hoped. My K students were smart and motivated for their junior years abroad. Seniors back from a year in Spain, Mexico, Central or South America inspired younger ones with stories of special people, places, and experiences. Their own improved oral proficiency was impressive, too.

Half the weekends that first fall, Bernie drove to Kalamazoo on Friday afternoon and left Monday morning, giving us two full days to discover appealing villages, restaurants, and painting spots.

On alternate Fridays, after my last class, I'd stop at the condo, pick up the kitty, head west on I-94 toward Lake Michigan, and loop south around the Indiana Dunes and the rusty remains of steel mills. Below the lake, I'd gain an hour and take the Chicago Skyway Toll Bridge before merging into rush-hour traffic on the south side for a long, tiring slog through the city to far-north suburban Cook County.

In normal weather and traffic, José and I would arrive about 6:30.

Coming in the front door, I'd listen for Bernie's *'S'at-CHOU?* and respond with my own *Itz-'SMEEE!* Then we'd go out for dinner while José Gato catnapped in one of his favorite spots at home.

Saturdays in Glenview were for cleaning, laundry, and grocery shopping. I'd make and freeze beef stew, Texas-style chili, or pasta sauce for Bernie to heat and eat after work over the next few weeks.

Saturday evenings were for socializing with friends.

Sunday mornings were for eating homemade waffles, watching *Meet the Press*, reading the *Chicago Tribune*, and playing a fierce game of Scrabble.

On Sunday afternoons, José and I would head east, losing the hour we'd gained on Friday. Those evenings in Kalamazoo, I'd prep for the next week's classes.

That routine left little time for rest and relaxation, but I was an energetic young woman motivated to make it work.

Throughout that fall semester, I felt I was handling it well.

As winter closed in, however, I realized for the first time in my life how time zones and weather patterns can impact one's mind and mood.

Several facts are important to understand.

Kalamazoo lies on the far-western edge of the Eastern time zone.

Chicagoland lies on the far-eastern edge of the Central time zone.

Which means the sun comes up an hour later at K than at NU.

Which means K classes that start at 8:00 a.m. in the winter are not like NU classes that start at 8:00 a.m. in the winter.

I'm usually an early riser, ready to go at dawn. At NU, I always had volunteered to teach 8:00 a.m. classes, so, naturally, I did the same at K. Imagine my surprise when I discovered that, in midwinter, Kalamazoo was still dark at 8:00 a.m. The sky would start brightening by the end of that hour, but neither my students nor I ever were ready to get started when classes began before dawn.

Southwestern Michigan winters were different, too. Almost every night, clouds built up over Lake Michigan, blew east, and dumped snow on Kalamazoo. They blocked the sun as well, so bitterly cold days at K were also gray and gloomy. By contrast, the colder it got at NU, the bluer the sky and the brighter the sunshine. Its lakefront campus literally sparkled as the sun's rays hit floating ice crystals.

I'd known the winter drives would be hard. Wind, rain, or snow would make them treacherous and slow. And they were. But the most-dangerous trips usually came on Sundays. Since I had to teach the next morning, I took more chances driving on snow and ice.

Once on the road in those pre-cell phone days, I couldn't tell Bernie where José and I were, what conditions were like, or when we might arrive in either town. There were many wait-and-see evenings for him.

In June 1984, Bernie relocated *AD PIX* and the Apple III to a nearby office space and hired a part-time secretary to handle the tasks that I'd been doing. Soon, another part-timer took over his page-layout work.

That same month, my parents drove to Kalamazoo to visit me and attend the graduation ceremony. They loved the campus and participated in several events. They had given me an academic robe with Northwestern's spectacular purple-and-gold doctoral hood. As a real college professor at last, I proudly wore that bit of traditional finery in the faculty procession. On that beautiful day, it was easy to believe I'd found my academic home.

Then, back in Chicagoland for the summer, normalcy returned.

Bernie and I partied with friends, savored our favorite ethnic foods, and attended concerts under the stars at Ravinia in Highland Park. We took a painting-and-loafing trip to the Oregon coast and another to visit Murray and his family in New England.

June, July, and early August were as lovely a summer as I could recall, which led to a new problem. I struggled from the first of August with the knowledge that I was obligated to go back to K for the fall semester.

Bernie's increasingly busy work schedule no longer allowed time for the same twice-monthly visits to southwestern Michigan, so throughout my second year at K, José and I drove home and back each weekend.

Over the winter, exhaustion turned the tide for me. I realized that I wasn't physically and emotionally up for sustaining that routine much longer, especially with no guarantee of tenure at the end. And even if I were to achieve that desired goal, could I keep up the grueling commuter-marriage lifestyle forever?

Another thing happened that December. Mutual friends told me that a young widow whom we all knew had been inviting Bernie over for weeknight dinners and encouraging her toddler to call him "Daddy."

"Is that true?" I asked Bernie one day.

"Yes. She likes to cook, and I like to enjoy a meal with someone, so it works out well."

"And does her son call you Daddy?"

"Sometimes. He misses his real dad, I guess."

I gave him a hard look. "This is a strange situation, Babe."

"I dunno. We're just friends, so it seems perfectly fine to me."

"Doesn't it feel like you're cheating?"

At that, he got huffy. "No, because if you were home like a normal wife, I wouldn't want to go to dinner at her place by myself. But you're not, and I do prefer eating with someone. Her kid's kinda cute, too."

"You know, I don't appreciate that you've been going to her house for weeks without telling me. It feels like something has shifted in our relationship."

Going into the spring semester of 1985, psychological and physical pressures piled up on me. As before, I saw several alternative paths.

Only this time, the decision was mine alone to make.

I could try again to find a position in Chicagoland before giving up my job at K.

I could stay at K and keep going home each weekend, wearing myself out even more in hopes that Bernie would appreciate my efforts.

I could stay at K, immerse myself in research, academic writing, and campus activities to ensure that my tenure decision went well, and let my seventeen-year marriage collapse.

Or I could abandon the career that I had aspired to since before Bernie and I met.

Nothing of interest to me appeared in Chicagoland's job market, so that door closed. And even if it hadn't, I knew my age—almost forty—was a strike against me in a field that rewarded youth over experience.

In the end, forced by circumstances to choose between the man I loved and the career I loved, I chose the man.

My feminist friends at K scolded me for that decision.

"Stand up for yourself!"

"Fight for your dream!"

"Stick with your career!"

But by then I realized that more was at stake than my career.

After growing up in a cold, quarrelsome, and judgmental family, I'd been fortunate in finding a warm, sweet, and easygoing man to share my life. I loved Bernie and knew he loved me.

There was no way I could slam the door on him now.

In February 1985, I met with the chairman for my first performance review but cut it short by telling him I had decided to leave at the end of the term. Personal reasons, I said. Nothing to do with the college.

As the news spread, my K students did what my NU students had done two years earlier. They gave me cards and hugs and teary good wishes for a happy future and promises to stay in touch.

Faculty colleagues mentioned that they'd watched my energy and spirits fade over the second year. They all knew the chairman was planning to discuss it with me.

I left Kalamazoo College with much warmer feelings than I'd had upon my departure from Northwestern. The people at K had treated me well and would have allowed me to blossom in the kind of academic environment that I craved. Under different circumstances—if I could have lived full time in Kalamazoo, for example, without commuting each weekend—I gladly would have taught there until my retirement.

That was my second truly momentous bet on Bernie, following my first super-easy decision to marry him.

Leaving K College was the exact opposite. It turned out to be the toughest decision that I ever had to make.

I had worked hard for many years, not just to earn the formal credentials but also to gain the life experience that allowed me to hold a professorship in such a perfect-for-me academic setting. And I had done my best during those last two years to make it work.

But it wasn't working.

The process of coming to that conclusion pained me, because I knew it marked the end of the career I had dreamed of for so long.

I went home for good in June 1985, saved my marriage, and never taught Spanish again.

Chapter 14
The Golden Goose of Gigs

1985–1992

By June 1985, Bernie was producing three different monthly or quarterly *AD PIX* titles. As he had predicted years earlier, those publications did establish him as a marketing and advertising guru in the burgeoning home-furnishings industry.

With an actual office and two full-time employees handling *AD PIX*, Bernie pursued lucrative consulting contracts. Increasingly, as his network of subscribers and clients expanded and his creative and production-oriented crew grew larger, retail executives around the country sought out the advice, talent, and capacity of what was now known as Marks and Associates.

In July, Bernie and I bought our first real house in the leafy Village of Riverwoods, just north of the Lake County-Cook County line.

Riverwoods is aptly named. It's a peaceful place where the Des Plaines River flows through a northern flatwood forest dense with native trees, shrubs, and wildflowers. The landscape naturally floods in springtime, but after those annual soakings, the understory explodes with white trilliums, wild pink geraniums, yellow marsh marigolds, and unique jack-in-the-pulpits. Then the woods fill with the preening, flirting, and singing of birds in courtship, followed by the plaintive *cheeps* of hungry nestlings. August nights resound with delicate choruses of tree frogs. Autumn colors accompany the rustle of migrating wings.

The log house was vacant when we first saw it, so we drove there several evenings in a row and sat for an hour in the driveway with our windows down, simply enjoying the ambience. No rowdies showed up. No noisy vehicles. No commercial ruckus. Nothing but the whispering leaves of tall white oaks and hickories and barred owls calling back and forth, "Who cooks for you? Who cooks for you all?"

We were sold.

Surrounding our shady acre were hundreds of others like it, many protected by the Lake County Forest Preserve District. The house itself was a flat-roofed, one-story ranch with a fireplace in the rustic den and a spacious screened porch that jutted twenty feet into the woods just off the kitchen. Like every other modest home in our small "Indian Trails" cul-de-sac subdivision, it nestled into its natural setting.

On anyone's first visit, I pointed out the house's uniqueness. "Wood walls. Wood floors. Wood beams. Wood ceilings. Wood kitchen cabinets with wood-tone appliances. Woods outside. Woods all around. This is the brownest house you'll ever see in your life."

Over time, we brightened it up with a remodeled kitchen and bathrooms. We raised the roof for a master bedroom suite. But we never expanded into the woods or spoiled the rustic character that we loved.

We also enjoyed the birds, butterflies, flying squirrels, and other wild creatures that lived in that oak-hickory forest. Bernie began sharing my passion for nature as Riverwoods and the Lake County Forest Preserves provided his first exposure to the concept of an "ecosystem." Daddy gave him his World War II submarine glasses so he could better observe all that wildness. I bought a Canon SLR film camera with two lenses, and started teaching myself wildlife and nature photography.

Bernie turned the larger of our two extra bedrooms into a studio and in his free time painted watercolors that he would sell at suburban art fairs the next summer… for fun, not because he needed the money.

I took the smaller spare room for myself. Apple's new Macintosh computer was garnering rave reviews, so I bought one and started work on my first historical novel, *Rubies of the Viper,* with characters that had been growing in my mind since my childhood visit to Pompeii, and also with a suspenseful family-saga plot that intrigued me.

Other than writing fiction, however, I had no idea what I would do in my post-academic life, and I didn't care. My Northwestern salary had carried Bernie and me through the early *AD PIX* years. So now, Bernie and *AD PIX* could carry me through this empty-feeling, post-teaching period of my life.

From the early '70s on, Bernie's mother and sister had lived near us. Rozanne had married in 1979, but she and her husband still were close by. So it was nice when, soon after our move to Riverwoods, my folks came north to reside in a neighboring suburb. Minnie always got along well with them, so it felt like we were a real extended family at last.

Mama, Bernie, Minnie, and Daddy in the den of our log house in Riverwoods, Illinois, fall 1985

Betting on Bernie

Starting in the fall of 1985, a series of unexpected and unsolicited freelance projects began coming my way. The first was from the world's largest telecommunications company, AT&T, which was about to launch a live, over-the-phone translation service for its customers around the globe. But before it could do that, it had to find and hire interpreters with guaranteed superior-level proficiency in at least two languages.

Enter the Oral Proficiency Interview, which I knew inside and out.

AT&T hired me to test and evaluate candidates' oral proficiency in both English and Spanish. Each week—from the porch, the den, or my desk—I interviewed by telephone, evaluated, and rated a dozen or so potential translators from all over America. I set my own schedule and controlled my own time. Didn't have to dress up or go anywhere and got paid in a timely manner for each batch of interviews. That neat gig lasted a couple of years.

Me about to devour homemade tacos on the porch, spring 1986

Meanwhile, the OPI movement was growing even faster than had been expected, so it became hard for the organizers to qualify enough trainers to lead the workshops that taught others to administer the test. When they realized that one of their longest-serving OPI veterans was usually available, I became their go-to road warrior in Spanish.

From the fall of 1985 to the summer of 1992, I traveled coast to coast and everywhere in between, testing students and training both professors and high-school teachers to test and rate their own students. Sometimes a Spanish department would hire me to evaluate their advanced students or to guide their teachers in switching from traditional teaching methods to the oral proficiency model. I also flew to Central and South American capitals to help the Peace Corps' own native-speaking teachers improve their American-volunteer students' oral proficiency and then evaluate them in a standardized way.

Then, even as I stayed busy with my novel, OPI workshops, and AT&T job applicants, another offer arrived that I couldn't refuse.

"No way, José," I told my kitty.

An editor at Random House's College Textbook Division called to ask if I would co-author with another professor a new second-year college Spanish textbook with a current-events theme. I jumped on it.

The book that resulted, *Al corriente* ("Up to date"), came out in 1989, along with a workbook and a teacher's guide that I had written.

Not long after, the same editor returned with another proposal. Would I write a third edition of a beginning college Spanish textbook that had been in print for a while and needed refreshing? I accepted, of course. A couple of years later, the updated *¿Qué tal?* ("How's it going?") and its workbook and teacher's guide carried my name, too.

Satisfying royalties began coming in from both books.

Bernie and José Gato shaking hands on the porch, spring 1986

Betting on Bernie   163

And then the biggest, best, and most-exciting opportunity of all knocked on my door.

In 1988, my publisher, Random House, sold its college division to another textbook publisher, McGraw-Hill. Soon, a new partnership emerged between McGraw-Hill; the Public Broadcasting System's Boston affiliate, WGBH; the Corporation for Public Broadcasting; and the philanthropic Annenberg Foundation. Their goal was to create a brand-new concept for a multi-media college Spanish course.

The same editor who previously had recruited me to co-author the two textbooks for Random House was now working for McGraw-Hill. She invited me to join yet another new team that would envision, develop, and write scripts and a book package for a series of custom-shot videos and audiotapes that would be integrated into the teaching program.

I jumped on that offer, too.

At the WGBH studios in Boston, we brainstormed ideas. I mentioned that, for all second-year classes at Northwestern, I'd created a Spanish TV-style soap opera—or *telenovela*—whose story line featured fictional characters in authentic cultures and settings. Others liked the concept, so it became the organizing principle for our new project.

Minnie, José Gato, and Mama in our living room in Riverwoods, spring 1989

Bernie and me spring skiing in Alta, Utah, April 1992

Printed materials and videos would use characters in a soap opera-like story to be shot in real Spanish-speaking locations around the world.

We divided into two separate teams that worked together over many months. One wrote fifty-two episodic scripts and later shot those videos on three continents with local actors. Based on those scripts, my co-author and I wrote the textbook, workbooks, audiotape scripts, and a teacher's guide to go with those final, edited videos.

When it was released in 1992, our *telenovela* called *Destinos*—which translates as both "Destinations" and "Destinies"—made a splendid splash. We had designed it to be practical and interesting for college classes, individual adult learners, and small study groups. PBS stations broadcast the videos, and libraries made them available for checkout. It was highly accessible to anyone who wanted to learn to speak and understand spoken Spanish and learn about Spanish-speaking people.

On the day when UPS delivered to our home a heavy box of *Destinos* textbooks, workbooks, teacher's guides, and audiotapes, Bernie took me to Charlie's to celebrate.

Those books, those tapes, and that dinner marked the end of my academic career and reminded me that my most-recent big bet on Bernie had been a winner, too.

By 1992, *Rubies of the Viper* had found a well-known agent in New York City but not a publisher, so I reclaimed it and shelved it.

About that same time, our much-loved, hand-shaking José Gato—who for over twenty years had filled the role of surrogate child for us—died. Bernie and I buried him deep in the woods behind the porch where we three and our family and friends had enjoyed so many happy times together.

Bernie and me mellowing out on a screened porch in Sawyer, Michigan, 1992

Chapter 15
A Fateful Getaway

1991–1997

In 1991, Bernie sold *AD PIX* to a competitor and ramped up Marks & Associates, drawing on his long experience and deep connections that reached far beyond the home-furnishings industry. Sophisticated multi-media marketing projects for corporations as diverse as Office Max, Coca-Cola, Sears, and the *Chicago Tribune* further enhanced his national reputation and generated ever-higher revenues.

My life took a turn that year, too. It was unpredictable. Nothing I'd ever aspired to do before. And yet, I found I had both a passion and a knack for something other than Spanish teaching, testing, and textbooks.

Even before 1985, the year we bought our house in Riverwoods, I'd watched suburban sprawl creep across the Cook County border into Lake County, consuming much of the lovely landscape that Bernie and I had enjoyed since our first explorations in 1969.

So now, as a Lake County resident, I joined grassroots efforts to preserve its finest remaining natural areas. In 1991, with other activists, I co-founded the Lake County Conservation Alliance (LCCA) to unite groups working to save oak savannas, flatwood forests, riparian corridors, wetlands, prairies, and wildlife habitats in every part of our large county. Over the next decade, LCCA promoted conservation and battled land developers, road builders, and the politicians who were too cozy with them.

Also in 1991, I decided to run as a "Teddy Roosevelt Republican" for an open seat—or two open seats, really—on the Lake County Board and Forest Preserve District Board. I soon learned how to explain that unusual situation. "It's a two-hat office. You vote for one person and you get an elected representative in two legally separate offices."

One wintry evening that December, in preparation for the March 1992 primary, I introduced myself to leaders of the Lake County Republican Federation and offered my "Green GOP" bona fides for endorsement. They all-but-laughed me out of the room.

One precinct committeewoman in particular was peeved that I hadn't made a pilgrimage to her house to seek her support. "Maybe next time you'll do it right," she sniffed after I lost the endorsement.

My sole primary opponent was at the event, too, of course. Bernie had gone with me, so naturally he struck up a cordial conversation with the candidate who had won the endorsement.

Later, as we headed to our car, my dear spouse wrapped his arm around me and kissed the top of my head. "How's my kid?"

"Just ducky."

"I've got a news flash for you. That poor guy's not gonna know what hit him."

I grinned up at Bernie. "That's my plan."

And I don't believe the poor guy ever did.

Every day from January 2, 1992 to the March 3 primary, I walked from one Republican-registered house to another, protected from the weather by a hooded, ankle-length, bright-red coat, plus black gloves, scarf, and boots. No one could avoid seeing me as I clomped through the snow drifts. I carried a bag of flyers on which I'd pre-written by hand my home phone number and "Sorry I missed you!" If nobody answered my knock, I wrote the date and time on a flyer and stuck it in a visible spot.

Some evenings, people actually called to apologize for missing me.

A week before the primary, in the residential neighborhood where my opponent lived, I approached a big corner lot bristling with his signs.

I almost skipped that house, then decided to stick with my plan.

They may as well know who they're voting against.

The door opened before I reached it, and a woman I'd never seen until then pulled me in. "I saw you hesitate out there," she said. "So glad you came on up. I've been wanting to tell you to ignore those signs."

"Ignore them?"

"Yeah. He's a VIP in this village. We couldn't say no."

My face must have looked blank.

"I'm telling you, Martha," she went on, "you'll get five votes out of this house and many more from our neighbors, even those with his signs."

She was right. The next Tuesday, I beat my opponent and learned two good lessons. Signs don't vote. Endorsements don't matter.

Despite the honchos' support of my opponent and his mass of signs, I won the GOP primary by 72% to 28%. Better yet, I soon discovered that the Republicans who had cast their ballots for me in that first round weren't the only people who ever would.

Bernie at the wheel of a rented convertible in a Fourth of July parade when I was the Republican nominee for the Lake County Board, 1992

Betting on Bernie   169

Throughout the summer and fall of 1992, as I knocked on non-GOP doors and met voters of all political persuasions outside stores, post offices, and train stations, dozens of self-described Democrats confided that I would be the first Republican they'd ever voted for. And sure enough, that November, running on a strong pro-conservation platform against a wishy-washy Democratic opponent, I won the two-hat seat with 78% of the bipartisan vote.

That night, Bernie kissed me and said, "Ya done good, Kid."

Meanwhile, he had been taking courses at suburban art centers. Since he preferred capturing human and animal figures on paper, he took figure classes. Usually, he was the only one working in watercolor. Over time, he got better and better in that difficult medium. By the middle '90s, every single piece he painted sold at local art fairs.

After traveling a lot in the '70s and devoting the '80s to work, we resumed traveling in the '90s. Memorable trips to Italy, Spain, Greece, France, Germany, Belgium, the Netherlands, the Pacific Northwest, British Columbia, Quebec, and Puerto Rico crowned that notably happy decade in our lives.

After that, the call of the Great American Southwest became too strong to resist. Especially after Beecham and Renate Robinson turned us on to New Mexico, USA, the Land of Enchantment.

Bernie and a friendly goat beside a road on the island of Crete in Greece, 1992

Renate and Beecham Robinson toasting the new year in our home in Riverwoods, Illinois, 1992

At Northwestern in 1981, I had brought Renate onto our Spanish-teaching team. Gradually, Bernie and I became close friends with her and Beecham, who was a professor at the University of Wisconsin, Parkside.

Once the Robinsons began visiting New Mexico, they'd send us postcards with just one handwritten line: "Another boring, partly cloudy day in Santa Fe." That became a running joke, because—as we later found out—there's absolutely nothing boring in New Mexico's three hundred days a year of brilliant sunshine. Or puffy white clouds sailing turquoise skies. Or rainbows rising as rainstorms retreat. Or breathtaking sunsets and sunrises over the Sandia, Jemez, Sangre de Cristo ("the Sangres"), and the state's eighty-four other named mountain ranges.

Bernie and I finally got to New Mexico in August 1994, at the peak of monsoon season. We flew through a torrent over the Sandias, landed at Albuquerque's Sunport, picked up a rental car, and drove north on I-25 for our first experience on *La Bajada*. That name, "The Descent" in Spanish, makes sense when you're heading down its 2,000' drop from Santa Fe toward Albuquerque, but not when you're ascending it, as most tourists do after arriving in the city that the locals—fondly or not—call "Quirky Burque" (which happens to rhyme with Turkey Jerky).

We stayed north of Santa Fe in the original *Rancho Encantado* ("Enchanted Ranch")—an old, traditional *hacienda* and dude ranch filled with the photos and spirits of movie stars who had frequented the place in its heyday—as the monsoon did its thing for a couple of hours each afternoon, treating us and the parched earth to long, gentle, soaking rains. On that first visit, we came to anticipate the distinctive smell of ozone that a summer shower acquires moments before it hits the desert floor.

Every night, we slept in our second-story bedroom with the balcony doors wide open under a star-studded sky that stretched from the Sangres in the east to the Jemez in the west. Some nights also indulged us with grand lightning shows that crackled as we snuggled under the comforter, sheltered from passing downpours by deep, unscreened porches called *portales*, which are architectural details characteristic of the area.

We agreed that—night or day, stormy or clear—New Mexico had the sweetest, cleanest, crispest air that ever had filled our lungs.

Over subsequent visits, we fell into a laid-back, bilingual state of mind, as often happens to visitors in that laid-back, bilingual state.

Our favorite activities in Santa Fe included slow *vagabundeos* around the Plaza and up Canyon Road, Santa Fe's main *distrito de arte;* leisurely *almuerzos al aire libre* on vine-covered *patios* as immense *nubes grises* billowed up over the *Sangres*; and slowly sipped *cocteles* with delicious *cenas* as we gaped at double *arcos irises* and gasped at brilliant *puestas del sol*.

We savored New Mexico's unique *sabores* and learned to answer its Official State Question: ¿*Rojo, verde o Navidad?* (Red, green or Christmas?)

Having already accustomed ourselves to Tex-Mex and True-Mex foods, we now got happily hooked on New-Mex cuisine as well.

In the summer of 1995, I co-founded with two other women—later known as the "founding mothers" of Republicans for Environmental Protection (rep.org)—a national nonprofit that I jokingly called "the world's funniest oxymoron." Of course, an organization with that name would have been neither a joke nor an oxymoron through most of the twentieth century, when Republicans were the acknowledged champions of natural-resource conservation and environmental protection. REP was a worthy effort, albeit somewhat akin to Don Quixote tilting at windmills.

In July 1996, my family members were planning a celebration of my fiftieth birthday when we learned that Daddy had stage 4 lung cancer. He had started smoking in World War II, and even though he stopped thirty years later, he still coughed a lot. He shrugged off our concerns until things got so bad that he couldn't deny it. Refusing everything but palliative care, he entered hospice in his and Mama's home.

I was in a big re-election fight and needed to campaign until Election Day, November 5. But Bernie and I did what we could to help my folks and visited several times a week.

Early that October, a friend took Daddy out to vote early. For me.

Daddy and Bernie raking leaves around our house in Riverwoods, Illinois, early 1990s

Betting on Bernie 173

On October 25, the evening before Daddy died at age 85, we gathered at his bedside. He was alert and made a point of telling Bernie, "You're the best son-in-law I ever had." In the context of his imminent death, that statement was at once sad, poignant, funny, and ironic, because, of course, Bernie was the only son-in-law he'd ever had.

But Bernie, Mama, and I all heard it as an acknowledgment of how badly Daddy had misjudged Bernie in the years before our marriage.

Toward the end, I leaned over and kissed him. "I love you, Daddy."

"I love you, too." Those were his last words.

Something remarkable happened as people came from around Lake County for the memorial service. As I spoke quietly with friends, an older man dressed in a suit and tie arrived alone, approached the open casket, and stood looking down at Daddy. He was the only one there I didn't know, so I introduced myself.

From his pocket, he pulled a faded photo of himself, clearly still a teenager, standing beside Daddy. Both of them wore uniforms. "Major Alford and I," he said, "served together in the Sixth Tank Destroyer Unit in Europe and also at the liberation of Dachau. I saw his obituary in the *Tribune* and had to come see if it really was the same Truman Alford."

"Yes." I pointed to the photograph. "That is my father."

The stranger smiled. "Fifty-two years ago, he saved my life. I wouldn't be here now if it weren't for him."

"How'd that happen?" I asked tearfully.

"In 1944, they asked for volunteers to go on a particularly dangerous mission, so I and several other enlisted men stepped forward. Major Alford accepted everyone else but told me no, because, he said, I was too young. All the others were killed, but I went home alive because of your father."

The stranger sat beside Mama and me through the service, holding that photo the whole time.

I had asked Beecham Robinson—an ordained Baptist minister who had become Daddy's friend as well as ours—to deliver the eulogy. Among other things, he mentioned several thoughtful conversations that he'd had with Daddy about love and life and other soulful topics.

At the end, after the stranger had hugged Mama and me and left, one of my good friends came close and whispered to me, "Until Beecham spoke, I never knew your dad was so deep and thoughtful."

"Oh, he wasn't," I whispered back. "I think our dear Beecham just wanted to make Daddy sound a bit more sensitive than he really was."

A few days later, Mama, Bernie, and I traveled to Many for Daddy's burial, with full military honors, beside generations of his family at Fort Jesup. That's an 1822 US Army base dating from the time when Louisiana was part of America's contested western frontier. It's now both a cemetery and a state historical park. Mama left the service with the widow's traditional, triangular-folded American flag.

While I was away, my allies in Lake County rallied to finish up my re-election campaign, so I wouldn't have to worry about it anymore.

And on November 5, I won a second term for two more years.

Not long afterward, the Robinsons bought a house in Santa Fe, moved, and encouraged us to visit. Come often, they said. So we did.

Their adobe-style home reminded us of special lodgings we'd enjoyed in Mediterranean countries. In summer, traditional *portales* blocked the midday sun while allowing windows to stay open for ventilation, even during hard rains. Thick wooden beams, or *vigas*, supported the flat roof and pierced its walls, allowing metal channels, called *canales*, to drop rainwater into barrels for irrigating Beecham's beloved flowers and pinyon pines.

In winter, heat gently wafted up from below terracotta floor tiles, spreading its silent, even comfort throughout, unlike the drafty, noisy on/off/on/off/on/off forced-air systems that we'd always known.

Each evening from fall to spring, heady aromas from freshly burned oak and pinyon logs in their *kiva* fireplace enveloped us and then lingered through the night and into the morning.

Each evening from spring to fall, their adobe-walled garden called us for margaritas, chips, salsa, guacamole, hummingbirds, and sunsets.

Daytime cries of pinyon jays and prairie dogs and nighttime hoots of owls charmed us year round, as did the yips and yaps and yowls from roaming packs of wild "song dogs," aka *coyotes*.

Their framed-up views of mountain ranges blew our minds.

To keep from feeling like moochers, we always treated the Robinsons to luscious lunches in town each day we were there.

Bernie also gave them three of his original watercolor paintings, including a portrait of them in their garden and another that Renate had "commissioned" for Beecham's birthday. It was a realistic portrayal, made from photos, of all their living and deceased dogs and cats on the rug and sofas of their living room. Beecham actually cried when he first saw it.

In 1997, as Bernie attended a watercolor workshop in Santa Fe and we again stayed with the Robinsons, I popped into a real estate office, asking to see buildable lots out of town. It took an agent and me just four days to turn up the perfect spot for a getaway cabin. Five and a half heavily treed, undeveloped acres atop a rise west of Santa Fe. Reasonable price. Superb views of the Jemez Mountains. Heaven on Earth.

Bernie warned the Robinsons and anyone else who would listen that this was an excellent example of the danger of leaving Martha alone with time on her hands. But he loved the lot, too, so after we went back home to Riverwoods, with a Santa Fe lawyer representing us, we bought it.

From then on, whenever we returned, we'd visit "our place." Relish its high-desert beauty. Savor its silence. Marvel at its views. Inhale its pinyon-juniper fragrance. Envision the cabin that we'd build there soon.

And with that, we planted our flag in Santa Fe.

Chapter 16

The Villa on the Hill

1998–2001

By 1998, the year Bernie turned sixty, Marks and Associates employed thirty marketing experts and creative talents. The company that he had built from scratch was doing well, which might have been enough success for most people.

But Bernard Marks still had a lifelong dream to fulfill.

It was August, our favorite month to be in our favorite city. The Robinsons had other plans for the day, so Bernie and I lunched near the Plaza, in the shade of a thick, twisted vine on the patio at The Shed.

He finished his usual green-chile something-or-other, set down his fork, and trained those too-blue-to-be-true eyes that I loved on my face.

"I've been thinking," he said.

"Thinking is good," I said.

We both laughed, but then his expression grew serious. "I'm thinking it's time to reorganize the company."

After thirty years of marriage, few things he said ever caught me by surprise, but that one did. "Sounds like a big project, Babe."

He shrugged. "The lawyers will handle it."

"Any particular reason for wanting to do that?"

"So we can move here the day after your third Board term ends."

I finished my usual red-chile something-or-other and let that idea filter through my margarita-marinated brain.

"You mean in December 2002? Assuming I get re-elected this fall?"

"You will, and we'll need that much time to design and build a house on the lot." Bernie leaned forward and lowered his voice, although nobody else on that Santa Fe patio knew anything about his business back in Chicagoland. "I'm thinking of elevating someone to partner."

"Can you maintain your income from the company if you do that?"

"I'll have to take a cut, but we'll be okay."

"And you've got a qualified person to serve as captain?"

Bernie's old twinkle returned. He'd always enjoyed playing around with sailing metaphors. "Plenty of talented sailors to pick from," he said.

"But unless you're gonna sell him or her—or them—the whole ship, you'll need to mind the sails."

"And keep an eye on the sky, the weather, and the rum."

"And grab the rudder on occasion."

"And return a few times a year to make sure the boat is still afloat."

"But really, Babe." I paused. "What if it doesn't stay afloat?"

"I'll launch an underwater rescue mission."

"Let's hope that never happens." I decided temporarily to suppress my worries. "What would you do with yourself as a retired sea captain?"

Of course, I knew the answer to that question before I asked it.

"Become a full-time, professional fine artist in Santa Fe," he said.

I realized where this talk was going. He was ready to roll the dice. Take serious chances with the business. Spin the wheel of fortune as our comfortable lifestyle and retirement security hung in the balance.

My gut clenched. I wasn't sure of the company's odds of survival without Bernie's magical combination of skills, smarts, and personality.

Besides, art was a notoriously iffy endeavor. Even though Santa Fe was packed with galleries, every third or fourth Santa Fe resident claimed to be a fine artist. From what I'd seen and heard, gaining representation in a reputable, well-established gallery often required more connections and luck than talent.

I also wondered if—at age sixty-four, which Bernie would be in November 2002—he could possibly drop into such a traditional, tight-knit community and compete with hundreds of other artists. He was untested in that way.

I needed to consider my own situation, too. Back in Lake County, I had a satisfying, well-paying, and reasonably secure elected position that I was good at. I felt sure I could keep it for as long as I wanted. Maybe even get elected to the legislature or Congress if I ever decided to try.

But if I left my job at the end of 2002, as Bernie was suggesting, my paid work life would end at age fifty-six. I couldn't do much to supplement iffy art sales if that ever were needed, and I wouldn't have enough in my IRA to retire securely on my own.

It would be hard for me to start over professionally in New Mexico, too, either in politics or as a Spanish teacher, unless I changed my name

Bernie and me hiking Bandelier National Monument in the Jemez Mountains of New Mexico, 1998

to "Marta Marcos" and mastered the lovely, lilting, four-hundred-year-old, unique-in-the-world, northern-New Mexico/southern-Colorado dialect. I would forever look, sound, and feel like a carpetbagging Anglo.

"I thought we were just gonna build a getaway cabin," I said, "not a full-time home. Not sure what I'd do with myself if we moved here."

"You'd find something good to keep you busy. You always do."

"Not sure what it would be."

"That's what you said when you left K College, and look at all those books you wrote and the political career you built and the thousands of acres of land that you and your friends are saving through the Lake County Forest Preserves."

"But I'm a lot older now. Can't keep reinventing myself forever."

"And I'm eight years older than you." As before, Bernie looked at me straight on. "If I don't do this soon, it'll be too late for me."

By "do this," of course, he meant to follow the dream that he'd first told me about in 1965 and postponed for so many years in order to be a good provider.

How can I tell him that I won't help him fulfill his lifelong ambition?

So I nodded. "I'm gamy, Babe, if that's what you really want to do."

In November 1998, I won four more years in office. We hard-working, outspoken, "Green GOP" activists had become a force, helping LCCA and other groups elect like-minded officials from both parties and take control of the County and Forest Preserve Boards. We then passed county-wide conservation policies and three bond referenda totaling $160,000,000 to purchase and restore high-quality natural land, protect riparian corridors, and build trails. Running on that platform, I had been elected three times (two four-year terms and one two-year term).

Despite having a Democratic opponent in each cycle, the same percentage of Democrats voted for me. The '90s may have been the last time when bipartisanship was both possible and popular in America.

Meanwhile, I kept busy running Republicans for Environmental Protection, serving as its volunteer, unpaid president and board chair.

Much of my "job" consisted of traveling the country to call attention to the organization, promote its goal of restoring the Republican Party's once-great conservation tradition, and raise the funds to pay its five actual staff members.

A major highlight of my involvement with REP came in January 2000, when we endorsed Senator John McCain before the GOP presidential primaries—mainly because of his early, enthusiastic leadership in addressing climate change—and then became actively engaged with his campaign. Unfortunately, that was a short-lived effort, but we never regretted doing it.

Senator John McCain and me on the "Straight Talk Express," his campaign bus, after REP's endorsement press conference in New York City, spring 2000

After Bernie reorganized his business, we visited Santa Fe often, always hanging out with the Robinsons, treating them to lunch each day we were there, and planning the retirement home we would build on our lot. In 1999, we chose a builder and paid a deposit for the design work.

And then, after much back-and-forth with that builder through the summer and fall, we settled in for another winter in Riverwoods.

One day in January 2001, the builder in Santa Fe called me at home in Riverwoods. "Martha," he said, "I've got good news and bad news."

I braced myself. "I'll take the good news first."

"Your house plan is finished, and it's a beauty. But now you need to hear the bad news. You and Bernie don't own the lot you think you do."

My brain failed me. I clung to the phone as he went on.

"We designed the house based on the plat you gave us. But recently, as part of our required due diligence, we went to the county land office and discovered the truth."

"But the Realtor that sold us the lot is supposed to be the best in Santa Fe."

"Maybe, but in your case it seems they screwed up."

My mind still balked at taking this in. "Bernie and I weren't in Santa Fe when the sale closed. We assumed the Realtor and the lawyer would get it right." I searched for a clear thought. "Do we own anything out there?"

"Oh yes, you do. The lot you actually own is five-and-a half acres lying alongside the five-and-a half acres that you thought you owned."

"So, maybe it's okay?"

"I'm afraid not. Instead of spanning the crest of the hill, where all those views that you love are, the lot you own wraps around the bottom of the hill. Mostly, it's a deep *arroyo*."

To New Mexicans, an *arroyo* is what Arizonans call a "wash" and most other Americans call a "gully." Although they usually look bone dry, *arroyos* are natural wetlands that carry water whenever storms occur in the vicinity. They can be especially dangerous in the monsoon season and therefore are not buildable.

I recalled all the times that Bernie and I had stood at "our place" looking out across that *arroyo*, never realizing that it was what we owned and very little else.

"Does that lot have any views?" I asked the builder.

"Almost none."

"Buildable acreage?"

"Hardly any."

"Will your plan work there?"

"No."

"Is it worth the price we paid for it?"

"Not even close."

A lawyer I knew in Albuquerque recommended a Santa Fe lawyer who specialized in real estate issues. "Be warned," he said, "the guy's a sonofabitch. People he sues hate his guts."

"Doesn't sound like someone we'd want to work with."

"Oh no, he's exactly the one you want on your side. If anybody can get your money back, it's him."

We made an appointment with the sonofabitch lawyer, who spent half an expensive hour telling us of New Mexican real estate deals gone bad in recent decades. Hearing all that, we felt lucky. At least we hadn't built our dream home on a lot we didn't own.

Ultimately, the sonofabitch lawyer sued the real estate company on our behalf. It took over a year, but we got our money back, plus legal fees. We tried to buy the lot we wanted, but its owner wouldn't sell.

So, in June 2001, we started searching for another lot that would fit the plan that we'd already had designed. Clearly, it was a backward approach, but we had to try. Our sonofabitch lawyer recommended a Realtor named Fred. "You can trust Fred," he said, and we did.

Santa Fe's land market was booming, so Fred had plenty of lots to show us. When nothing worked with our existing plan, he invited us to visit some newly finished spec houses. One morning, he opened a gate into the courtyard of a brand-new one in a small subdivision named *Colinas Verdes* ("Green Hills").

This place was almost twice the size of the cabin I'd wanted to build. Its two-acre, tree-covered lot was one of the highest anywhere around and much closer to town than the other one had been. It also was loaded with finer touches than we had meant to include.

Its long foyer, sporting the silkiest plastered walls we'd ever seen, separated the living room, kitchen, and master suite from the den and two guest suites. Such accommodations are a common feature in the area, nearly a requirement for upscale homes, because when you live in Santa Fe, everyone you know comes to visit.

Its unobstructed 180-degree western view of the Jemez Mountains promised spectacular sunset panoramas year round. Its views toward the Sangres in the east—through pinyon pines and junipers on an adjacent lot and from a spacious brick patio with an outdoor fireplace—meant that sunrises and stargazing would be exceptional, too.

Its one-story layout—with extra-wide hallways and doorways, plus smooth brick floors throughout—meant that we could live comfortably there for the rest of our lives, even if we needed walkers or wheelchairs.

We could negotiate a price and start enjoying it right away without all the hassles, delays, and cost overruns associated with custom construction, especially when done from a distance.

I've chosen to describe a few special things about that house, not to brag about them but to point out that, for us, it was deliberately more than just basic retirement digs. We saw it as a reward for our many years of hard work and a sign of how far we'd come from that tiny apartment in Northbrook where we'd lived for almost a decade. For sure, we hadn't inherited the money to buy this new place.

In 2001, being able to own such a home meant that sixty-three-year-old Bernie Marks—who, when I first met him in 1965, could boast of no work experience beyond engraving trophies and cigarette lighters and drawing furniture, and who possessed little formal education beyond high school—had done quite well for himself… and for me.

And also, we knew that—after our bad luck in losing a building site that we'd bonded with and a house plan that we'd managed to get just right for us—we now had the good luck of finding a far nicer place than we ever would have set out to create for ourselves.

We loved every single thing about that house from the moment we walked in. All Fred had to do was stay out of our way as we talked each other into it. That afternoon we made an offer. We got a counteroffer and made one of our own. Before nightfall, we had it under contract.

We closed on the house on August 1, 2001, represented at a Santa Fe title company by Fred and our sonofabitch lawyer, two men we totally trusted to make sure nothing got screwed up this time.

And then, approaching mid-month, over three days and nights, we towed a one-way rented trailer south through Illinois and west through Tulsa and Amarillo on historic Route 66, bringing our first load of household goods. We spent the last half of August making the empty space livable. I called it "playing house."

Each evening, as the setting sun turned the monsoon clouds to flame and the Jemez Mountains into a dark, stark silhouette, we ate dinner on our west-facing *portal*. Since New Mexico's high desert has few mosquitoes, sitting out at night under the silent stars without screens, sprays, or zappers is a total treat.

Bernie painted several of those stunning sunsets. Two panoramic watercolors of the Jemez Mountains became the first framed pieces that we hung on the walls of what we now were calling our villa on the hill.

During that pleasant interlude, Bernie made a business trip to visit a potential consulting client in Houston.

While he was away, Fred called me to say that the vacant two-acre lot bordering our property on the east had just come on the market. "It's yours if you want it," he said. "Not terribly expensive, and a great way to protect your privacy and views of the Sangres."

"But," I countered, "we've still got a house in Illinois, and this house to furnish, and the worthless lot in the arroyo. We're house poor and land poor and can't afford to buy anything else at this time."

"But," Fred countered, "all those other issues will go away and then you'll own a fabulous four-acre estate atop that hill. Nobody's bidding on that lot right now. It's fully developed. It'll never be cheaper. And you can sell it easily enough if you ever need cash."

"I'll discuss it with Bernie when he gets back."

Two evenings later, in the arrivals lane at Albuquerque's Sunport, Bernie gave me his biggest smile ever. "How's my kid?"

"Loving our villa. How's the new client?"

"Very nice. He's a smart young guy with a great future ahead of him. And we're getting the contract."

I drove on north toward Santa Fe as the sun sank into fat, pink clouds over the Jemez Mountains to our left. To our right, the dramatic Sandia Mountains turned their Spanish-namesake watermelon color.

Bernie actually gasped as we rounded a bend and spotted a bright double rainbow arching over the closest cliffs as a rainstorm slipped away behind them.

"The native people around here say double rainbows are a good omen," he told me. "So now, I'll boldly predict that hundreds of thousands of dollars worth of Marks and Associates' work products will soon be on their way to Houston."

And with that celestial setup, I told him of Fred's call.

All the way up La Bajada and farther on toward the blood-red Sangres, we discussed the idea of buying the adjacent lot. By the time we pulled into our driveway, we'd decided to take a chance on it.

Call it yet another bet on Bernie, if you like.

A week later, we drove our car back to Riverwoods, arriving just a few days before September 11, 2001.

And then, forever after, we recalled that blissful period at our villa on the hill in Santa Fe as the last time America seemed normal.

Chapter 17
A Full-time Professional Fine Artist

2002–2008

Minnie Marks remained mentally sharp into her nineties, even as her overall health failed. Every Saturday for years, Bernie visited her in the nursing home, still joking with her. She died at 93 in October 2002. Her three children and their spouses traveled to New Orleans to bury her alongside Sid.

Early in December 2002, after a decade in the two-hat county office, I retired when my third elected term ended.

Minnie Marks on her eightieth birthday at our house in Riverwoods, 1989

Bernie had to keep working for a while longer, so I escorted Mama and Sugar, the tiny-tiger kitty who had been our baby for the previous ten years, through O'Hare Airport en route to our new home.

Early in 2003, Bernie joined a group of watercolor artists and then, with them, began

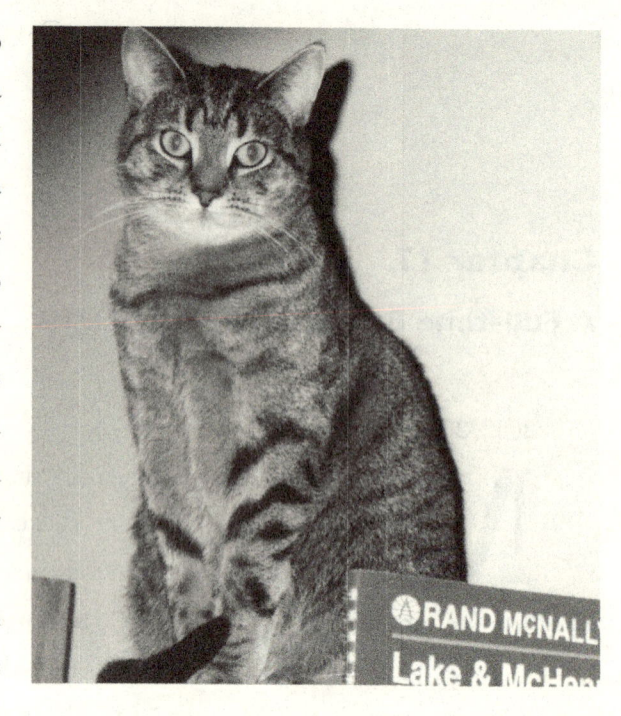

Sugar, our second kitty, atop my desk in Riverwoods, Illinois, 2000

visiting and painting *au plein air* (outdoors, on site) a wealth of high-desert landscapes that he might never have discovered on his own.

In 2004, with a new friend in Santa Fe filling the all-important role of cat sitter, we started exploring the "Four Corners" states: New Mexico, Arizona, Utah, and Colorado. It's a vast, still-wild region that contains more natural beauty than most people are likely ever to see in a lifetime.

In 2005, Bernie took a chance in selecting his dramatic watercolor "The Colorado in the Canyon" for submission to *International Artist Magazine*, which was holding a world-wide competition organized around the theme of "rivers." The magazine published it as a runner-up.

And with that, Bernie Marks was on his way to the top.

Such excellent recognition, plus previous statewide awards and his professionally framed, ready-to-show pieces, landed him precious wall space at a high-quality art gallery on Canyon Road in Santa Fe.

On the day Bernie's work went on display—the same day I took the photo below, which explains the modestly proud, non-grinning expression on his face—I reminded him how, on our first dinner date forty years earlier, he'd told me of his ambition to become a "superfine artist" selling his work in "superfine galleries in superfine cities with superfine reputations for selling superfine art." Now, he had done it.

From then on, even in Santa Fe's competitive environment, Bernie's lively, colorful watercolors of people and places, including the two shown here, sold like fresh-made pistachio ice cream on a hot New Mexico day.

It wasn't long before galleries in Pinetop, Arizona and St. George, Utah also displayed Bernie's pieces. In fast-growing St. George in particular, new-home buyers snapped up his wonderful paintings of southern Utah's national parks and monuments.

Bernie and two of his paintings in his first-ever gallery on Canyon Road in Santa Fe, New Mexico, 2005 (His award-winning "The Colorado in the Canyon" is over his shoulder. It sold that same day, his first from any gallery.)

Betting on Bernie

And on one exciting day, the owner of a statewide bank in Utah bought five of Bernie's largest framed pieces to display in his branches.

With that start, less than three years after we moved to New Mexico, Bernie achieved his dream. He was now a full-time professional fine artist selling his work in multiple galleries around the Southwest.

Also in 2005, twenty years after José Gato and I had returned from Kalamazoo and Bernie and I bought the log house in Riverwoods—and despite all our happy memories of families, friends, felines, and festivities associated with that fabulous place—we sold it to someone else who loved it, too. Finally, we were denizens of the desert and nowhere else.

At some point, the gallery owner who had been representing Bernie's work exercised her right to change her specialty, so Bernie and other southwestern artists left for different galleries.

The owner of the venerable Waxlander Gallery urged Bernie to switch to oils and acrylics, which sold for higher prices than watercolors and tended to be more in demand. Once he did, she exhibited his work.

That change turned Bernie's creativity loose. Working in different media inspired him to punch up his colors, play with textures, and produce significantly larger pieces. He still used watercolors for field studies but never again made a finished watercolor painting.

By hanging his artwork on their walls, those gracious female owners of two important galleries became the latest in a long line of people who had taken a chance on Bernie and been rewarded for it.

One evening in January 2008, as the Great Recession gained momentum—with a fire crackling in the fireplace, classical music filling the air, and a bottle of wine waiting to be finished off—we discussed our finances and plans for the future. As Bernie's income from art had increased, he'd steadily reduced what he took from Marks and Associates.

I had earned nothing since leaving Lake County in 2002, so our income was dependent on Bernie's ability to keep painting and selling his work. That scared me. But still, we owned our house outright, so our costs were relatively low. Our investments had been in good shape until the recession tanked the economy. Bernie assured me they would come back soon.

"Personally," he said, "we'll be okay, but the company is another matter. I'm not sure how long it can survive."

"What are your options?"

"Let the few who still are there struggle on or just pull the plug."

"Which would you prefer?"

"Pulling the plug."

"Good idea. And I'm ready to end my involvement with REP, too."

"Can you be out by the end of this year?"

"Right after the election."

"So," he said, "other than enough cash flow to live on, what do we need to make our 'golden years' the best part of our lives?"

"To be honest, I'm fed up with those ratty old motels in the middle-of-nowhere places where you like to paint and I like to photograph."

"But those towns don't usually have more than one motel."

"The parks provide campgrounds, so if we had an RV—"

Bernie cut me off. "I don't want one of those big monstrosities."

"Me neither, but even a small RV would be an improvement."

"Well, I can't keep painting forever in our bedroom sitting area. I need a real studio with storage and space for a taller easel."

"And you deserve that, but I don't see how we can afford both an RV and a studio. I vote for the camper. We'll enjoy it together."

"And I vote for the studio, so I can keep growing in my art."

"Dukes!" I punched my fists into the air. "Who's gonna win?"

"Oh, we both know the answer to that." Bernie flashed his big grin. "You'll win, Kid. You always do."

"You know what, Babe? I bet we both can win."

Betting on Bernie

That March, Mama died at 94 in a memory-care center in Santa Fe. While still in Illinois, she had lost her sight in both eyes, but luckily she kept her wits long enough to enjoy sharing much of our life in Santa Fe for a few years. We buried her next to Daddy in the Alford plot at Fort Jesup in Many.

Mama and me having fun on her last birthday, 2008

The Great Recession ended Marks and Associates even before Bernie had time to pull its plug. He personally paid off everything the company owed to employees, clients, suppliers, and creditors. Ever the nice guy, he took his business down as gently as possible, without bankruptcy or internal chaos, doing the right thing for those who had worked with him and for him.

At the end of 2008, I turned my "job" at REP over to others.

Finally, Bernie and I were free of outside obligations and ready for retirement. Along the way, we concluded that he could have his studio *and* we could have our camper. We just needed to spread those expenses out a bit.

Within three years, we had them both.

And all was well.

Until it wasn't.

Chapter 18
BluCon and the Calm Before the Storm

2008–2011

In August 2008, Bernie developed bronchitis. He coughed almost constantly and fought a fever for two weeks, during which time I had little to do but keep him fed, hydrated, and comfortable.

And research high-quality, small-size motorhomes.

I soon narrowed it down to three brands with good reputations and intriguing names: Born Free, Chinook, and Lazy Daze. All were 20'-30' and built on a modest scale, not mass-produced. Any one would satisfy our needs. But first, we needed to rent something similar to see if we liked the camping experience at all. So I researched those options, too.

After Bernie recovered, I gave him a report. He agreed to try a test-run camping trip in a rented Class C, to see what it was like.

In December, we drove from Santa Fe to Los Angeles to pick up our rented 24' home-on-wheels with "like new" amenities for the next week. After that, we were a two-vehicle convoy: me in our car up front as Bernie followed in the rented RV, or "the rig," as RV aficionados tend to call them.

For me, trying to navigate while maintaining visual contact with Bernie in the rig—and not losing him on LA's freeways as he coped with a large, unfamiliar vehicle—echoed our 1969 journey from Shreveport to Chicagoland. This time, at least, we did have cell phones and seat belts.

I had bought each of us a sleeping bag, and we were grateful for them once we reached our reserved campsite at Joshua Tree National Park. Bernie used his on a lumpy, not-too-fresh mattress tucked into a corner space beside the bathroom.

I used mine atop a thin cushion that barely softened the lowered tabletop. That sleep-on-the-dinette arrangement may work in better-quality campers, but it didn't in our rented one. At least once a night, when I rolled over, my "bed" would slip off its narrow railing and plunge to the floor. Each time, I laughed it off. Those falls didn't knock out my teeth, break my bones, or give me a concussion. They just kept us both on edge, never knowing when I might doze off, roll over, and crash.

Nevertheless, we loved stargazing beneath the darkest skies we'd ever seen, and sleeping with the windows cracked open even in early winter, and breathing the crisp night air.

Bernie noted how sweet it was to experience nature like that, as opposed to being miles away, hermetically sealed up in a motel room. Each day we were there, he chose to skip his morning coffee in order to paint the unique Joshua trees and rock piles at dawn, while I set out with my camera to "shoot" birds and critters in the same perfect light.

That outing convinced us that if we decided to keep on camping, we would want to buy our own motorhome with really new—not "like new"—mattress, sheets and towels, kitchen and bathroom gear. We would invest in a high-quality brand, not the popular-because-it's-cheap variety. And then we would store our sleepwear, underwear, outdoor clothes, hiking shoes and poles, and basic supplies in it, all ready to go.

Studying a map of southern California on our last morning at Joshua Tree, I noticed that the Lazy Daze factory was just a two-hour drive away. We had to go that direction anyway to return the rented rig. Why not take a look? Bernie agreed, so we did.

The rest of the story is predictable. We liked the layouts, build quality, interior details, huge windows, and retro look of the Lazy Daze models. Compared to the tired thing we'd been sleeping in at the park, a brand-new Lazy Daze would be a sublime way to venture out into nature.

Bernie preferred one specific 27' floor plan that had well-cushioned beds for two people. He especially loved it in blue and white, and so did I.

The drive back to Santa Fe was a blast.

Heading west across northern Arizona on I-40, we brainstormed clever names for our potential motorhome. Two cute finalists—"Wild Blue Yonder" and "Rigadoon"—vied for the win.

But then, as we approached New Mexico, Bernie slowed down and glanced over at me. "How'd we happen to camp so near the factory?"

"I wanted us to see Joshua Tree, and Fate put Lazy Daze nearby."

"Doesn't seem too likely that Fate had anything to do with it."

I shrugged with all the nonchalance I could muster and kept mum.

So Bernie went on. "Does kinda seem like I've been conned."

"Conned?" I fanned my hands in front of my face, as if fighting off hyperventilation. "You think a sweet, simple little thing like me would try to con a big, strong man like you into buying a Lazy Daze?"

He flashed his broadest grin. "I don't *think* so. I *know* so."

We both fell silent again. But then, as we crossed the state line near Gallup, he slowed the car once more. "Hey, Kid." His eyes twinkled as he glanced over at me. "I've got it."

"Got what?"

"The perfect name for our new blue Lazy Daze. Are you ready?"

I gripped my seat as if bracing for a bombshell. "I'm ready."

"So, Martha, the perfect name is…" In equally perfect silence, he let the suspense build.

"Is what?" I asked, still holding on. "Tell me quick, before my fingers break off."

Finally, he uttered the secret word. "BluCon."

I relaxed my grip. "What?"

Betting on Bernie

"BluCon. One word. Spelled just like it sounds, but without an e."

"Okay, but… why BluCon?"

"Because it'll be blue, and you've conned me into it."

Before we got home, we had agreed that, come springtime, if our investments were holding up, we would place an order for BluCon.

By mid April 2009, with the country still in the grip of the Great Recession, the RV industry was in such doldrums that our order went to the head of the Lazy Daze production line, as opposed to the usual years-long wait.

Late in June, we flew to Los Angeles to pick up BluCon.

Over the next two weeks, Bernie drove her through Nevada, Utah, Arizona, and on to New Mexico. Then, for twenty-eight more months, accompanied by Sugar the Camping Cat, we ventured out for weeks at a time, high and deep into the western and southwestern wilds.

Bernie painting beside BluCon in Wyoming, August 2009

Bernie painting at Mirror Lake, 10,500' high in Wyoming's Snowy Range of the Rocky Mountains, August 2009

We camped at 10,000' elevations in the San Juan, Sangre de Cristo, and Snowy Ranges, all of which are part of the Rockies; below sea level in Death Valley; all over the Mojave, Chihuahuan, and Sonoran deserts; and along the Pacific and Gulf coasts; and everywhere in between.

My photo portfolio of wild birds and other creatures and Bernie's inventory of oil paintings peaked during that time. I also produced six full-color issues of an e-newsletter that I called "Two for Art," which I emailed to friends and family. Even though that was my first-and-only attempt at travel writing, recipients seemed to enjoy it. They reacted especially well to seeing Bernie's paintings and my photos of the places we visited and the diverse creatures and wildflowers that we saw.

In the early '90s, my novel *Rubies of the Viper* had found an agent in New York but not a publisher. I'd saved its file on floppy disks, stashed them away, and moved them to Santa Fe in 2002.

So now, in 2009, recently retired from REP, I decided to look at the manuscript again. My newer Mac couldn't read the old floppies, but after I found a tech with a Mac SE like I'd used in the '80s, the text reappeared on his monitor in its original format. He updated the Word version and returned it to me on a CD.

Back at home, reading my creation on-screen for the first time in almost twenty years, I decided it needed work but still had merit. So for the next eight months, using feedback previously received from publishers and the agent, I rethought, restructured, rewrote, and reformatted it.

Amazon's brand-new self-publishing technology allowed me to release *Rubies of the Viper* in my own name as both author and publisher for the Kindle e-reader. In 2010, I reformatted it for a paperback edition and offered it for sale that way, too. Gratifying reviews and sales followed, so I never regretted going that route.

Bernie and me in one of his two full-room displays on opening night for his first art show at Waxlander Gallery, October 2010

On October 8, 2010, Bernie's first show began at Waxlander Gallery and ran for several weeks. Paintings featured were mostly large oils from places we'd recently visited in BluCon. Having an event like that on Santa Fe's iconic Canyon Road was the final fulfillment of his lifelong dream.

For both of us, that opening day was probably the second-proudest of our lives, following his graduation day at the University of Chicago.

Also in 2010, we began designing a freestanding studio to be built a few feet away from our house. Bernie's job was to make it work for himself as an artist, with great natural light and storage. My job was to make sure the same 800 square feet would work as a *casita* (guest house) —with a full living room, kitchenette, bedroom, bathroom, closet, and fireplace—in case some future buyer preferred that to a studio.

A builder turned it into reality, and in July 2011, Bernie moved all his painting gear from the house into his dream studio. He was as happy that day as I had ever seen him.

In August 2011, Sugar—our dear, well-traveled, tiny-tiger kitty—died at age twenty. We mourned her for a month, and then, at the Santa Fe Humane Society, found Smokey, a dapper green-eyed, gray-and-white tuxedo cat who filled our hearts and took to RV travel well, too.

Smokey, September 2011 (Bernie liked to say, approvingly, "He's Smokey Dokey.")

As a Waxlander Gallery artist, Bernie loved participating in the annual Canyon Road Paint Out. Coming in the glorious middle of October, it's a day when artists affiliated with the galleries in Santa Fe's main art district set up their easels and show their stuff.

In 2008, 2009, and 2010, he had painted in front of Waxlander's entry garden. So now, as Saturday, October 15, 2011 approached, he was looking forward to doing it again.

Our plan was that on Friday, we would drive to BluCon's storage spot in Albuquerque, bring her home, and park her beside the new studio.

On Saturday, as Bernie painted in the garden, I would shop for food and other essentials and stock the rig.

On Sunday, we would leave for a six-week painting-and-shooting trip to Utah and Idaho.

Bernie in front of Waxlander Gallery during the Canyon Road Paint Out, October 2009

Over breakfast on Friday, Bernie told me that he'd had a headache all night. Ibuprofen in the wee hours hadn't helped, but he took two more anyway as we set out for Albuquerque.

I drove the car down and back, but he brought BluCon up the steep La Bajada, even as the throbbing in his head persisted.

An artist friend was opening a show that evening. We'd promised to go, and we did, even though Bernie didn't feel well enough to drive.

"Sure you're up for painting tomorrow?" I asked when we left the show early.

"No stupid headache's gonna stop me."

On Saturday morning, I was at my desk in the den when he came in to give me a kiss. His eyes betrayed the pain that was now raging into its second day.

"Maybe you shouldn't go, Babe," I said.

"But they're giving me the prime spot in the garden this year, on the path between the gate and the front door. Everyone who comes in will stop to watch me paint. How can I pass that up?"

He walked to the end of the hallway, then turned to wave.

I waved back. "Call if you need anything, okay?"

It seemed he made a special effort to flash his big, bright Bernie smile in my direction.

That was the last time I ever saw it.

PART III

BETTING ON BERNIE IN SICKNESS AND DEATH

Chapter 19
Unusual Activity in the Brain

Saturday, October 15 to Sunday, October 16, 2011

I had just finished unloading food and supplies onto the store's conveyor belt when my phone buzzed in my handbag.

"Where are you?" Bernie's voice sounded far away.

"Grocery store, checking out. Where are you?"

"In the…" His words drifted off.

The cashier was chatting loudly with someone at the next register. I waved at her and pointed to the phone at my ear.

"Tell me again, Babe."

I detected a chuckle, which suggested he was chagrined.

"The ER," he said.

"Why? What happened?"

"Blacked out." His voice shook.

As the cashier rang up my purchases, I heard nothing more from Bernie, so I went on. "While you were painting in the garden?"

"Yeah." Still faint.

"Did they call an ambulance for you?"

"Don't remember."

I paid the cashier and checked my watch. It was 2:15.

"How're you now?"

"Sick to my stomach."

"And your head?"

"Still hurts."

Betting on Bernie   205

My own head remained in traveling-to-Utah-tomorrow mode. "Listen, Babe, I'll take this stuff home, then come find you."

On the telephone answering machine in our kitchen, I listened to a report from the director at Waxlander Gallery.

People in the garden where Bernie was painting had seen him suffer what appeared to be a seizure. He'd collapsed onto his easel, which broke under his weight and tore up his left arm as he fell through it. His head hit the pavers, then his body jerked hard for several minutes. The director said she had called 911, and Bernie was now on his way to Christus St. Vincent Hospital. She didn't have my mobile number but hoped I'd get this message soon.

I found Bernie in a curtained ER cubicle with his head and arm bandaged. The moment I walked in, he gave a manic laugh and pointed to the wall. "Smokey, silly guy, jumping around up there."

I stared at the plain, pale-green wall, trying to figure out what could possibly look like a big gray cat jumping around. But Bernie continued cackling. Talking to himself. Hallucinating.

A nurse whispered to me that the meds they'd administered for the nausea and headache might be causing him to see things that weren't there.

Bernie kept giggling over what he clearly saw as Smokey's ongoing gymnastics atop the cabinets. Various medical personnel came and went.

A doctor arrived to perform a lumbar puncture. When he suggested I step outside, I did and then, from the hallway, called Bernie's brother Murray to let him know what had happened and ask him to pass the news on to their sister Rozanne. As they wheeled Bernie out for an MRI, I went to the hospital cafeteria for some food to keep me going.

Much later, after they moved Bernie to a regular room, I went home to feed and cuddle the real Smokey.

On Sunday morning, instead of setting off for Utah with Bernie and Smokey in BluCon, I returned to the hospital.

Bernie had a high fever and didn't speak to me, but at least he was awake and, apparently, not hallucinating.

After a while, a doctor I'd never met before entered and introduced himself to me. I'll call him "Dr. N" for neurologist.

Calmly and quietly, Dr. N began explaining in simple terms a few things that he said I needed to understand. In a small spiral notebook that I kept in my bag, I jotted down the words in quotation marks below.

The MRI had detected "unusual activity in the brain."

Dr. N wouldn't know for sure what "the insult" was without further analysis, so he was sending "a vial of spinal fluid" to a lab for testing. He expected to have "results by the end of the week."

He asked my permission to start Bernie on "a drug called acyclovir." If he did not have what Dr. N suspected, Dr. N would stop giving him the drug. But if Bernie did have it, "getting him on acyclovir right away could save his life."

Although Bernie was awake, his glassy eyes and glazed-over facial expression suggested that he hadn't grasped much of that. "We'll fight it" was the only thing he said that whole morning.

As for me, I was stunned by this development. Bernie was seventy-three, slim, strong, and sharp. He took good care of himself. Ate well. Exercised regularly. Never abused his body. In the four-plus decades of our marriage, he'd never spent a single night in the hospital until now.

Even as I made notes, I didn't have the wits to ask Dr. N what he meant by "unusual activity in the brain" or "insult," much less what mysterious malady he suspected Bernie might have.

My befuddlement didn't last long, however. Dr. N had indicated that Bernie's life was at risk, so I had to be strong of heart and clear of mind to help the medical professionals save him.

"Yes," I told Dr. N, "you have my permission. Please do start that treatment right away."

I'd never heard of acyclovir and had a hard time holding the word in my head. I finally got it by conjuring up the curious image of a virus riding a bicycle.

After receiving his first intravenous infusion, Bernie slept the rest of the day. Hours later, he was still asleep and unresponsive as I kissed him goodbye and left for home to face down my fears.

That Sunday night, as an experienced researcher on many topics but never anything related to afflictions of the brain, I turned to the internet to learn the basics.

Dr. N had provided a few clues, so I focused on those.

Specifically, I went looking for some kind of intersection between spinal fluid and acyclovir. To keep track of what I feared might be a mass of confusing data, I grabbed a larger spiral notebook and started writing in longhand.

"Spinal fluid is tapped as a way to diagnose meningitis, encephalitis, bacterial tuberculosis, fungal infections, etc."

That wasn't very helpful, just a starting point.

"Acyclovir treats viruses only."

From that, I concluded that I could drop from my list of concerns all non-viral maladies.

"Acyclovir is commonly prescribed for viral infections like chickenpox and its offspring, shingles."

I knew Bernie had contracted chickenpox as a child, just as I and most other kids did until a vaccine for it became available in the '90s.

I'd even endured the misery of shingles on my back during my last semester at Centenary, which was an abnormally young age for it.

But Bernie never had had shingles.

"*Acyclovir is also used to treat life-threatening viral infections like meningitis and encephalitis.*"

Now I felt like I was getting somewhere.

"*While meningitis is an inflammation or swelling of the protective membranes that line the inside of the skull and the spine, viral encephalitis is an inflammation or swelling within the brain itself.*"

The words used there, "swelling within the brain itself," matched Dr. N's description of what Bernie's MRI had revealed: "unusual activity in the brain."

Viral encephalitis. Bingo.

Next, I dug into the most-common symptoms of viral encephalitis: headaches, seizures, hallucinations, high fever, and consciousness disorders, such as being comatose and unable to open the eyes or communicate. Over the past two days, Bernie had exhibited them all.

I turned up a connection between viral encephalitis and a nasty little something called *Varicella-zoster virus* (VZV):

- VZV originated in ancient times and, traveling under the name of chickenpox, came to America with the first European explorers, who spread it far and wide among the native population, causing millions of deaths.
- VZV lurks forever in the bodies of those who survive chickenpox and often pops up later in life as shingles.
- Much less often, VZV reappears as a dangerous infection (or inflammation, or swelling) of the brain.

I learned of another nasty little something, *Herpes simplex virus* (HSV):

- HSV jumped from monkeys to humans a million years ago.
- HSV causes cold sores and genital herpes, a sexually transmitted disease passed from one human to another.
- Like VZV—but even less often—HSV also reappears as an infection (or inflammation, or swelling) of the brain.

Betting on Bernie

At first, I had trouble keeping VZV and HSV straight.

I learned that they're both part of a family called *herpesviruses*, which has over a hundred mutated members.

Within that family, VZV and HSV are part of a subset called *human herpesviruses*, because they can infect humans.

That night, I had no idea which of the two might be Bernie's assailant, but VZV seemed the more likely since he'd had chickenpox as a child. So far as I knew, he'd never had sex with anyone but me, and neither of us had ever showed signs of a sexually transmitted disease, which seemed to rule out HSV.

While reading on, I perked up at the knowledge that acyclovir saved from death most patients with encephalitis caused by either VZV or HSV, assuming they received the drug quickly. Which, of course, explained Dr. N's urgency to get Bernie on it right away.

Another encouraging discovery was the existence of international online support communities for survivors and their families. Just as cancer is often called the "Big C," people with personal experience in dealing with viral encephalitis tend to refer to it as the "Big E," or simply "E."

Throughout that long, sleepless night, I kept conjuring up scary hypothetical scenarios.

What if Bernie's grand mal seizure had hit on Friday as he drove BluCon north from Albuquerque, up La Bajada towards Santa Fe, instead of on Saturday as he painted in a small garden surrounded by people?

What if it had hit on Sunday morning as he drove us in BluCon back down that steep slope, heading west to Arizona and Utah?

What if it had hit a few days later near Grand Staircase/Escalante National Monument, on our planned drive across "The Hogback," a notoriously treacherous 10,000'-high ribbon of road with sheer drop-offs on both sides?

What if it had hit while we were camping in some remote spot with no hospital within hundreds of miles, much less an expert neurologist who could make an accurate diagnosis of the extremely rare Big E and know how to treat it?

In any of those scenarios, either Bernie alone or both of us almost certainly would have died. We might even have taken others with us over a cliff.

If there was any bright light to be found in the crisis we now were facing, it was that none of those terrible things had happened.

Chapter 20

Do You Know Who I Am?

Monday, October 17 to Monday, November 7, 2011

On Monday morning, I found Bernie still comatose, receiving acyclovir and other meds and fluids intravenously, getting oxygen, and being fed through a tube. Our friends Renate and Beecham Robinson arrived, too, although we had little to do but share information gleaned from the internet, ponder the quirks of Fate, and sweat the small stuff.

One bit of small stuff that I sweated that day was that BluCon had been in our driveway since Friday. Our homeowner association covenants limited RVs to three nights on a property, so we were now in violation. It wasn't a terrible infraction, but we did try to be good neighbors.

So, before going to bed that evening, I sent out an email informing the neighbors of what had happened to Bernie and promising that BluCon would be gone just as soon as I found someone to return her to her storage spot in Albuquerque.

While I was at it, I then copied the "what happened to Bernie" part of that message, pasted it into another email, and blasted it out to a few close friends and family members around the country.

On Tuesday, while I was at the hospital, over a dozen people left messages on our home answering machine, including some who hadn't been on my original list. That evening, it took me forever to listen to them all, and most ended with some version of, "I want to know more, Martha, so please call me back."

But by then, I was exhausted, with neither the energy nor the desire to call anyone back. Clearly, I needed a new communication strategy.

That night, I sent another blast promising to keep them all updated via nightly Bernie Reports and to add new emails to the list as requested. "Feel free to share my reports with others," I wrote, "and email me if you need more information. But please don't call."

People honored my request, which I repeated on each new message. As my distribution list grew to well over a hundred names, circulation loops became obvious. Our friends in Chicagoland, Santa Fe, and elsewhere were sharing them. Bernie's far-flung family and mine. His former employees, colleagues, and clients. Gallery staffs and fellow artists in towns where his work was displayed. Writing nightly Bernie Reports served as a useful de-briefing, head-clearing exercise, too, so I kept it up.

I knew little of brain diseases and injuries in October 2011, when my world shifted on its axis. In the days, months, and years that followed, I learned a lot. Since I'm not a medical doctor, however, I never grasped everything that Dr. N and the other specialists, therapists, and counselors explained to me in the heat of many battles to save Bernie's life. Through research, I filled gaps in my knowledge from the most-reputable online sources until I felt I knew enough to make wise decisions on his behalf.

The narrative that follows quotes from my contemporaneous notes and accurately reflects my understanding of events as they happened in real time. These are my true personal experiences, as I lived them, kept from being a fuzzy blur now by my saved nightly Bernie Reports. Any lack of medical precision here is due to my ignorance and no one else's.

On Wednesday morning, October 19, I was alone with Bernie in a regular hospital room. He remained nonresponsive, in a natural coma.

Then, abruptly, his whole body went rigid. Moments later, his limbs began thrashing as his head jerked back and forth sideways.

I dashed to the nurses' station. One of them returned with me while Bernie was still flailing. She checked her watch and packed the side rails of his bed with pillows to keep his head from hitting them.

By the time the doctor, a hospitalist, arrived, Bernie's seizure had ended and the nurse had propped him on his side with the same pillows.

"He stiffened first," I told the doctor, "then started jerking."

"Did you see it?" he asked the nurse.

She nodded. "It was a tonic-clonic. Went on for two more minutes after I got here."

With that confirmation, the doctor said to me, "It's good that you got help for him so fast. And we needed to know about this episode."

The nurse stayed after he left. I was agitated and grateful for the opportunity to talk with her. "You called it a tonic-clonic," I said. "Is that the same as a grand mal seizure?"

Again, she nodded. "It's a newer term. 'Tonic' refers to the first stage, when someone loses consciousness, stiffens, and falls. Once the jerking starts, that's the 'clonic' stage. There are other types of seizures, too. Have you ever seen him stare blankly into space? Or smack his lips together or chew on something that's not there?"

"Yes, he does that sometimes, but I never thought anything of it."

"Those were absence seizures," she said. "He'd probably had them many times before the first tonic-clonic hit. You might not have noticed the other types either, but it's likely he's had them all at different times."

After she left, it took me a while to process what she'd said.

The "big one" didn't hit Bernie out of the blue on Saturday.

He'd been having seizures at home that I never recognized.

Did he have them even when he was driving?

If so, how dangerous was that for him, me, and other people?

Could I have gotten help for Bernie earlier if I'd known what to watch for?

I resolved to learn more about brain injuries and seizures.

Dr. N arrived soon, fully up-to-date on Bernie's latest episode.

"What if I hadn't been here when that happened?" I asked him. "What if it happens again and nobody's in the room to call a nurse?"

"I'll transfer him to the ICU. More eyes there to watch him." Dr. N paused as if thinking, then looked at me once more. "But there may be something even better that I can do for him. Please wait around today. We may need you here later on."

The sun was setting when Dr. N entered Bernie's ICU room.

"I have colleagues," he said to me, "at UNM Hospital. At my request, they're holding a bed for Mr. Marks in the Neuro-ICU. That's a specialized facility for patients with life-threatening brain injuries."

"Like viral encephalitis?"

Dr. N didn't seem surprised by my use of a term that he hadn't yet mentioned to me. I took his nod as confirmation of my amateur diagnosis.

He went on. "Here, we can only perform one EEG per patient per day. But the Neuro-ICU does it around the clock. They have the best team and the finest equipment in the state. Once Mr. Marks is hooked up there, they'll know exactly what's going on inside his brain, and if something happens they can address it right away. I'll need your written permission to get him admitted." He handed me a printed sheet and a pen. "If you agree, we'll transfer him tonight."

I signed the document and stayed with Bernie until the EMTs arrived. They lifted him onto a gurney with all his drip bags and tubes.

I followed them to an ambulance waiting outside in the dark.

"I love you, Bernie," I called as they locked the gurney down inside, but with little hope that he, deep in his coma, had heard me.

At home, I sent out a Bernie Report, then began researching what neurologists call "insults" to the brain. Over the course of that evening, I learned two important terms.

Traumatic brain injuries are caused by external forces like bullets and motorcycle crashes. They damage the all-important organ within the skull and leave visible scars. Often, the damage is permanent.

Non-traumatic brain injuries—like viral encephalitis and seizure disorder (a newer term for epilepsy)—come from within the body. They leave no external scars, because all the damage is internal. They can be permanent, too, and equally devastating.

My first thought was that, assuming Bernie survived, it would be better that he'd had a non-traumatic brain injury. He wouldn't be disfigured, so other people wouldn't gawk at him or recoil from him.

That turned out to be true.

But the very invisibility of a non-traumatic brain injury can also be a curse of sorts, because the lack of external signs of injury doesn't mean that unexpected and unpleasant behaviors can't happen. It just means that other people don't anticipate them and may not be prepared for them.

It's an hour's drive from Santa Fe to the University of New Mexico Hospital (UNMH) in Albuquerque, so Bernie's new location altered the rhythm of my life. I no longer went home during the day to feed Smokey and myself. I left a house key and cat-care instructions with a neighbor in case something ever prevented me from getting back.

I did make it home almost every night, because I wanted to relax with Smokey, send out Bernie Reports, and sleep in our bed. Throughout that ordeal, I felt Bernie's presence at our villa on the hill and clung to hope that he'd soon return as good as new.

The UNMH is New Mexico's only Level 1 Trauma Center. It's also the only academic teaching hospital and the top medical center within hundreds of miles. Its Neuro-ICU has twenty-four beds divided into two wards at the secluded end of a high-level floor. For seventeen days and nights, the superb staff cared for Bernie in both wards.

He spent the first thirty-six hours in a tall, high-tech bed connected to a tower of monitoring equipment unlike any I'd ever seen, all within an isolated, silent, wedge-shaped, glass-fronted enclosure.

The only other item in that chamber was a single straight chair that suggested visitors were not encouraged to linger. Even so, I sat with him, sporadically reading, all day Thursday.

Outside that space, a long, curved bank of identical glass-fronted wedges faced a semi-circular work station where technicians monitored each patient, ready to summon immediate help if needed.

Bernie remained comatose as electrodes all over his scalp produced nonstop graphs of his brain's electrical impulses for the techs to monitor and the docs to analyze. It was a confidence-inspiring situation, and I trusted the science to pull him through.

But still… sitting there that day, I couldn't escape dark thoughts.

What if he dies of this?

What if he lives on but remains comatose forever?

What if he comes out of it with a badly damaged brain?

What if he winds up in a vegetative state?

As the hours passed, my dark thoughts turned inward.

What do I do if he dies of this?

What do I do if he lives on but remains comatose forever?

What do I do if he comes out of it with a badly damaged brain?

What do I do if he winds up in a vegetative state?

I saw only one path for myself if any of those awful situations should arise. If Bernie died, I would put our real estate up for sale and travel full-time with Smokey in BluCon. If Bernie lived but remained in a comatose or vegetative state, or if he emerged badly brain-damaged, I'd get him into the best nursing-care facility I could find and follow the other plan for myself.

Odd as it may seem, coming up with that simple strategy did more to get me through that dreadful week than anything else.

After I drove home that Thursday night, I opened our wedding album and spent an hour with those forty-three-year-old photos. For reasons that I'll never understand, doing that comforted me. I cried a lot, but it did bring Bernie back to me, as good as new, if only in my heart.

Bernie and me on our wedding day, January 27, 1968

Looking at those photos made me think, too.

When two people are young, strong, and healthy, the traditional vow "to love, honor, and cherish, in sickness and in health, till death do us part" may sound like a dusty cliché from some Brothers Grimm fairy tale.

But when life-shaking crises arise—as they now had for us, four-plus decades later—those promises take on real meaning. We were just lucky on that sweet January morning of our wedding that such troubles were unforeseeable, unknowable, and unimaginable.

Late Friday morning, having monitored Bernie's brain around the clock since Wednesday night, the staff transferred him to the other ward, a large, rectangular room with curtained beds on both long sides.

The most amazing thing to me was how noisy that ward was. I soon learned that patients with brain injuries have little self-control, so they often shout or curse, and quite colorfully, too, as was the case with one woman who was there while Bernie was.

After waiting all week for the test results on Bernie's spinal fluid, I rejoiced when they arrived that day. It wasn't that I was glad to learn he did have viral encephalitis, but because I now knew that Dr. N's early, accurate diagnosis and quick action in getting him on acyclovir had given Bernie his best chance of avoiding an incredibly painful death.

Nobody ever told me which specific human herpesvirus was the culprit in his case. I assumed it was VZV, given its connection to chickenpox and the fact that Bernie never had suffered from the cold sores and genital herpes associated with HSV.

As with all teaching hospitals, UNM's medical students accompany their professors on rounds. So, early that afternoon, the neurologist who was now in charge of Bernie's care stopped by to get acquainted.

"Viral encephalitis is so rare," he told me, "that many physicians, and even some neurologists, go their entire careers without ever seeing or treating a patient who has it."

"And yet," I said, "my husband has it. What are the odds of that?"

"Incalculably small. Which means, the opportunity to study him would be a priceless gift to my students. Would you let me bring them in to meet you, observe him, and discuss his chart among themselves?"

I agreed, of course. Soon, half a dozen doctors-to-be filed in to stand around the bed, casually chatted with me, and began analyzing Bernie's condition as a group. The neurologist stood by to answer questions or suggest ways to improve their assessments.

After they finished their group analysis, I pushed for information that would help me. "Can you tell at this point if he's going to live?"

"No," the neurologist said gently, "but he's breathing. He's nourished and hydrated. He'll receive acyclovir for twenty-one days. So, his odds look pretty good to me."

The students nodded, clearly eager to reassure me.

I addressed another concern. "We have friends who went through a similar experience. The wife suffered an aneurysm and was comatose for weeks. When she came to, she didn't recognize her husband for months, and neither her personality nor her behavior ever was the same."

The doctor invited his students to respond.

"That's common with brain injuries," said one.

"The results are unpredictable," said another. "Some do have issues like that, others don't. Actually, the problems can vary a lot."

"So, it's possible," I said, "that Bernie won't know me? And that he'll come out of this a very different person?"

"Time will tell," said a third student.

Around four o'clock that same afternoon, Bernie moved. It wasn't herky-jerky like a seizure, but almost normal, as if he'd just gotten tired of lying in one position and needed a change.

I stood, leaned over him, and touched his stubbly face. He must have noted my presence, because he lifted his hands.

I took them in mine, gently pressed them, and started talking to him. "Bernie, can you hear me? I'm right beside you, Babe."

Moments later, his crusted eyelids cracked open. I hardly dared believe it, because in my darkest hours I'd steeled myself for the possibility that he wouldn't ever wake up.

"Can you see me?" I asked.

He grunted.

"Oh, I do believe you see me."

Another grunt.

"Do you know who I am?"

A gruff voice replied in a tone of great umbrage. "Of course."

"Of course," I echoed. Then, from some hollow deep inside me, I dredged up a relieved laugh. "Of course, you do."

"Martha," he said. "My kid."

And with that, my self-control cracked. Tears welled and streamed down my cheeks as I sobbed in loud, uncontrollable relief.

We won't have to go through what our friends did.

"I love you, Bernie."

"Love you."

It wasn't much of a conversation, but as the ward nurses told me when they gathered around his bed to see this miraculous development for themselves, it was the best possible sign that he was going to live.

I cried on and off for the next hour and all the way driving home.

When I entered the ward the next morning, the nurses cheerfully informed me that they'd given Bernie a sponge bath and a shave, so he was looking and feeling better. He'd eaten oatmeal, too, his first real food in a week. And he was talking, they assured me.

I held my breath and pulled the curtain aside.

Bernie looked at me and waved a hand around. "Where?"

"You're at the university hospital in Albuquerque. It's a good place, Babe."

"How?"

"You're asking how you got here?"

He nodded.

"By ambulance. Three days ago."

"Don't remember."

"You were unconscious."

"How long?"

"You were unconscious for six days."

"Why?"

Throughout this exchange, his voice and facial expression remained flat. No hint of a smile or a chuckle. No twinkle in his eyes. But still, his curiosity seemed a good sign that some part of his brain was working.

The nurses had warned me not to provide many details, because he wouldn't be able to grasp them and any confusion could upset him.

So I kept it simple. "A little bug messed you up."

"Bug?"

"The same bug that gave you a bad headache. Remember that?"

"No."

"That's how this started. We just didn't know it at the time."

On Monday, Renate and Beecham drove from Santa Fe to Albuquerque to engage Bernie with cheerful banter. Fortunately, there had always been plenty of merriment among us, so it almost felt like a normal visit. While they were there, a physical therapist arrived to get Bernie on his feet for the first time in ten days. She wrapped a gait belt around his chest and stood him up.

At that moment, the tiniest hint emerged of the funny guy I had loved for decades and soon would come to think of as "Old Bernie."

Standing now, he looked around and exclaimed, "Ta-da."

Normally, a big, bright Bernie grin would have accompanied such a celebratory comment, but this time it didn't. Still, the rest of us, including the therapist, laughed in response and cheered him on. That glimmer of wit offered hope, to me at least, that a trace of Bernie's usual personality still lurked somewhere within his virus-infested brain.

Over the next few days, self-imposed stresses piled up on me.

For over a week, I'd been leaving home too early. Staying too late at the hospital. Driving a long stretch of the too-lonely, too-dark I-25 by myself. Eating too much junk food. Spending too many hours at the computer. Sleeping too little.

I knew I was abusing myself but didn't realize how badly until the morning of Bernie's second Thursday at UNMH.

In that long, large ward, as I walked between the parallel rows of curtains with my eyes focused on those around Bernie's bed, the room seemed to start spinning. An instant later, I dropped like a limp rag, heard a *thud* as if from somewhere far away, and lost consciousness.

Awareness returned in waves of isolated sensory impressions.

Nurses. Hovering. Kneeling. Above me. Beside me. Taking my pulse. Rolling me onto my back. Calling for orderlies. Tut-tutting at this odd occurrence on their ward. Orderlies. Talking. Lifting me onto a gurney. Wheeling me into an ice-cold elevator. Leaving me in a corner of a noisy waiting room. Transferring me into a bed. More nurses. Hovering. Pinching me for an IV. Attaching drip bags. Bringing me soft food. Helping me eat it.

Slowly, it dawned on me that I was now the patient in the hospital bed. The one hooked up to the tubes and wires. The one whose brain felt flat. The one who wasn't thinking clearly.

But I did remember that I had a cat at home. Groggily, I called our neighbor and asked her to care for Smokey.

It all seemed surreal. I didn't want to be there but was too tired to resist. I slept straight through that day and night.

The next morning, I woke up rested and ready to go.

"My husband's a patient in the Neuro-ICU," I told the nurse who brought my breakfast, as if that would impress her. "I gotta get back."

"You're not going anywhere till the doc says it's okay."

I raised my voice. "So, where is he?"

"Gee, I dunno." She fiddled with a tube dripping some kind of fluid into me. "Taking care of two hundred other patients, maybe."

When the doctor still hadn't showed up by noon, she brought me lunch. After that, I was ready to depart, with or without permission.

"I think I'll head upstairs now," I told her as the afternoon wore on.

"Nobody's gonna stop you, honey. But you'll have to pay every penny of your bill here, 'cause insurance won't cover it unless you're officially released. And trust me, thirty hours in the ER ain't cheap."

Her wisdom convinced me.

Finally, late that afternoon, word came that the doc had agreed to discharge me, but only on the condition that I promise to eat a hearty and healthy restaurant meal right away and then check into a nearby hotel, at least for one night, if not more. Needless to say, I agreed. Our neighbor was willing to continue Smokey-sitting, so I followed the doctor's advice.

Those two nights were the only ones when I didn't get home to sleep. From then on, I allowed myself to doze longer each morning. I ate better meals, shortened my visits, and experienced no relapses.

Monday, November 7, 2011 felt like a graduation day of sorts.

Although Bernie still never smiled or spoke more than isolated words and phrases, he had finished three weeks of acyclovir. He and I had learned enough teamwork to get him shuffling around the ward with the support of a gait belt. With that essential preparation, he could go home.

Before Bernie was released, the neurologist and his med-student flock made a last visit to his bedside. The students thanked him for what they'd learned from him and wished him well in his ongoing recovery. Others were there, too: nurses, techs, orderlies, and therapists.

I passed around a print of the photo that Mama had taken of us in Linden in 1966 and also our wedding portrait. If there had been no context, few in the group would have recognized either of us—young and slim and dark-haired and carefree—in those old shots.

"This is what you've saved," I told them with tears in my eyes. "A long-time love affair and a really good marriage. Bernie and I want you to know how grateful we are."

As we bid them all goodbye, mine weren't the only eyes that were wet.

Chapter 21

The Most Awful Day and Night

Monday, November 7 to Thursday, November 17, 2011

Before bringing Bernie home, I'd stocked up on his favorite foods and beverages. At his request, I also bought a big box of crayons and a drawing pad, plus a pair of flat-top wooden TV tables for him to work on. I took up all our area rugs. Had a wheelchair and several gait belts at the ready. Laid in a month's supply of his now-essential, prescription anticonvulsant drug.

But even after all that preparation, the prospect of living with an epileptic husband gave me pause. After studying first-century cultures for my novel, I knew the Romans had considered epileptics *lunaticus*, meaning "under the influence of the moon." Spanish literature had taught me that medieval Europeans believed epileptics were demonically possessed. Like lepers, they were shunned, forced to live and beg on the streets, or expelled from society into isolated camps. Even in later centuries, epileptics were often locked up with criminals and "other insane people."

Now I had a new set of fears to stare down. Bernie was going to live. He knew who I was and had the intellectual capacity to communicate with me. There would be no reason to sell our home and travel full-time with Smokey in BluCon. But still, did I have the physical and emotional strength to cope with a brain-damaged, seizure-prone husband?

It was one thing to sit at his hospital bedside as a host of medical professionals ably cared for him, and quite another to be his at-home caregiver. His only caregiver. Maybe for the rest of our lives.

I'm not a nurse. Never wanted to be a nurse. Nursing was probably the last career I ever would have chosen, so I won't pretend that I was enthusiastic about the prospect of taking care of Bernie full-time at home all by myself.

But by setting an alarm clock to ring every six hours—interrupting our sleep at least once a night no matter how I timed it—I kept him on his massive four-pills-a-day, 4,000-mg anticonvulsant schedule.

I cooked his favorite meals.

Helped him get dressed, brush his teeth, and eat.

Eased him back and forth to the bathroom with a gait belt.

Escorted him into the car and out to appointments that same way.

Undressed him, got him showered, and redressed him for bed without losing my grip and banging his head on the floor tiles.

The brain injury had left his skin highly sensitive to both hot and cold water, so any deviation from lukewarm provoked a panic attack. He had to test the temperature on both forearms for several minutes before he'd even consider stepping into the shower stall. And once he deemed it perfect, he wouldn't let me turn it off for fear the temperature would shift. That meant I had to undress myself for his shower, too, because both of us would get soaked as I clung to his gait belt, eased him over the raised edge, and maneuvered him onto the bench as the water ran.

Fortunately, he remembered how to soap up and shampoo all by himself. Once he'd rinsed away the suds, I'd shut off the water, towel him dry inside the warm enclosure, and help him back out over the raised edge onto the bath mat.

The process of getting Bernie undressed, bathed, dried off, into his pajamas, tooth-brushed, and medicated took an hour.

The hardest thing for me to accept was how foolishly he acted. How childish he was. Nothing about him was normal. Not his sensory perception. Not his judgment. Not his thinking process. Not his reasoning. Not his verbal and motor skills. Not his hand-eye coordination. Not his grasp of his own limitations.

In almost every imaginable way—even attempting to have sex—my husband had turned into a four-year-old. He wanted to call friends but couldn't. Wanted to write them notes but couldn't. Wanted to dress and undress himself but couldn't. Wanted to tie his own shoes but couldn't. Wanted to feed himself but couldn't. Wanted to go to the bathroom alone but couldn't. Hardly any aspect of his brain or body worked right, and neither one of us was prepared for that.

As I told a friend, "I never wanted a child, but now I have one."

Bernie did enjoy his crayons though. At his request, I'd move the TV tables around the house so he could color different rooms and views. I saved a drawing that he signed and labeled "Smokey" in printed letters, which was how he wrote forever after.

For me, it was gratifying to see him having fun with crayons, but also agonizing to compare his new

Bernie's crayon drawing of Smokey, November 2011

(Background: bright orange. Cat: gray and white with green eyes, darker-orange whiskers, and black tail.)

Betting on Bernie

"artwork" with the exquisite oil paintings that he'd made up to the very moment of his seizure in the garden.

Our lives improved a lot when a fine team of physical, speech, and occupational therapists began coming to our home, along with a nurse who checked on Bernie twice a week. Soon, he progressed from a wheelchair to a walker. He developed enough sensitivity in his fingers to identify by touch objects buried deep in a bowl of dry beans and pull them out. He learned to speak in short, halting sentences.

But still, when we were alone, I had to watch him all the time.

One day, I caught him trying to steer his walker with one hand as the other clutched a long-bladed kitchen knife.

After that, I hid our knives and scissors.

Another day, he started auto-dialing people at random on his cell phone, but when they answered, nothing he said made sense.

Temporarily, I hid his phone, too.

On yet another day, I heard a noise in the dining room. I found him teetering on a chair, trying to remove a burned-out bulb from the hanging fixture over the table. The process of getting him safely down almost killed us both.

And on a particularly cold and snowy morning when he was nowhere close to steady enough even to navigate the house without a walker, I spotted him out on the far edge of our white-coated patio without his jacket, hat, gloves, or walker. I grabbed a gait belt, raced out, strapped it around his chest, and guided him back into the house.

"Why'd you go out there, Babe?" I asked once we were inside.

"I'm okay."

"But you might have slipped and cracked your head again."

"I'm okay."

"What if you'd fallen in the snow and I hadn't seen you?"

"I'm okay."

His voice kept rising with each "I'm okay," exhibiting the baseless bravura that I now recognized as the latest, new-but-not-improved, post-E version of Bernie.

I yelled at him then, for the first and only time in my life. "You are not okay!"

Bernie's birthday was November 14, a week after he came home, so I invited our neighbors and the Robinsons to a party to celebrate.

My childlike husband refused to use his walker while others were there. I was terrified that someone would forget his fragility, congratulate him with a sharp clap on the back, and knock him over.

Fortunately, it turned out to be a fun, uneventful evening.

Early in the afternoon of Thursday, November 17—ten days after Bernie took his first at-home doses of the anticonvulsant drug—we were walking with a gait belt down our main hallway when his body abruptly seized up and went rigid for a few seconds. I was new at dealing with seizures, but still I realized what was coming next.

Desperate to keep him from collapsing and hitting his head on the brick floor, I wrapped my arms around his torso from behind, interlaced my fingers, braced myself against a wall, and held on tight until he stopped jerking. Then I guided him into a cushioned armchair in the living room and called 911.

At Christus St. Vincent Hospital, an ER doctor tapped Bernie's spinal fluid for lab testing, ordered an MRI of his brain, and started him on acyclovir again. "Just in case," he said.

Back in an ER cubicle like the one where Bernie had laughed at Smokey's imagined antics a month earlier, he now was unusually quiet.

He said nothing when I asked how he felt.

Maybe some sense of peril is sinking in.

But then he began talking in his new halting pattern. "Want you...," he said, "to know." And then he stopped.

"Know what, Babe?"

"Long time ago." Another full stop.

"Yes?"

"In Shreveport." Another stop.

I nodded. "While we were living in Shreveport?"

"And later." Another stop. "In Waukegan."

"When you worked in Waukegan?"

He seemed reluctant to say more, so I prompted him again. "What happened in Shreveport and Waukegan?"

He remained silent.

"Babe, keep on telling me what you want me to know."

"Two women."

Those simple words knocked the wind out of me. I struggled to breathe. My mind needed time, too, to roll them around. Process them. Absorb them.

Something happened. Two women. Shreveport and Waukegan.

Then he started up again. "Waukegan... didn't last... long."

Realization hit. He was confessing to me, as if I were a priest inside a dark wooden booth and he a penitent outside on his knees. Or as if it were a deathbed confession. Maybe he believed he was about to die and needed to get his worst sin off his chest.

I didn't probe any more, just let him tell me in his own way, at his own speed, what he wanted me to know.

"Two women..." Long pause. "Worked for me. Only in..." Long pause. "Office hours. Didn't..." Long pause. "Love them. Loved..." Long pause. "My Martha." He stopped cold and shrugged.

After a longer interval, he went on. "Not much time in Waukegan." A heavier-feeling silence was followed by, "Respected my Martha too much."

At that point, apparently having reached the end of his confession, he stopped. I had no more words either. We spent another hour together, not speaking, as the staff came and went.

Sitting there, I realized I wasn't surprised. A man couldn't marry a girl as inexperienced as I had been and expect her to turn into a practiced sexpot on their wedding night. Or even soon thereafter. Or ever, really. Maybe he'd just needed a bit more fun than I could provide.

Instead of surprise, I felt hurt. The wound burned.

Around seven, an orderly entered the curtained cubicle with the greenish walls. "I've come to take Mr. Marks to his room," he said.

I simply stared at Bernie. "See you in the morning, Babe."

In the gathering darkness, I stopped at a fast-food joint before heading home. The route from downtown Santa Fe took me north to an exit ramp leading to New Mexico State Road 599.

I knew my car was leading several others as we came off that ramp, because their headlights glowed in my rear-view mirror. The sky was black by the time I reached an isolated stretch with no street lamps.

I was still ahead of the other cars, nearing a curve in the road, when my headlights picked out the figure of a man not far ahead of me.

A man walking down the center of my lane.

A man walking with his back to the traffic.

A man walking in the same direction as we drivers were moving.

I did the only possible thing. I swerved hard and fast into the empty oncoming lane. And then, having avoided hitting him, I pulled off onto the shoulder and reflexively turned to watch in horror.

Other drivers with less time to react weren't so lucky as I had been.

I heard a heavy *thump* as the car that had been behind me hit the man straight on. I saw the following line of cars either run over his body or swerve away as I had.

Then, sitting in my car on the side of the road, shaking almost as hard as Bernie did when in the grip of a tonic-clonic seizure, I called 911. My already awful day had just gotten much worse.

For two hours, we drivers sat in our cars on both sides of the road, running our engines for heat as the police did their investigation. They stopped traffic in both directions, covered the body with a tarp, and with flashlights walked a straight line across the highway, looking for evidence. Also with flashlights, they inspected the tires and front grilles of all our cars, looking for more evidence. They talked individually with us and asked us to fill out written reports.

At last, a female officer came to my window to thank me for my call to 911, which she said was the first one received for the incident. She said that my car was "clean," other drivers had confirmed my swerve, and I was free to go.

She seemed concerned for me personally, too, so I told her how that call to 911 had been my second of the day. How I had dialed it earlier, seeking help for my epileptic husband. How I was just going home after being at the ER with him when I spotted the man in the road.

Around ten p.m., I pulled into our garage, still grappling with three terrible truths, as I had the whole time I waited alongside the road.

I couldn't doubt that Bernie had viral encephalitis again.

I couldn't unhear what he had confessed to me in the ER.

I couldn't unsee the back of the man in my headlights.

Once inside our kitchen, instead of flipping on the light, I dropped to the floor and released an earsplitting primal scream. Long. Loud. Gut wrenching. Terrifying, even to me. Poor Smokey raced off to some distant part of the house and stayed there till morning.

Throughout that awful night and many more like it—as the sleepless hours and exhausting days dragged on—I went pretty damn close to crazy.

Chapter 22

Beating the Odds in the Worst Possible Way

Friday, November 18 to Thursday, December 8, 2011

Even as I struggled to recover from that unbelievable day and night, Bernie's latest spinal-fluid analysis came back. He did have the Big E again. He had relapsed.

Now I was confused. Previously, I'd assumed that UNMH's doctors had cured him. They'd sent him home, after all. But he wasn't cured, and he couldn't remain at home.

I had to understand why, so I dug deeper.

What I learned this time around stunned me.

While viral encephalitis has afflicted people throughout time, the chance of its ever hitting any one individual is mind-bogglingly low. And the odds that it hits the same person twice are almost nil.

Only two out of every million humans ever get viral encephalitis in their entire lifetimes. Historically, 75% of them died dreadful deaths from uncontrolled swelling of their brains, trapped within their skulls. All it took for me to comprehend the horror of that was to imagine Bernie's skull-splitting headache growing worse and worse and never stopping.

After the 1974 discovery of acyclovir—by two American scientists who later shared the 1988 Nobel Prize in Medicine for proving that a drug could stop a virus that already had infected a body—the numbers flipped. Now 25% died and the rest lived. So, Bernie was "lucky" in contracting the Big E after acyclovir came along. The drug had tripled his chance of survival.

While grateful for that medical miracle, I still struggled to grasp the concept of viruses.

One basic fact seemed totally nuts. Viruses aren't alive, so they can't be killed. I couldn't wrap my head around that.

Over time, I came to picture a virus as if it were a packaged grocery product with a shelf life of three weeks. Whether sitting on a store rack or rampaging through Bernie's brain, its goal is to replicate itself as many times as possible before its sell-by date.

Or, to put it another way, each virus's potency lasts about twenty-one days, during which time it wildly copies itself to keep its kind going. Acyclovir shuts down its ability to replicate. So, after three weeks of treatment, there should be no more viruses capable of replicating.

And thus the infection stops. In theory, anyway.

But if even a single sneaky virus eludes that onslaught of acyclovir, it starts copying itself again, and those copies then copy themselves, and so on and on and on. That explained why the infection had roared back in Bernie's brain after he came home from his three weeks of treatment.

And there was more.

Out of the already-tiny pool of people who had endured the Big E and lived, 8% would relapse. By relapsing, "Lucky Bernie" had joined the 8% of the 75% of an initial minuscule number of encephalitis patients.

Talk about the workings of Fate.

Fortunately, some things improved that second time around. During the next three weeks, Dr. N personally cared for Bernie at Christus St. Vincent in Santa Fe. Closer to home now, I returned to a semi-normal life. More friends were able to visit Bernie and cheer him on.

He was not comatose this time, and yet—with a new crop of viruses replicating inside his brain—the second assault left him with more cognitive damage and new personality changes on top of the earlier ones. Neither physical therapy nor acyclovir nor anything else would repair the previous and ongoing wreckage. We had entered new territory.

Over the next week, the *Santa Fe New Mexican* and the *Albuquerque Journal* identified the man I had swerved to avoid. Columnists and readers pondered the question of why he was walking down the middle of a dark road, marveled at how the first driver had managed to dodge him when others couldn't, and noted that nobody was charged with his death.

Still traumatized by that experience, I longed to talk it over with Bernie, as I always would have done before. But that was impossible now.

That same week, awake but confined to his hospital bed, Bernie needed things to do. He'd always worked the Sunday *New York Times* crossword puzzles with ballpoint pen in blue ink and in a single sitting, so I bought him a drugstore book of much-simpler ones. At first I feared he'd take offense, but he welcomed them and jumped right in. He insisted on using a ballpoint with blue ink, despite my urging to start in pencil.

The book I'd bought had one puzzle grid and clue set per page, so no matter where Bernie opened it, he saw grids and clues on facing pages. The layout was clear to me, but the moment he began, reality intruded.

When he opened a spread and confronted those two mirrored grids and clue sets, he didn't realize that each puzzle was unique. He'd pick a clue on the left page and look for a place to insert a word into the grid on the right page. But none of them fit. No matter how many pages he flipped through, none of the left-side clues fit into the right-side grids.

I explained it time and again. "Look, Babe. The clues on the left page go with the grid on the left page, and the clues on the right page go with the grid on the right page. They are each separate puzzles."

Bernie would nod and go right back to what he'd been doing, flipping from spread to spread, seeking a puzzle that was "right." Then he'd seethe with frustration and fury because, of course, all of them were "wrong." He got mad at the publisher for screwing it up. And at me for bringing him a "bad" book.

So I bought a clipboard, tore out one puzzle page, fastened it face up, and handed it to him. Surely, I thought, if he saw only one puzzle at a time, he'd figure out how to make it work. And he did, briefly, until a new problem arose.

Instead of putting the letters of each word in separate boxes on the grid, he'd stack them all into one. Blue letter upon blue letter, precisely printed on top of each other. He'd end up with one box solid blue and the rest blank. No amount of coaching induced him to spread the letters across all the available boxes.

I noticed, too, that it didn't help to show him or tell him how to do something. His brain no longer seemed wired to imitate an action or to listen to and follow verbal instructions.

A bit later in that first week after his relapse, Bernie asked me for a newspaper. I bought that day's *Santa Fe New Mexican*, which pleased him. He successfully read aloud to me the headlines and the photo captions. My heart rejoiced that he still could do that.

Frustration set in for us both, however, when he moved on to the articles. He was furious that the newspaper typesetter, like the designer of the crossword puzzle book, had screwed up the layout.

It took me a while to realize that he was trying to read the text straight across the columns, instead of letting his eyes track down the first column on the left, then the column to the right of that, and the next column to the right, and so on. He read and understood the words, but the instant his eyes leaped across the vertical gaps between each column, nothing made sense. Obviously, the typesetter was stupid.

I explained that in the past he'd always read the newspaper column by column and tried to show him how to do that now. But no, he insisted, he couldn't, because it wasn't laid out correctly. I tried covering up all the columns to the right, so he'd only see the first one, hoping he would learn to read down it, instead of always looking across to the right for more text. But that only made him madder. For the rest of his life, he rejected my efforts even to get him to hold a newspaper again.

While Bernie was still stuck in that hospital bed, I went online in search of some non-verbal way of engaging him cognitively. One website provided free downloadable mazes at every difficulty level, from colorful ones meant for toddlers—"Help the bunny find the egg in the nest!"—to others complex enough to confound an atomic physicist.

Before leaving home each morning, I printed out ten copies each of two of the easiest mazes, so when Bernie goofed he had an unmarked-up sheet to start over with.

On the first day, when I gave him a pencil and a "bunny and egg" maze attached to the clipboard, I offered basic instructions. "Bernie, can you draw a line from the bunny to the egg?"

"Of course." Umbrage again, which I now recognized as the sign of a fragile ego easily offended by any suggestion that he might not be competent. He ignored the obvious pathways radiating out from the bunny in the center and drew a line straight across them all, essentially "flying" the bunny to the egg in the nest on the outside edge of the maze.

"Oh, you handled the pencil so well," I gushed, since he actually had done what I'd asked. But even as I bubbled with enthusiasm at how well he'd handled his pencil, my heart sank under the weight of realizing that he no longer remembered what the point of a maze was.

He repeated the "flying bunny" trick several times as I babbled on, praising him for doing what he understood from my directions.

But soon, my need to see progress intruded. "Now, Babe, would you like to try doing it a different way?"

"Okay."

"Let's pretend those lines and spaces on the paper are roads."

"Okay."

Betting on Bernie

On a clean sheet, I demonstrated with my fingers how, instead of flying *over* the roads, the bunny naturally would hop *along* a road until he reached an intersection. At that point, he would need to choose the next on-the-ground route to hop along to get to the egg in the nest.

So now, starting at the bunny, Bernie would draw a line along one "road" until he reached the first intersection, at which point he'd zoom his pencil straight to the egg on the edge… "flying" the bunny again.

It took all ten copies of that one maze before he started getting the idea. And with that, we cheered and quit. It was enough for one day.

The next morning, he had forgotten. In trying to "Help the baby kangaroo return to his mother's pouch!" he flew the joey over all the roads that separated them.

But still, we made progress. By the end of that week, he could solve the easiest mazes, so I gradually upped the level of difficulty to keep it interesting for him.

Bernie's best experiences of that entire final quarter of 2011 came in his last two weeks of acyclovir infusions, when he moved into Christus St. Vincent Hospital's excellent in-patient physical rehabilitation center.

After spending so much time in hospital beds, he relished the freedom that a wheelchair gave him to move around a cheerful, open area on his own. He was happy to strengthen and rebuild his body.

Once the staff realized that he was an artist whose work was, at that very time, represented by the famous Waxlander Gallery, they brought in an art therapist to work with him in various ways. Bernie loved that.

He also made friends with other patients, two of whom stand out in my mind. One was a young Native American woman who treated Bernie and me with special kindness.

The other was an older man, an evangelical who talked nonstop to Bernie of Jesus, repeating the same words and phrases: "Jesus loves you. Jesus is the highest angel. Jesus sits at the right hand of God. Praise

Jesus." Over and over. Every waking hour. Every day. I appreciated the man's desire to help Bernie spiritually, but he created a problem for us.

During those two weeks, I began thinking of my husband as if he were two completely different men.

There was the "Old Bernie" of my happy memories. Quick to have fun with words, crack a joke, smile, grin, and laugh. Smart and clever in tackling challenges. Deft with a pen and a paint brush. Slow to anger.

Then there was this "New Bernie." Flat in expression, emotion, and personality. Good at remembering the therapists' names. Bad at retaining the skills they taught him. Unable to acknowledge his own weaknesses. Quick to take offense at the slightest hint of criticism and to blame others for the things he couldn't do.

More than anything else, the latter issue got to me. Bernie never had been one to blame anyone else for his mistakes, but now whatever he didn't understand or couldn't do was someone else's fault. The puzzle-book designer. The newspaper typesetter. A young therapist. Me.

After a while in rehab, Bernie did begin wisecracking and horsing around a bit. Faint hints of his old personality started to emerge.

But even then, something struck me.

Old Bernie's way of laughing involved his bright eyes full of twinkle and tease. His sparkly smile. His quick-flashing grin. His keen wit paired with a gentle nature that never meant to hurt.

None of that was in evidence now.

New Bernie's way of laughing was to shake his shoulders while his face and eyes remained impassive. His lips no longer parted except to speak and eat. They no longer even curled up. They never smiled.

More and more, I found myself longing for Old Bernie. Aching for the guy I'd loved since 1965. The sweet, funny fellow I'd trusted and depended on. The one person on Earth who would never let me down.

New Bernie was an ongoing frustration. I hoped we would still be able to love each other and someday live as happily as before, but the longer his problems lasted, the harder it was to see how he'd ever recover from the Big E's double-whammy "insults" to his brain.

I had stayed reasonably strong throughout our ordeal. Increasingly, though, I felt myself at risk of cracking and crashing. I mourned our compounding losses. Saw no way out. Cried all the time. In public. In private. Everywhere.

Bernie was happy in rehab, but now I was the one who needed help. For the first time in my life, I was seriously depressed. Suicidal at times. But I had no choice. I had to keep going for him, if not for myself.

Through my many conversations with a rehab-center counselor, a new term, *metabolic encephalopathy*, entered my vocabulary.

I soon learned that, while *encephalopathy* looks and sounds like *encephalitis*, the two are not the same. That difference felt like something I needed to understand.

Eventually, I grasped it in a way that may not have been scientifically precise but made sense to me.

Encephalitis, "an inflammation or swelling of the brain," describes what happens when an infection rising from within the body "insults" brain tissue.

Encephalopathy, "an acquired brain injury," refers to the detectable changes in a survivor of any kind of "insult." Those changes may include personality shifts, memory loss, seizure disorder, coma, and death. Bernie now had experienced everything but death.

Metabolic encephalopathy refers to those same changes when they result from a brain injury specifically caused by an infection within the body.

In a nutshell: Encephalitis was the cause. Metabolic encephalopathy was the effect.

Then, as if that weren't enough, I learned about *toxic metabolic encephalopathy*, which describes those same changes when they are caused by external agents, like the anticonvulsant drugs used to control seizures.

In another nutshell: The medication that Bernie needed to survive with epilepsy might continue damaging his brain.

It seemed that "Lucky Bernie" just couldn't win, no matter how hard he might try to play the game.

I also learned that predictable problems for those suffering from metabolic encephalopathy—toxic or not—include dementia, language and speech disorders, failure of the brain's all-important executive functions, a strange behavior called "left neglect," and a dire prognosis only slightly camouflaged by its Latin name, *status epilepticus*.

In one of my nightly Bernie Reports, I described a terrible irony. "Bernie never smoked. Never did drugs. Drank alcohol in moderation. Rarely ate red meat. Preferred fish, chicken, and veggies. Worked out three times a week. Kept his strength up and his weight down. Did everything right in his life. So what does he get now for all that good behavior? A brain disease. It only goes to show there's no justice in this world."

During Bernie's last week in rehab, the staff counselor who had been advising me on how to cope with his condition suggested that I find a nursing facility for him, because, she believed, caring for him by myself in my current emotional state would overwhelm me.

When I said I wasn't willing to do that, we discussed how to adapt our home to his new needs.

She also arranged for the same Medicare-provided occupational, physical, and speech therapists and nurse to continue working with him as soon as he was able to go back home.

Sooner or later, she said, I would need to hire an in-home care company to provide light housekeeping and respite breaks for me a few hours each week... and also a private personal trainer for Bernie... and also a psychotherapist for myself. Eventually, I did schedule all that professional assistance, although paying for it busted our budget.

That December, while Bernie was still receiving acyclovir infusions and both physical rehabilitation and art therapy at Christus St. Vincent, I visited El Castillo, a lovely pueblo-style retirement community right downtown in Santa Fe, three blocks from the historic Plaza.

El Castillo is a high-quality, stand-alone, non-profit operation that offers apartments categorized as independent living, plus individual rooms for patients in assisted living, nursing, and memory care. For the most part, its residents are active, well-educated, and mutually supportive. It offers the services that seniors need to live securely and comfortably to the end of their days, come what may.

So I felt confident that if Bernie or I ever needed more care than we could give each other in an independent-living apartment, El Castillo could provide it. That winter, without mentioning it to him, I put us on the wait list and started checking out apartments as they became available.

I ached at the notion of doing that entirely by myself, without consulting Bernie. Normally, neither he nor I would have done anything like that alone, but nothing was normal now. For the first time in our marriage, every bit of the daily- and long-term planning and decision-making fell to me. Bernie no longer had the capacity to be a full partner, not even in such a major, expensive, and permanent decision.

During that heartbreaking winter, spring, and summer of 2012, I cried every time I visited El Castillo, even though I knew it would be a good future, final home for us.

Or maybe because I did know that.

Chapter 23

Highest Angel. Praise Jesus. Coffee Pot.

Friday, December 9, 2011 to Friday, January 27, 2012

On Bernie's last Friday in the rehab center, I sat off to one side of its practice kitchen like a spectator at an odd sort of final exam.

The counselor encouraged Bernie to show me how well he had learned to fix and eat a bowl of cereal and milk without help. And make instant coffee in a microwave; wash and dry utensils, glasses, and dishes; take off and put on his shirt, belt, socks, and shoes; use a walker to stand up, sit down, and get around by himself; and so on. All were good achievements for him, so I cheered and applauded loudly.

But the counselor had saved the two thorniest issues for the end.

One was "left neglect." Two insults by the Big E had badly damaged the right side of Bernie's brain, causing him to lose awareness of things on his left side. He wasn't being deliberately obtuse or klutzy. From his perspective, nothing existed there, so I should expect him to bump into furniture on the left side of a room or hallway. And ignore food on the left side of his plate. And disregard sounds coming from his left side. And never look at, listen to, or talk to anyone on his left side.

I especially needed to understand this, she said, given his tendency to blame me for whatever went wrong. If he bumped into a table or chest on his left side, it would always be "Martha's fault" for putting it there.

As part of his "exam," she asked Bernie to write the numbers 1-12 on a blank clock face. He positioned them with precision, top to bottom, on the right half—as if the left half didn't exist—and proudly held it up for me to see. I cheered his precise markings, of course.

But seeing that broke my heart, because after Mama's long slide into dementia, I knew that the inability to draw a traditional clockface reveals an impairment of the frontal lobe's executive function. It's generally considered to be evidence of cognitive decline.

The other thorny issue involved a jigsaw puzzle that was spread out on a table. As a longtime puzzle fan who, in the past, often had enticed Bernie to join me, I'd spotted it right away. This one featured brightly colored, cleverly drawn animals on twenty extra-large pieces. A big red band marked the straight edges, three of which were already connected. Seventeen other pieces lay face up, easy to see.

The counselor asked Bernie to resume his work on the puzzle. But even with three frame pieces in place, he didn't recognize other pieces' straight red edges as clues. He couldn't match up any of the center pieces either, despite their unique shapes, lines, and colors.

Old Bernie would have solved that kindergarten-level puzzle in seconds. New Bernie froze on sight of it, which floored me.

The next morning, an orderly wheeled Bernie out into the cold air, helped him settle into our warmed-up car, belted him in, bid us a Merry Christmas, and departed with the wheelchair.

Sitting in the driver's seat, I glanced over at Bernie before pulling away from the curb. He was staring straight ahead. His eyelids fluttered. His lips smacked. He chewed on something that wasn't there. He was having an absence seizure, the kind I'd failed to notice when he'd had them at home early in October, before his big seizure in the gallery garden.

This was my first time to recognize one as it was happening.

What should I do about it?

Moments later, he moved his head in a sign of consciousness.

"You just had another seizure," I said.

He didn't look at me or react to my voice.

Of course not. I'm sitting to his left.

So I got out, went around the car, and opened the door. "You just had another seizure."

"No."

"You don't remember it, but you did."

Not remembering is another sure sign of absence seizures, so for a few moments I considered what to do next.

"Stay here where it's warm, Babe. Don't leave the car, okay?"

"Okay."

I zipped into the rehab center, reported the seizure, and asked to have the orderly bring him back to where he'd spent the last two weeks.

"He's been discharged," the receptionist said. "We can't take him."

"But he was just here."

"Go to the ER. They'll readmit him."

I returned to the car and stood outside, looking back and forth from Bernie to the ER in the distance. Every part of me—mind, heart, gut—balked at taking him back there.

Six weeks in two hospitals.

Six weeks of infusions and monitoring for seizures.

Would they have discharged him if he was still having them?

Maybe he didn't have one just now.

Maybe I was wrong about that.

I couldn't do it. Couldn't take him back. I took him home instead.

Over the next week, Bernie's capacity for speech dwindled even more, reduced to listing things in a room and other mindless mutterings. He didn't communicate with me any more, just babbled nonstop.

The worst thing, in my view, was his robotic parroting of the evangelical patient's oft-repeated mantras: "Jesus loves you. Highest angel. Right hand of God. Loves you. Loves you. Right hand of God. Highest angel. Praise Jesus. Loves you. Highest angel. Loves you. Right hand of God. Jesus. Jesus. Jesus."

Coming from my resolutely secular Jewish husband, that constant burbling noise made me want to run screaming out the door.

Before breakfast one morning, as we sat in our bathrobes in the kitchen watching the snow fall, smelling the percolating coffee that got Bernie going each day, I called Murray and his wife Pat, a retired nurse practitioner. They had been following our situation from afar and knew all but the latest developments.

Not wanting to prejudice them, I asked if they would talk with Bernie and give me advice.

They agreed, so I handed the phone to Bernie.

Murray and Pat later told me that they'd tried basic questions like "How are you?" and "What's going on?" and "How's the weather?"

Regardless of the question, Bernie's answers went like this:

"Sink. Stove." Long pause. "Jesus loves you."

"Fridge. Praise Jesus. Highest angel." Long pause.

"Pencil. Magazine. Praise Jesus." Long pause.

"Right hand of God." Long pause. "Door. Loves you."

"Window. Jesus." Long pause. "Jesus."

"Highest angel. Praise Jesus. Coffee pot."

At some point, Bernie stopped talking and began staring into space with his eyelids fluttering and his mouth making idle chewing motions.

I grabbed the phone as it slipped from his hand. "He's having another absence seizure," I told Murray and Pat on the other end.

"Get him to the ER," Pat said. "Fast."

"I can hardly stand the thought," I said, "but I guess I gotta do it."

"You do," Murray said. "Keep us posted."

I hung up and tried to tug Bernie to his feet to dress him. He wouldn't budge. A lead weight fused to the chair would've been more mobile. So I called 911 and scooted to my closet. At least one of us would be properly attired when the EMTs arrived.

They whisked Bernie off in his bathrobe, pajamas, socks, and slippers.

For the first time in that miserable fourth quarter of 2011, I didn't follow the ambulance to the hospital. Instead, I made breakfast for myself. Savored the quiet. Thought calm thoughts. More than ever in my life, I needed a peaceful break, if only for a single hour.

They hadn't admitted Bernie to the ER. I tracked him to a regular hospital room where he was sitting on the edge of the bed, sock feet dangling, fiddling with the hem of his hospital gown as a nurse chatted to him without receiving any response.

I introduced myself to the nurse.

"He needs toys," she said. "Something to play with."

"For what age?"

"Toddler. Walmart has plenty to choose from right now."

So off I went to a festively decorated aisle where I picked one of those cone-shaped thingies with colorful plastic rings in graduated sizes, which seemed designed to develop hand-eye coordination. A few other items landed in my cart, too. I checked out, returned to the hospital, and slunk into the room, embarrassed to be seen carrying toddler toys to my seventy-three-year-old husband.

Bernie spent a few more days in that room, playing with his toys, as Dr. N sought again to end the seizures once and for all.

His two previous hospitalizations had been tough to get through, but this one shattered me. No online research and no human I talked to suggested that he would get better or that I might yet be able to keep him at home. I almost convinced myself to put him in a nursing home.

I didn't write a Bernie Report during that time. Couldn't bring myself to share such dismal news with friends at Christmastime.

I was alone, sad, depressed, and suicidal. Ready to end my lousy, losing life. Disappear. Die. Just go away. Never be seen again.

I jotted down ways to kill myself. Did online research about it. Picked the best way for me. Once during that week, I came close.

What stopped me was a single inescapable question.

If I do that, who will take care of Bernie and Smokey?

A few days before Christmas of 2011—as I remembered all those years of tree-decorating that Bernie and I always had enjoyed so much—I decided that, instead of killing myself, I would go alone to buy a tree.

And so I did.

I hauled that fairly large tree tied atop the Subaru, wrestled it inside by myself, coaxed it into a stand, and then—with some well-spiked eggnog to sip on, a few chocolate-chip cookies to munch, and my favorite holiday music to brighten my mood—I decorated it to the nines. Simply doing that, even with Smokey as my sole companion, did a lot to lift my gloom.

Somehow or other, by December 23rd, when the hospital discharged Bernie again, I was psyched up enough to take him home. Never again, despite the tough times that still lay ahead, did I contemplate suicide.

Consciously or not, I had made another bet on Bernie. I would stick around to get him—and myself, too—through this nightmare.

If it had been anyone other than Bernie who wouldn't stop talking of Jesus, I'd have thought he merely was caught up in the spirit of the season. But he *was* the one who endlessly blathered that same "Jesus,

Jesus, pillow, right hand of God, towel, TV, highest angel, lamp, coffee pot" nonsense, even as I tried to sleep at night.

Please understand. Those weren't conversations. We weren't two intelligent people engaged in a spiritual discussion. It was just Bernie talking to himself non-stop. Not waiting for my response. Not asking if I had anything relevant to say about Jesus.

The problem was, I couldn't leave him alone at night and go sleep by myself elsewhere. He still had to take a big 1,000 mg pill four times a day, precisely on schedule. He wouldn't remember to do it, and he wasn't steady enough to get to the bathroom by himself. If he tried, he'd likely fall and crack his already messed-up head on the brick floor.

He wasn't sleeping. I wasn't sleeping. If this continued, we'd both be back in the ER.

So the week after Christmas, I called an in-home, nursing-care company and asked for a male nurse to stay overnight for the next week, keeping Bernie safe and on his meds in another bedroom while I slept undisturbed in ours. It was an expensive and intrusive experience, but by having quiet again, I was able to sleep.

Even so, at random hours, I'd wake and hear Bernie and the nurse guy talking and laughing. All night long. Once, I got up, went there, and pointed out that Bernie's brain needed sleep as much as mine did. Probably even more. But he kept talking, so I went back to bed.

On the nurse's last morning in our home, he gave me a sympathetic hug and whispered in my ear, "I couldn't believe you paid me for so many overtime hours just to listen to him rattle on about Jesus and name all the items in the room."

In the first week of 2012, the speech therapist returned and noted Bernie's deteriorated conversational skills. From the trunk of her car, she produced a simple but clever tool called a "talking stick" to help Bernie relearn how to speak when it was his turn and to not speak when it was not his turn. For several weeks, we three would sit facing each other, as if playing a children's game. The therapist made the rules clear. When it was our turn to hold the stick, we could speak without interruption. When we had said what we wanted to say, we had to hand the stick over so someone else could talk without interruption.

It took Bernie a good long time to grasp the basic concept of "conversation," but eventually he did. And as his interpersonal-communication skills improved, his Jesus talk faded away. That boosted my spirits in more ways than I ever could have imagined before.

Another step in the process that I now thought of as "rebuilding Bernie's brain" was to work on jigsaw puzzles at home.

Online, I ordered a table built just for that purpose, plus several puzzles ranging from the same twenty-piece kind that he'd frozen up with before, all the way up to sixty pieces.

Putting them together became our main daily activity.

At first, Bernie didn't notice that each piece was different and only fit into another one that had a matching cut and design. His preferred technique was to choose two at random and crush them together, whether they fit or not. After that, it wasn't clear that they ever would work with other pieces, because he had mutilated them. He would fume at the "defective" products or blame me for buying him "cheap" puzzles.

After squashing another three or four pairs of pieces, he'd shove the mangled ones aside and select more, which he would then mistreat in the same way. I tried several times to get him to use his eyes before grabbing pieces, to hunt for matching cuts and colors and lines. Invariably, he'd forget those suggestions minutes after I made them.

It took a week or so for him to accept my many layers of clichés that—when it comes to jigsaw puzzles and most other things in life—easy does it, gentle beats rough, patience is a virtue, practice makes perfect, and slow and steady wins the race.

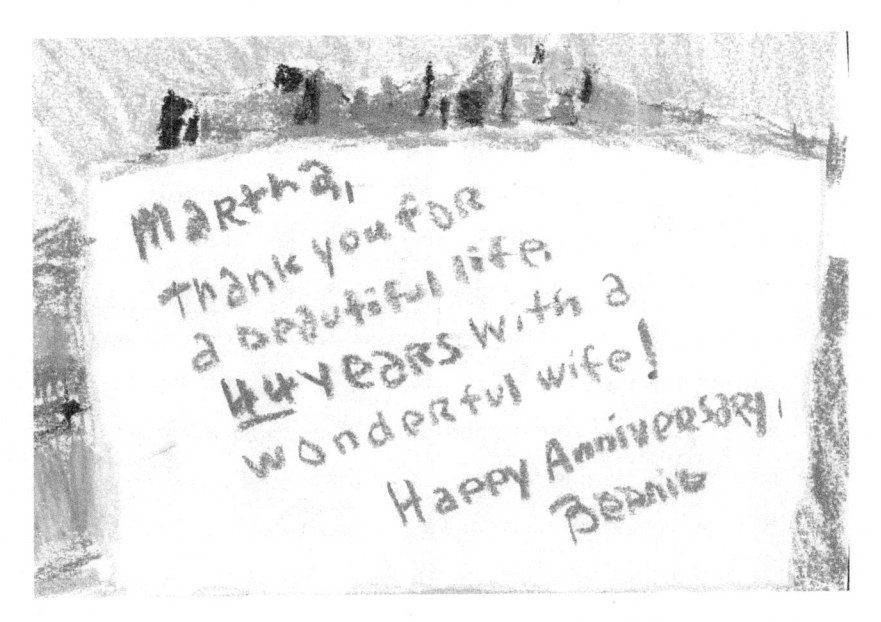

Bernie's handmade card for me (On the reverse, he wrote, "To my dearest.")

On January 27, 2012, our forty-fourth anniversary, Bernie gave me a "card" that he'd sketched out in pencil, then brightly colored and printed in crayon on a sheet of white paper.

I wasn't expecting such a thing at all.

I hugged him and cried and displayed his precious hand-crafted gift in our kitchen for a week before stashing it in the photo album along with his creatively colored portrait of Smokey. Both were keepers.

By now, Bernie finally grasped the concept of printing individual letters into individual boxes and could complete in one sitting an entire crossword puzzle from that same "faulty" book that I'd bought him weeks earlier. For him, it was a proud accomplishment, and from then on, at his request, I bought puzzle books of increasing difficulty.

Also, working entirely on his own, he had progressed to sixty-piece jigsaw puzzles and was eager to tackle new challenges. So we celebrated our anniversary and his improving skills with a fine Ravensburger-brand puzzle that I'd tucked away for some special moment like this. It consisted of a hundred large pieces with an illustration of Mayan stone ruins complete with a twisty serpent, which provided a fine excuse to reminisce about our long-ago travels to Mexico and Guatemala.

Bernie recalled trip highlights that I didn't, and vice versa. We both laughed a lot and genuinely enjoyed being together, as we always had before. That also was our first normal-feeling conversation since October, and thus highly notable.

Something else I found significant that morning was that—on his own initiative, not waiting for me to do it for him—Bernie unpacked all the pieces and positioned each one face up on the table, as I'd been doing for him until then. When that first step was finished, he turned to me. "For our anniversary, let's work it together."

I kissed him. "Good idea, Babe."

Side by side, we finished that Mayan-themed puzzle in one sitting and had so much fun that we redid it in the afternoon. Only that time, at Bernie's insistence, we hid the box and reconstructed the entire picture from memory.

That was our happiest day in months.

Chapter 24
Living the Post-E Life

2012–2020

Early in the spring of 2012, for some reason that I never understood, Bernie became paranoid. He didn't want me going in with him to see any of his doctors, even though I had to drive him to their offices. It wasn't worth a fight, so I'd wait in the car as he went in with his walker.

Likewise, he refused to share with me any postal mail addressed to him. He'd hide bills in his desk, then forget to pay them. After a few embarrassing in-person encounters with a bank-box manager and other unpaid local vendors, I solved that problem by making sure future bills came addressed to me. Bernie never noticed the change.

The rehab counselor had provided a list of Executive Function Disorders (EFDs), all potentially caused by damage to Bernie's frontal lobe, so I was watching for them.

The first I'd seen was his inability to number a clockface.

The second showed up as he began printing everything he needed to write. He couldn't even replicate his previous signature, because his cursive handwriting was gone forever.

The third was his extremely short attention span. Even after the talking stick helped him converse again, he'd leap from one subject to another. No amount of prompting enticed him to stick with a topic for more than one round, so engaging with him felt more like a TV quiz show than a normal chat.

With jigsaw puzzles, he'd work one section and almost finish it, then jump to a different area. Likewise, right in the middle of gathering his dirty clothes to wash, he'd lose focus, do something else, and forget the laundry. He wouldn't even recall that his clothes needed washing.

The fourth EFD became obvious when I saw that he no longer had the ability even to make a multi-step plan, much less hold it in his head and carry it out to completion. His short-term memory was impaired.

Always in the past, before going into town, we would discuss what needed doing and make a short mental list in logical order, such as: bank, cleaners, gas, lunch, groceries. Old Bernie would have them memorized at once. New Bernie just recalled the first one. Following the bank stop, he had no clue what came next. Even after actually stopping at the cleaners and the gas station, he'd only remember that we meant to go to the bank.

Two of those EFDs—zero attention span and predictable memory lapses—merged in April 2012 when we made our first post-E camping trip. We both were stir crazy and needed a getaway, so we took one.

Since that would be my first time driving BluCon, we wouldn't tow the Subaru as we had in the past. With Bernie now learning to walk with a cane, two new challenges per trip would be enough.

Or so I thought.

Back in the day when Bernie always drove, I always had navigated. But now, on our planned weeklong outing with Smokey to southern New Mexico and west Texas, those roles would be reversed. Before leaving, we made a short test run in the car with a paper road map, to see how Bernie handled the navigation side of things. But the map made no sense to him. He couldn't locate Santa Fe on it, even when he was still there.

So I marked our city with a black circle and a large yellow X, then highlighted the entire upcoming route in yellow and superimposed every road number in bold, black ink. My concern wasn't getting us to our planned stops, since it was an easy route that I could drive from memory.

But still, I hoped that Bernie would acquire the basic navigational skills that we would need for more-complex journeys to come. Several times before leaving, we went over our upcoming super-simple route. Sitting in the car, one last time before departure, I reviewed the route for the umpteenth time, showing him with my index finger how he could track our progress along the way. "Just follow the yellow line with your finger, Babe."

"Okay."

As we neared Albuquerque, I tried to engage him in the process. "We'll drive straight through the Big I," I said, using the local name for a tangle of flyover ramps where the north-south I-25 crosses the east-west I-40. "Then we'll take the first exit to pick up BluCon."

"Okay."

"Do you see the Big I on your map?"

"No."

"So, find Albuquerque, then look for the spot where the two big highways cross."

"Okay." His finger picked out the black circle and bold yellow X marking Santa Fe and traced the yellow line south to Albuquerque.

"Good job, Babe," I said with one eye on the road and the other on his finger.

"What do I look for?"

"The spot where the Interstates cross."

"Okay."

He located the Big I as we passed through it. "We're there," he said.

"You did it!" I crowed. "Good job, Bernie."

"Thanks."

Without counting on him to recognize the correct exit to pick up BluCon at her storage facility, I just took it with minimal explanation.

Soon, in the RV, we two and Smokey headed south again.

Betting on Bernie

A couple of hours later, I initiated a similar process. "Now let's start watching for our Las Cruces exit."

"Okay."

"Can you find Las Cruces on the map?"

His finger returned to the black circle and bold yellow X marking Santa Fe, which we had left three hours earlier. From there, he traced the yellow line south to Albuquerque, through the Big I, and on south.

"What town are we looking for?" he asked.

"Las Cruces."

"Okay, we're there," he said after a while.

Again I cheered his success. He did remember Las Cruces at last, and he recognized it once we got there.

Upon arrival at the campground in Las Cruces, my super-talented husband—who for decades had painted and sold fine images on paper and canvas—lacked the hand-eye coordination needed to hook up the RV's two hoses and electric cord.

Making it worse was the fact that he knew he *used to* be able to hook them up, but he couldn't do so now. Obviously, these connections had been installed wrong. Or some previous campers had messed them up.

I saw why it wasn't working for him. Old Bernie always had squared up the connectors that locked together when turned. New Bernie held them at an angle, rather than straight. They weren't going to lock together that way, no matter how many times he tried, but he couldn't accept that.

Then there was his ego. "It's a man's job," he said when I offered to help with the hookups.

"Not really, Babe."

"But you're the driver now."

"I can do both, you know," I said. "I can drive on the road and also hook up in the campground."

"That's a man's job."

But then, again, he failed to do it. When I tried to show him how, he got upset. "That's not how *I* do it."

"It *is* the way you *used to* do it. What you're doing *now* won't work."

"But that's how I do it *now*." Such circular logic—or illogic—drove me bonkers.

That night, fortunately, we already had what we needed on board.

The next morning, Bernie resumed trying to hook things up his way. "They're just not set up right," he concluded after a while.

"Bernie, honey, hand them over, please, and let me do it."

Finally, he accepted the fact that I did know how to hook up, and from then on we had electricity, water, and sewer connections.

But he wasn't happy. He told me every day of that short trip that traveling this way wasn't fun. He wasn't sure he wanted to do it anymore.

Bernie sketching in Guadalupe Mountains National Park, April 2012

Two days later, we left Las Cruces for El Paso. Old Bernie would have homed in on the New Mexico-Texas border south of Las Cruces. New Bernie had to find Santa Fe first. Then his finger had to follow the yellow line south to Albuquerque, through the Big I, and on to Las Cruces and El Paso, forty-six miles farther on.

The pattern repeated two days later when we left El Paso and went straight east toward the Guadalupe Mountains. It also repeated when we left there and turned north into New Mexico, toward Carlsbad Caverns.

To figure out each upcoming leg of the trip, Bernie had to find Santa Fe's black circle and bold yellow X and trace the yellow line the whole route from there. He couldn't remember our most-recent stop or our upcoming one. Just as when we ran errands around town, only our initial departure point and our first stop stuck in his mind.

Bernie, happy to be walking with a cane, and me in the main cave at Carlsbad Caverns National Park, April 2012

So, on the day we set out for home, Bernie had to locate Santa Fe and retrace the entire route that we'd already driven to find our current location. I actually challenged him to find a road on the map leading straight north from Carlsbad to home, or to seek a reverse route directly from Santa Fe south to Carlsbad. But he couldn't do either one.

Likewise, he had trouble following side roads on the map. He only ever wanted to go straight. That real-life experience reminded me of the "bunny and egg" maze that he had struggled with in November. Like that silly rabbit, BluCon couldn't fly over roads, towns, or mountains. We had to stay on the road, with all its angles, curves, and intersections.

After that trip, I bought a GPS device and taught myself to use it, which simplified our future outings. I also got pretty good at hooking up the Subaru by myself and towing it. Our friends and family worried about us the first few times we were out like that, but I enjoyed doing it and appreciated the freedom to explore that the "toad" (towed vehicle) gave us after we reached our destinations.

In June 2012, a "large" 1,200-square-foot, two-bedroom, two-bath, independent-living apartment that appealed to me opened up at El Castillo. Bernie's progress appeared to be stalled, so the idea of moving to a place that also offered assisted living, nursing, and memory care if either of us ever needed it seemed wise. We each would be independent residents for as long as we had the physical and mental capacity to live that way. Meanwhile, in that pleasant place, I could keep on assisting his living as I had at home, for as long as I was able.

For months, I'd been telling Bernie about El Castillo. Engaging people. Superb amenities. Good food. Gorgeous grounds. Perfect location in the heart of town. Easy walks to restaurants, museums, galleries and the two events he most enjoyed painting, Spanish Market and Indian Market.

But he still hadn't been there.

So one day, I dredged up our old-favorite line. "Bernie, are you gamy to go check out an apartment at El Castillo?"

I wasn't sure if he would remember that after so many years, but one corner of his flat mouth tilted up. "As gamy as I'll ever be."

The decision to leave our home and his barely used studio in order to move to El Castillo was hard for me to make alone. Throughout our marriage, we always had discussed and decided the big steps together. But Bernie couldn't do that now, so the burden did fall entirely on me.

I pored over the "life plan" contract, figured out the finances, and informed him that we were going.

His options boiled down to saying yes or no to that specific apartment and either printing his name on the contract or not.

Luckily, he liked the apartment as much as I did.

Throughout the previous decade, we had treasured our villa on the hill, which was purpose-built for entertaining. We'd hosted parties of all sorts and houseguests galore. With overnight accommodations for two couples or three singles at at time, it worked great for special events.

Never for a moment did we regret buying the extra lot, because that house on those four hilltop acres was the most marvelous property we ever owned. But when life got a lot more complicated and we needed a chunk of money to buy into El Castillo, our Realtor Fred came through as promised. He helped us sell the second lot as quickly as we had bought it, and for a good price, too.

I assumed the same thing would happen with the house and its nearly new, freestanding *casita*/studio, once we were ready to move out.

So together we paid El Castillo's entrance fee and signed a contract for continuing care at whatever level we might need going forward.

And then from mid-June to September 10, 2012, our move-in day at El Castillo, the logistical, physical, and emotional challenges of downsizing from 3,800 square feet to 1,200 nearly killed me.

Old Bernie would have been a big help. New Bernie was not.

He couldn't pack a box, wipe a shelf, or focus on anything for ten minutes. The best he was able do, in short spurts, was shred the years of old tax returns that had been stored in the garage. But that needed doing, too, so I was glad he could and would do it.

We would only have one parking space at El Castillo, and we needed room in our garage now for packed boxes and stuff to be hauled away. So we agreed to keep my Subaru, which was set up for BluCon to tow, and sell Bernie's larger SUV, which hadn't been driven in almost a year.

Soon after, Bernie took it upon himself to clean the floor *under* and *behind* a tall, wheeled storage unit standing beside a wall in the garage and tried to move it without telling me. But it was loaded and heavy, so instead of rolling, it tilted and crashed down onto the driver's side of the Subaru, crumpling the door and shearing off the outside mirror.

I was working inside, heard the crash, and came running. Bernie felt terrible about it, of course, and my first instinct was to wring his neck. But still, I couldn't get mad at him. He had no capacity to plan ahead and lacked the judgment to see that the car needed to be moved from the garage and the upper shelves emptied before either of us rolled the storage unit.

Insurance paid for the bodywork to repair our car and provided a rented sedan with less cargo space, which made it even harder to clear out the house. We didn't need that inconvenience and interruption.

The Realtor had reserved some items for staging, but everything else that wouldn't fit into the apartment went to friends, consignment shops, and charities. Whenever Bernie had an appointment with a doctor or his personal trainer, I got rid of stuff. Somewhere. Somehow. Someway. For example, in a busy restaurant parking lot, I gave away two dozen nicely potted, lovingly tended cacti simply by leaving the car doors and trunk open and offering them to passersby.

"Free to good homes," I said through tears.

My grief at losing Old Bernie and the many treasures that we'd collected in our travels and the beautiful home that we'd expected to enjoy for the rest of our lives… was nearly unbearable. Months of therapy helped me more than my good therapist probably realized, but even so, I cried nonstop until we finally settled into our apartment.

Moving to El Castillo turned out to be the best thing I could have done for myself. Its administrators, cooks, dining-room servers, cleaning crew, and maintenance team eased my burdens. Its warm, supportive resident community revitalized me and relieved my depression.

But much more important than that, by engaging Bernie in upbeat, intellectually stimulating, and non-judgmental conversations and creative activities—like the writing group he joined—the community helped erase his paranoia and insecurity.

Since his non-traumatic brain injury had left no external scars, it was easy for those new friends to accept him simply as "Bernie," without the "old" and "new" comparisons that I never managed to overcome. They hadn't known him before, so they didn't see the differences that I saw.

Brisk walks around Santa Fe's lovely, historic downtown restored us both, emotionally and physically. Festivals on the Plaza plus everything else we already loved about "The City Different" brightened our lives more than I had dared to hope. Autumn drives into the nearby mountains and to Bernie's longtime-favorite painting spot, Pecos Canyon, lifted our spirits, too, and made our lives feel almost normal again.

Also that September, we leased another studio, fifteen minutes by car from El Castillo. The year before, Bernie had barely had three months to enjoy the one that we'd had designed and built for him. Finding a good replacement was the key to his future happiness, and so we did.

Professional movers hauled all his gear—including his prized brand-new, extra-large, extra-tall easel—up an exterior flight of eighteen steps to a big, high-ceilinged, north-facing loft with a bathroom.

Talk about making a bet on Bernie. Wow.

As a gamble, it was a doozy, because that space wasn't cheap and at first it took a major effort on his part even to get up those stairs. Signing a year-long contract for a studio in addition to our other expenses was a clear financial risk, but it did the trick. He worked hard to regain his painting skills, and climbing stairs improved his physical condition, too.

Literally, that studio gave him something to live for.

In December 2012, fourteen months after his initial big seizure in the garden, our primary doctor signed the papers needed for the state to restore Bernie's drivers license, so he could get himself back and forth to the studio and doctors' appointments on his own. Finally, I saw some real joy in his otherwise-expressionless face. He was a free man again.

Bernie actually put himself on a schedule. After breakfast each weekday, he'd set off to paint until noon, which had the added benefit of giving me quiet time to start on my second novel, *The Viper Amulet*. That winter of 2012–2013 was a calm, restorative, and productive time for us both.

By the summer of 2013, Bernie's artistic talent was on the rebound.

By the summer of 2014, his work was almost as polished as before and much more soulful. Even his new titles reflected an emotional shift. He gave the revealing name "A Time of Tranquil Water" to an oil painting that he once would have identified more prosaically as "The Green River in Dinosaur National Monument." Another, "The Persistence of Beauty," reflected his emotional bond to a prickly pear cactus blooming alongside a dead, fallen saguaro in the Sonoran Desert.

His disappointment at losing gallery representation in Santa Fe and elsewhere after seven years was profound, yet even he realized that he couldn't recover everything the Big E had taken from him. Gone was his ability to paint fast enough to satisfy gallery owners and managers, as well as the social skills needed to schmooze with customers at shows.

What he still could do was create beautiful artwork and seek out new ways to sell it. The rise of online art outlets gave him his first route out of what one artist friend called the "gallery grind."

With that in mind, Bernie and I worked together in 2014 to build a new website, bernardmarksfineart.com, to give him a strong presence on the internet. Thanks to that site and larger ones, collectors in America and abroad began discovering and purchasing his new paintings.

Unfortunately, fewer people were able to buy original art during and after the Great Recession. So, with or without a gallery, painting was an even-dicier way to earn a living.

For the first time since the '70s, I began worrying about cash flow.

My royalties from the three Spanish textbooks had arrived twice a year for almost two decades, but that ended as each one inevitably went out of print. My income from the other golden gigs of the late '80s and early '90s was gone, too, along with revenues from his business and art. And I'd earned no salary since we left Lake County in 2002, as I'd worried in 1998 when we first discussed moving to Santa Fe.

We had quickly cashed out our side lot in 2012, but efforts to do the same with our villa on the hill ran into a buzzsaw of hundreds of other equally beautiful places waiting to be sold during the recession's long tail end. Our next-door neighbors' spectacular home was for sale the whole time ours was. Many others had been built as high-elevation summertime getaways for wealthy Texans from the oil patch, which was still deep in the doldrums. House prices had dropped catastrophically, yet few sold.

It took twenty months for ours to find a buyer, during which time we paid out much more in taxes, maintenance, and insurance—plus our monthly fees at El Castillo and the studio rental—than we could afford. Our investments kept us afloat but took a hard hit.

In June 2014, to make the sale, we essentially gave a buyer the *casita/studio*, which had turned out to be more of a negative than a plus. But at least—and at last—we were done with home ownership.

In the summer of 2015, with deep sadness, we also sold BluCon. Bernie had driven her a few times after getting his license back, but that was nerve-wracking for us both. The other oft-repeated problem was that he didn't enjoy being a passenger, especially one who never could do the hookups. We weren't using her enough for it to be worth keeping her.

A lucky couple from Fort Worth claimed our beautiful Lazy Daze the day I listed her for sale, as a package with the Subaru that was set up to be towed behind her. They gave her a name more meaningful to themselves and have enjoyed her as much as we did, and for years longer.

We bought a new car and drove back to Chicagoland, but Bernie soon tired of road trips. We'd already been everywhere, he said, and he had a stock of photos and *plein air* watercolor sketches to paint from.

All through that recovery period, together and separately, we finished scores of jigsaw puzzles. On his own, Bernie maxed out at five hundred normal-size pieces. Given where he'd started in the rehab center, that was an excellent accomplishment. He had come a long, long way.

Likewise, it took a couple of years for him to reach the level of the Sunday *Times* crossword puzzles that he once had taken pride in doing in ink in a single sitting. But by 2015, he had plowed through several books of them and was almost back to his old crosswording self… and in blue ball-point ink. The only difference was that he needed more time to finish them. But that was okay. Speed wasn't the goal. Cognitive recovery was.

Also in 2015, a friend in Santa Fe began representing Bernie's work, both older and newer pieces, by placing them in upscale resorts, hotels, and restaurants around Santa Fe; Scottsdale and Sedona in Arizona; Vail in Colorado; and similar places.

One day in 2016, a person unknown stole Bernie's *newest* oil painting off the wall of a hotel lobby in Santa Fe. Insurance reimbursed him, and after that he had a funny new slogan: "Bernard Marks, a modern-day Great Master whose paintings are well worth stealing."

That same year, *International Artist Magazine* began publishing Bernie's new paintings again, after choosing his brilliant "Aspens with Mountain Maples" as a world-wide competition finalist. In 2017, they ran a ten-page how-to article that Bernie had written and illustrated with some of his own gorgeous recent works.

In 2019, based on Bernie's reputation for painting public lands, the superintendent of Glen Canyon National Recreation Area invited him to spend two weeks there as Artist in Residence. At age eighty, Bernie drove himself to Utah and back and thoroughly enjoyed the experience.

He had re-emerged from the Big E as a fine artist with both national and international reputations and markets for his work. And that recovery—as he often had joked to me in different contexts—was a miracle. Only this time, the miracle was no joke.

Over the five decades of our marriage, I'd never had a reason to recall the third promise that I'd made to myself before our wedding in 1968: to protect Bernie if virulent anti-Semitism ever endangered Jews in America, as it had in Europe in the '30s and '40s and in Russia for a hundred years before that.

Beginning in 2016, however, synagogue shootings and the menacing "Jews will not replace us!" rally by torch-bearing Nazis in Charlottesville, Virginia reminded me of that promise and made me mad as hell.

But Bernie shrugged it off, as if to say, "It can't happen here."

So I asked him: Did he think he was immune to that kind of hatred and violence? Could he see how others might feel threatened, even if he didn't? Was he so assimilated into a non-Jewish culture that he didn't realize how badly this new breed of homegrown haters could frighten other Jewish people whom he knew and cared about?

Bernie had no answers to my questions. I assumed that his passivity was the result of age and cognitive decline. Maybe he no longer had the capacity to grasp the risk to people just like him. But I did.

For that and more reasons than I care to describe here, I'm no longer a Republican. Despite my having proudly served as a GOP elected official in the '90s, the direction the party began taking in that decade and carried to extremes in recent years has pushed me away, probably forever.

In 2017, I self-published on Amazon *The Viper Amulet,* the sequel to *Rubies of the Viper,* in paperback and ebook formats. In both cases, the chances I took paid off in good reviews, visibility, and sales.

That same year, I started work on *The Ruby Ring,* the final book of my Ruby-Viper Trilogy. When done, that third novel will complete the first-century family saga that started growing in my head in the years that followed my childhood visit to Pompeii.

In 2018, as the "Me Too" movement erupted, I finally told Bernie the real reason why I'd left the faculty at Northwestern thirty-four years earlier. His normally placid face flushed red. "Why didn't you tell me when all that was going on?"

"Because I had a good job that I loved, close to home. Despite my frustrations there, I would've stayed if only the guy had left me alone."

"I'd have busted his nose."

"Which is why I couldn't tell you."

Surprisingly, even at a time when we and others discussed the abusive sexual relationships that dominated the news from workplaces, politics, and religious communities, neither Bernie nor I ever raised the subject of his affairs with two women in Shreveport and Waukegan.

But in my heart, whenever I recalled the naive, trusting girl who had defied her parents to marry the man she adored, and then uprooted with him to a vast metropolis full of strangers, and then given up for him the college-teaching career she loved and had worked hard to build, and then, again, had given up for him her second career as an elected official, which she also enjoyed and was good at… his revelation still stung.

Sometimes in the wee hours, my mind recalled his confession in the ER on November 17, 2011 and ran amok with questions. He had made a point of telling me that the Waukegan fling "didn't last long" and was "not much time." Did that mean the Shreveport fling *had* lasted a long time? Did it start before we married? Was that why he didn't push me for premarital sex? Did it continue after our wedding?

Was his affair in Waukegan really the last one? Were those two female employees willing participants in their intimate relationships with him? Or were they—like me at Northwestern—trapped in otherwise-good jobs with a sexually aggressive superior?

Did he have similar relationships with any of our female friends and neighbors in the places where we'd lived? Or those consulting clients whom he traveled to "advise"? Or the widow who kept inviting him to dinner while teaching her toddler to call him "Daddy"? Or someone I never knew during my Kalamazoo years, when I was away every week? Or while I traveled the country promoting language proficiency?

Was the herpesvirus that had caused his encephalitis in fact HSV—the one spread by unprotected sex—and not the chickenpox-related VZV, as I had concluded earlier? And if so, had he given HSV to me? If so, did that increase my own odds of contracting the Big E someday?

I came to realize that trust, once lost, is devilishly difficult to regain.

As for Bernie's overall memory, attention span, and verbal skills… they did improve but so gradually that it was hard to see the changes in real time. However, whenever I compared him to the late-2011 version of himself, I saw progress. Even so, his once-keen ability to envision, focus on, plan, and execute a strategy leading to a desired goal—be it building a business, cleaning out a garage, or hooking up a rig—those critical "executive function" skills never returned. Neither did his beautiful smile.

But still, during our time at El Castillo, Bernie gave back to the community. For five years, as his brain improved, he lent his ingrained business expertise to the Residents' Association (RA) Finance Committee, which monitors the corporate investments, balance sheets, and audits. Likewise, for seven years, I interviewed and photographed a hundred or so new residents and wrote their bios for publication in El Castillo's monthly newsletter. I served as the RA president for two years.

To celebrate our fifty-second wedding anniversary, January 27, 2020, we flew to Phoenix Sky Harbor Airport and used my brand-new Uber app to get to Old Town Scottsdale, where for a week we enjoyed warm air, al fresco lunches, and a visit with a longtime friend from Chicagoland.

Bernie enjoying an al fresco lunch on our last trip together, January 2020

On our flight home, other travelers wearing masks reminded us that a dreadful new virus was starting to kill people in China.

Early in March, along with the rest of the country, El Castillo went into quarantine. Throughout the pandemic, our staff heroically prepared and delivered meals to us each day and maintained essential services. Once tests became available, the nurses tested us regularly. At the height of the crisis, when seniors in particular were dying around the world, to my knowledge, we didn't lose any El Castillo resident to Covid.

To keep us safe, Bernie offered to sacrifice the thing that meant the most to him. "Should I stop going to the studio?" he asked me.

"No reason to do that, Babe, since you're the only one there. Just don't go anywhere else."

"But we're gonna need stuff."

"So, we'll keep a list, and then I'll grab my face mask and go shopping. I can dash in and out of a store a lot faster than you can."

We had planned to travel to celebrate Murray's eightieth birthday, but the pandemic squashed that idea. My greatest regret is that Bernie and Murray never got to enjoy what would have been their last reunion.

For the next six months, Bernie kept painting and we both kept writing. Late in the summer, as Covid eased, we again enjoyed al fresco lunches. Life felt normal. It was a short interlude, but relaxed and happy.

In August, he needed a photo of himself for a writing-group project, so we went outside with my camera. The brief, fleeting, slightly parted-lips moment that I captured in this shot was the closest to the big Old-Bernie smile that I had seen in nine years.

It wasn't easy to get, but I coaxed it out of him. I'm glad I did.

Bernie at El Castillo, August 2020

Chapter 25

You Married a Lemon.

Tuesday, October 13 to Tuesday, December 8, 2020

For me, mid-October carries a heavy emotional load that dates from October 15, 2011, when Bernie suffered his first major seizure in the gallery garden on Canyon Road. Nine years later, as that anniversary drew near, he suggested that we take a half-hour trip east of Santa Fe to the Pecos River Canyon, which he had loved and painted in every season for over a decade. It would be especially beautiful then, at its peak of autumn color.

"Let's just pick a day and go," he said.

The day we picked was Tuesday, October 13, 2020.

In the little town of Pecos—set into a lush green valley that has been populated at least since the eighth century—we lunched at a long-time favorite eatery, Frankie's at the Casanova, which is locally famous for its traditional northern-New Mexico food. The indoor dining room was closed due to Covid, so they seated us outdoors at a picnic table under an old cottonwood tree. Bernie noted with pleasure the artistically perfect combination of blue sky and orange leaves.

After lunch, I drove the winding two-lane road along the river, up into the narrow, golden-glinted canyon, past an adobe monastery, an historic one-room adobe church, and a handmade sign commemorating the area's 1804 Spanish land grant and the killing of its "last grizzly" in 1934.

We reached the headwaters of the storied Pecos River, which is famous (as they say) in song and legend. Many times before, we had camped along its banks in both New Mexico and Texas.

Once there, we poked along as Bernie pointed out favorite locations that he'd painted. We parked near a rickety, long-abandoned bridge and walked on foot beside the river, shooting images meant for his future paintings and my stock-photography portfolio. After six months of Covid quarantine, it was wonderful being outside in nature together again.

As we approached an immense boulder that stars in his largest-ever painting, called "The River and the Rock," he took my hand and kissed it.

I mention such details to point out that this was a special pilgrimage for us, to a place with personal meaning. I remain amazed that we chose to revisit that particular place on that particular day, and also that those hours were as fun, happy, and affectionate as any we had known for years.

Because, mercifully unbeknownst to us at the time, it was Bernie's last good day.

Months later, I discovered an image of him still in my camera. While each of us was doing our own photographic thing along the Pecos, he had stepped into a shot that I'd meant simply to show the river, trees, and scenic drive. That "accidental last photo" is precious to me now.

My accidental last photo of Bernie beside the Pecos River, October 13, 2020

The next day, Wednesday, October 14, started off fine, too.

Bernie spent a normal morning in his studio. Drove back and forth. Then, after what would be our final al fresco lunch together at El Castillo, we walked across town and voted early.

Everything still seemed normal.

But as we turned toward home, cutting diagonally across the Plaza, he veered off the sidewalk and staggered onto the grass.

"What's wrong?" I asked.

"I'm okay." He returned to the pavement.

Two blocks farther on, he clearly wasn't okay. He staggered again and slumped against a low wall surrounding the patio of a café.

"Must be having a stroke," he said. "Weird feeling."

Moments later, a tonic-clonic seizure hit, his first in nine years.

I grabbed him as he stiffened, maneuvered him onto a bench inside the patio wall, and kept him from crashing onto the weathered tiles as he flailed. Once it passed, I called 911.

Bernie's weird feeling was what's known as an "aura" or harbinger of seizures. When the EMTs arrived, I mentioned it, and his history of viral encephalitis, and how it all had started "exactly nine years ago tomorrow."

At the hospital, as usual, an ER doc tapped Bernie's spinal fluid.

Days later came the wonderful news that he did not have viral encephalitis, so he could go home. The bad news was that Dr. N needed to replace the original anticonvulsant, which apparently had stopped working, with a stronger anti-epileptic drug.

Back at home with him that night, I researched the new drug's many known side effects. Headaches. Stomachaches. Nausea. Diarrhea. Weakness. Lack of energy and appetite. Abrupt weight loss. Swollen feet. Narcolepsy. Depression. Suicidal thoughts.

Bernie soon experienced them all.

Betting on Bernie

A home-care nurse and a physical therapist began arriving in hazmat suits to protect us and themselves from Covid. Over several weeks, they did their best to keep Bernie well and mobile, but they couldn't counter the new medication's dreadful side effects.

That strong anticonvulsant stopped Bernie's seizures immediately but made him miserable. "I can't keep on like this," he'd tell me several times a day. "This is no way to live."

On Thursday, November 12, we visited Dr. N in his office. Bernie wanted his dosage lowered, but the doc was reluctant, for reasons that I didn't understand at the time but absolutely do now.

In response to Bernie's pleading and my solemn pledge to monitor him closely, Dr. N agreed to a three-week, controlled-reduction plan, starting the next Monday. He wrote down three dates and gave them to me: November 16, 23, and 30.

On each of those Monday mornings—*assuming all went well*—we could lower Bernie's dosage by a specific amount and then—*assuming all went well*—hold that level through the week.

Each subsequent Sunday evening, I would call Dr. N's office and leave a detailed message describing how Bernie had fared on the lower dosage over the previous week. Based on my report, Dr. N would respond on Monday morning, approving another reduction, or not.

I swore to do my job: to give Bernie the correct dosage and make sure he didn't cheat by taking less than what Dr. N specifically prescribed.

Dr. N made sure we understood that, after those three weeks, there could be no further decrease. *Assuming again that all went well*, Bernie would have to keep taking the stronger anticonvulsant at the lower level that he reached in that third week.

Bernie's birthday was Saturday November 14. He now wore thin compression socks for edema, so I gave him cozy slippers for warmth.

That day, he told me he was ready to give up his studio. He no longer had the strength and steadiness even to climb the stairs, much less to stand up and paint for several hours.

I said I would start clearing it out.

So every day after that, I brought home two or three of his original paintings and propped them around the walls of our apartment. Getting them all home and then finding permanent storage would take time.

His dosage reduction began that Monday, November 16. The next Sunday evening, I reported to Dr. N that Bernie had felt little difference that week. No better, no worse.

Dr. N called back on Monday the 23rd with permission to proceed with the second reduction.

On Thanksgiving Day, with our quarantine in full effect, El Castillo's staff delivered a fine feast to our door. For the first time ever—on what always had been our favorite holiday to gather with family and friends and even host my college students when they were far from home—we were all by ourselves.

But Bernie ate well and seemed upbeat.

That Sunday evening, my second report to Dr. N was that Bernie felt better and had enjoyed Thanksgiving dinner.

So on Monday the 30th, Dr. N approved the final reduction.

Throughout that third week, Bernie's mood improved even more. His appetite returned. Most of the bad side effects vanished. He kept his food down and had enough energy and motivation to bundle up and walk around outside our building, holding my hand or the railing. He stayed awake all day, every day, and slept well every night.

As the weekend approached, we were almost giddy.

I looked forward to telling Dr. N on Sunday evening that we had hit the sweet spot: a lower dosage that controlled Bernie's seizures while making his life worth living again.

Betting on Bernie

Still feeling good on Saturday morning, December 5, Bernie said he wanted to go once more to what he called his "artistic man cave."

The day was warm and beautiful, so I agreed to take him.

After slowly and carefully making his way up the eighteen outdoor steps, he was amazed at how much I'd cleared out of the space over those three weeks. "I can walk across the room," he joked, "without tripping over anything."

Before we left, and also at his request, I called a nearby restaurant and ordered two to-go servings of our favorite green chile chicken stew with tortillas on the side. Ten minutes later, we pulled into the parking lot and paid the masked server who brought out the food.

We carried the containers home, sat at our table, and started eating.

Halfway through, Bernie abruptly stopped, put his spoon down, and raised his eyes to me. "Something's happening." His voice quaked.

It turned out to be another aura… and also the first time ever that he recognized an oncoming seizure in time to alert me before it hit.

I jumped up and, right before he went rigid, leaned down behind him, slid my arms under his, and wrapped them around his chest. Within moments, the chair began rattling and jumping as his arms and legs flailed and his head jerked from side to side. Once it stopped and he regained consciousness, I led him to his recliner and again called 911.

Bernie interrupted me while I was reporting what had happened. "It wasn't a seizure," he said loudly, as if trying to speak over me to the dispatcher, "just a mini-stroke." He repeated that, too, after I hung up. "It wasn't a seizure, just a mini-stroke."

"No, Babe," I said, "it definitely was a seizure."

At that, he released the longest, most-mournful moan I'd ever heard. "Ohhhhhhhhhhhh nooooooooooo."

Silently, I moaned, too, because we both knew what that seizure meant. The lower dosage of the stronger anticonvulsant wasn't working.

He'd almost made it the full three weeks. We'd been so hopeful. But now that hope was gone.

Moments later, another seizure hit. This time, all I had to do was make sure he didn't fall out of his cushioned recliner.

As he regained consciousness, we heard the shriek of a siren in the distance. "What a dreadful sound," I whispered.

"Especially," Bernie said, "when you know they're coming for you."

By the time the ambulance crew pulled into the El Castillo driveway and found their way to us, Bernie had suffered two more seizures. The second one was still going on when the EMTs arrived. I described to them what had happened. Four seizures in quick succession. Unlike anything I'd seen before.

I held our front door open as they wheeled Bernie out on a gurney.

He extended his hand to me and spoke the last words I ever would hear from him.

"You married a lemon."

The same ER doctor who had treated Bernie in October recognized me. "It's *status epilepticus*," he said.

"Say that again."

"*Status epilepticus.*"

I tried several times to say the unfamiliar word *epilepticus* and failed to get it right, as if my own worn-out brain refused to admit it.

But the doctor went on. "We call it *status epilepticus* when seizures start and don't stop. Your husband suffered four in your home, a few more in the ambulance, and even more after he got here."

"What's happening to him?"

"His brain is bombarding itself with electrical currents far greater than it's designed to tolerate." The doctor gave me a compassionate look. "Mrs. Marks, his condition is critical."

Before I arrived, the ER staff already had begun administering anticonvulsant infusions which, they informed me, had a strong sedative effect, so I shouldn't expect Bernie to respond to me now.

Later, they moved him to the ICU.

At home later on, reviewing my notes from 2011, I saw that I'd stumbled across the term s*tatus epilepticus* during my research into encephalitis, encephalopathy, and epilepsy. Now I dug into it again, in greater depth, but nothing I read encouraged me.

From that Saturday afternoon to Monday morning, the doctors attacked Bernie's epilepsy with every known treatment, which reduced the strength and the frequency of his seizures but didn't stop them entirely.

But then, on Monday morning, December 7, something happened that I will hold in my heart for the rest of my life.

I reached Bernie's ICU room while his daily EEG was in progress, waited outside, and thanked the technician as she left.

Once alone with Bernie, I noticed that his oxygen mask and feeding tube were still in place, but the IV drip bag was not. Its absence had to mean that he was no longer sedated.

Despite his closed eyes, I sensed a vibe.

Could he possibly be more awake and aware than before?

I approached the bed, wearing a mask as the hospital required. It was part of a cheerful set of good-quality, multicolored, heart-patterned, fabric masks that I'd ordered online during the previous summer and washed and re-worn dozens of times.

For sure, Bernie would recognize this mask if he saw it.

As I drew near, his right arm and hand moved slightly. No similar action came on his left side. That arm and hand lay inert on the mattress.

I pulled a chair up to his right side, took the hand that had moved, and leaned forward. "Bernie, this is Martha."

The staff had warned me not to expect any response from him, so it astounded me when the crusted lids of his right eye—and *only* that eye—parted just enough to allow a beam of light from the ceiling fixture to strike his eyeball.

After decades as a wildlife photographer, I instinctively welcomed that bright spot, which one always aims to catch in the eye of a bird or beast, because it makes a photo come alive.

So now my own eyes focused on that catchlight in Bernie's right eye. "Oh," I said to no one but myself, "that's Bernie's eye!"

At that moment, quite unexpectedly, the lids of that eye opened in full, revealing a clear blue iris. It was eerily similar to that joyful day in 2011 when he'd emerged from his coma at UNMH, except both of his eyes had opened then.

But still, just I had done on that earlier day, I began to cry.

Through tears, I spoke to him without actually thinking he might hear me. It just felt like the thing to do. "I love you so much, Bernie. I've always loved you. I'm here for you, Babe. I'm not leaving."

His eye didn't move. Didn't look around. Didn't blink. Just gazed straight at me from his blank face.

So I kept talking. "Oh, Bernie, I see your eye! Can you see me?"

The eye stayed open and still. I couldn't assume he saw anything, or that he was aware of anything, and yet...

Gently, I squeezed his right hand. "Press my hand, Babe, if you know I'm here. If you see me."

His hand responded, softly but unmistakably pressing mine.

After that, I kept holding it, stroking it, talking to him, asking for another squeeze that never came.

And yet his eye still stared at me.

That astonishing moment stretched on and on until a nurse entered the room and noticed his open eye. "Oh, that's creepy," she said as she reached over and closed it.

I was devastated. Barely refrained from screaming at her. Maybe it had been a little creepy, but still… how could she do that when we were looking at each other for what might be the last time?

To be honest now, I can't swear that Bernie heard me or saw me or squeezed my hand.

Maybe an involuntary reflex caused his eye to open in two stages at the precise moment that I happened to be sitting there talking to him.

Maybe a lingering seizure produced the pressure that I took for a squeeze.

Maybe the nurse knew something I didn't.

But I, who never believed in much of anything that I couldn't see or hear or touch… I have chosen to believe.

I believe he did hear me and respond to my voice.

I believe he did open his one functional eye and look at me.

I believe he did recognize me, if only by my colorful heart mask.

I believe he did squeeze my hand as an affirmative act of love.

I believe we did share a brief, ineffable conversation of sorts.

Believing those things helped me get through what was to come.

When I told Dr. N what had happened, he proposed an experiment. "We do one EEG per day," he said, "starting before visiting hours. I'd like you to come an hour early tomorrow and repeat what you did today. Wait until the technician signals for you to start and then, a few minutes later, she'll signal for you to stop. From the resulting graph, we'll know if Bernard responds in any way during that time that you're talking and touching him. Can you do that?"

"Yes, I can."

"Good," he said. "I'll tell the guards downstairs to let you in before visiting hours."

I entered the ICU at seven a.m. on Tuesday, December 8.

Bernie's eyes were closed, but he breathed steadily through an oxygen mask. He didn't react as the technician attached electrodes to his scalp.

I sat in the same spot and awaited her signal to begin talking and touching and pressing his hand. At her next signal, I stopped.

Despite my fervent hopes, Bernie lay still the whole time. His eye remained closed.

Later that morning, I saw that the EEG had recorded nothing but a flat line randomly interrupted by tiny, erratic blips. Nothing correlated to my presence, touches, or words.

I don't recall everything that the medical professionals and counselors and I discussed over the course of that day. But the gist of it was that, during thirty hours of excessive and destructive electrical bombardment, the malfunctioning neurons in Bernie's brain had burned it out.

He had just turned eighty-two. Not young, but not terribly old either. He would have wanted to keep living, but not with a dead brain.

Medical technology could have kept his body alive, in a vegetative state. I knew, however, from our discussions and his written advance directive that, given the current circumstances, he would not want that.

The gentle ICU doctor and an equally compassionate end-of-life specialist explained what would happen if I decided to let Bernie go.

Modern medicine does this very well, they said.

It would be private, peaceful, and painless, with no surprises.

But still, nobody could tell me what to do. The decision to remove Bernie's oxygen mask and feeding tube was entirely mine to make.

So I returned to his room and spent another hour with him. Talked to him some more. Allowed myself to cry.

And then I signed the consent forms.

A nurse entered the cool room, injected into Bernie's right arm something to ease this final journey of his life, and turned to me. "We're right outside if you need us," she whispered. She further lowered the already-dim lights and pulled the door shut, leaving a thin white rectangle shining through from the hallway.

My eyes soon adjusted to the dark.

Bernie continued breathing on his own without an oxygen mask. I held his hand, stroked his arm, repeated that I loved him. Over the next hour, his breath gradually slowed until it stopped.

My mind heard his old lilting call, "Is that you?"—pronounced with two syllables, *'S'at-CHOU?*—as if I'd been away and just walked into the house.

My mind answered with the same cheery cadence, "It's me!"—pronounced, *Itz-'SMEEE!*

That call and response was one of the many bonding rituals that we'd built up over fifty-two years and ten months of marriage. But since Bernie no longer possessed the ability either to call or to respond, I had to content myself with the echoes of his voice in my head.

Bernie in 1980, fifteen years after we met, twelve years after we married, and forty years before his death

CONCLUSION

On that cold December night, I returned home, fed Smokey, showered, snuggled into my PJs and warm robe, and spent the hours until dawn, dry-eyed and sleepless, in Bernie's recliner. All I felt was numb.

After sunrise, I called Rozanne and Murray, who were sorrowful but not surprised. It seemed we all had been channeling Bernie's spirit through the night.

The world was drowning in Covid that month, even as word spread of Bernie's sudden, unexpected death from something entirely different. Neighbors at El Castillo left cards, notes, and sweets at my door. Friends elsewhere called, emailed, and snail-mailed. But there could be no in-person visits, no warm hugs, no timely memorial service.

Sixteen days later, El Castillo's kitchen and dining-room staff brought a Christmas feast to my door. Except for treating Smokey to a few morsels of turkey, I ate it all alone.

Dr. N sent me a handwritten note: "I am sorry for your loss of Bernard and the decisions forced upon you. The right thing was done."

I appreciated that, because it kept me from second-guessing myself forever.

During the last three weeks of 2020, I finished removing Bernie's paintings and gear from his studio. Another artist was eager for the space, so if I could clear it out by December 31, the landlady would release me from the long-term contract.

I did, and she did.

Early in 2021, at our CPA's suggestion, I incorporated as Bernard Marks Fine Art LLC. Bernie should have done that for himself years earlier, but he never had. At first, it felt like I was stealing his name, but it *was* his name on all those paintings, not mine.

Also, on our lawyer's advice, I voluntarily went through probate to establish my copyright on the painted images that Bernie had created during his life.

Next, I catalogued all his remaining original pieces and took them to a professional photographer of art. Those large digital files now enable me to have top-quality giclée prints made from them.

After that, the originals went into secure storage.

Then, I had small and medium-size giclées made of the watercolor, oil, and acrylic paintings that Bernie had sold through galleries in the '00s and early '10s. It was exciting to bring those beauties back and offer them again to fans of his work.

From mid-2021 to mid-2023, I updated bernardmarksfineart.com, wrote *Betting on Bernie*, and built bettingonbernie.com to go with it. I see this book and those two websites as my best memorials to him, replacing the in-person service that the pandemic made impossible.

I also see this multi-year, multi-prong project as my last brave bet on Bernie. I've expended time, energy, money, and tears on it, because I believe his art is worth showing and our story is worth telling.

Bernie would be pleased, I think, at what I've done in his name.

So now, having thought, remembered, and written my way through our life together, I'm left with a few **Realizations**. I hope that some of them will resonate with you.

And if any of them *do* resonate with you, I'm going to invite you to tell me about your own similar experiences and any others that changed your life. Writing can be good therapy. Believe me, I know.

REALIZATION #1: ON ACCEPTING LIFE AS A GAMBLE

My life with Bernie Marks was a bet from beginning to end. I just didn't know or care about that when I married him at age twenty-one.

The main realization I have to offer now, after all these decades, is that, for most of us as human beings, life is an immense gamble.

In our twenties, we feel powerful and in control. A vast future lies ahead, ready to be seized, savored, and shaped to our liking.

In our forties and fifties, while we may be a bit beaten down, we still tend to see ourselves as the masters of our fate and the captains of our souls, to paraphrase "Invictus" by William Ernest Henley.

By the time we reach our seventies and eighties, we surely know that we owe more to chance and luck than we anticipated in our youth. We've gambled on beliefs, politics, creative endeavors, love, work, ourselves, and other people. The best odds probably came when we wagered on ourselves. When we rolled the dice on others, it was a riskier venture.

In my case, I made the biggest bets of my life on one man. We had five and a half decades together, and I was fortunate in that way. I don't regret the choices I made over those years, even though they weren't always easy to make, accept, and get through at the time.

So now, I'll ask you: Have you found parallels between my hardest decisions and your own? Or between the more-casual chances I took and those you took? Or between the kind of bets on other people that most of us have to make? What big risks have you taken in your life?

Please email me at the address below. I'd love to hear your story.

REALIZATION #2: ON LIVING WITH A DREAMER

From Bernie's earliest years, he had one goal: to be a professional fine artist. If he hadn't married me when he did, he might have achieved his dream a lot sooner. For sure, he had the talent and motivation to do it.

But still, his academic and business successes brought him personal satisfaction plus admiration, appreciation, and affluence, too.

I don't feel at all guilty about prodding him in that direction.

But still, "I thank whatever gods may be"—another unforgettable line from "Invictus"—that Bernie did finally achieve his dream of becoming a full-time professional fine artist.

And yet, much sadness lingers for me that he didn't have the benefit of a longer life to make it happen. Had viral encephalitis not hit him in his early 70s, his reputation-building time in galleries could have tripled. It's no stretch to say that he might have painted into his 90s.

What's amazing is that he did as well as he did between our arrival in Santa Fe at the end of 2002 and his illness at the end of 2011. In nine years, he perfected his craft, produced hundreds of stunning pieces, and made a name for himself in one of America's top art towns.

Even after the Big E hit him so hard, he not only brought his artwork back to a professional level but also learned to sell it via the internet. These days, I often whisper to his spirit a variation of something that he used to say to me at key moments: "Ya done good, Babe."

So now, I'll ask you: Have you experienced life with a dreamer? Was there an aspirational artist, writer, singer, songwriter, dancer, or other talent in your life? Or were you that dreamer? If so, how did it turn out?

Please email me at the address below. I'd love to hear your story.

REALIZATION #3: ON CHOOSING TO BE CHILDLESS

Looking back, I've noticed that the circle of our young, newlywed friends seemed to split apart after two to five years of marriage. Some couples followed the traditional track of having children. Their lives, as far as I can tell, have been happy and fulfilling. I wish them joy with their grown children, grandchildren, and more. For sure, most of them would not have done it differently.

Other couples, taking advantage as we did of the brand-new Pill, chose to remain, as I called it back then, child-free. Their lives, as far as I can tell, also have been happy and fulfilling, just as ours were.

But the interesting thing is that, over time, we grew closer to our friends who also were child-free and less close to those who had children.

Likewise, all our friends who had children gravitated toward others who also had children, which was logical since they shared concerns about the kids' health, day care, swimming lessons, schools, car pools, summer camps, scouts, sports, colleges, careers, and so on.

Meanwhile, we and our friends who had no such concerns developed other interests.

From my current decades-long perspective, I believe that we and our childless friends traveled more for fun (not necessarily for business) and engaged in a wider variety of social, recreational, and cultural activities with our spouses. We invested in ourselves, our homes, our trips, and our careers. We treated our spouses as the most important people in our lives. We had more time for one another. We made decisions with relative ease. We didn't argue over disciplinary matters, or how to deal with teachers our kids didn't like, or which summer camp or sport or school or college was best for them. To me, the childless couples usually seemed less stressed-out. More fun to be around. Happier.

I don't believe a single one of the childless-by-choice couples that I know now feels they missed out. But I can say that, in recent years, three different women—all long-time, dear friends of mine who raised great kids—have confided to me that they wish they'd done as I did.

I used to admit, when someone asked about it, "Yes, I know I'll be the lonely old lady that nobody ever comes to visit in the nursing home." And that may yet happen, but I don't think I'll care, because from childhood on, I've been a master at entertaining myself.

So now, I'll ask you: Did you consciously choose to have children, or not? Do you regret having—or not having—kids? Are you forever grateful that you do have them and the descendants that they have given you? Or, if you took the other path, do you now fear being left all alone?

Please email me at the address below. I'd love to hear your story.

REALIZATION #4: ON COPING WITH LOSS

Grievous loss, like useful wisdom, tends to come with age. Barring wars, pandemics, crimes, accidents, or natural disasters, we usually die one at a time of age-related causes, leaving others behind to grieve. Bernie's case feels unusual in that I lost him twice and to conditions that few know about. We've all lost friends and loved ones to cancer, heart disease, Alzheimer's, and the like. But how many do you know who suffered from viral encephalitis and died of *status epilepticus*? I only know of one.

My first loss came from Bernie's two back-to-back bouts with the Big E. Fortunately, he survived them, but from then on, each of us struggled with physical and emotional issues that we hadn't experienced before. Gone were the activities that depend on two sound minds and well-functioning bodies: meaningful conversations, equal decision-making, hiking together, and even sex. There hasn't been a single day since October 2011 when I haven't mourned what we lost that fall.

Then came December 2020. My second loss.

They say time heals all wounds, and I must admit that time is slowly healing mine. I'm enjoying life again without feeling guilty, including the freedom of living alone after years of taking care of Bernie.

Before his illness, I would have sworn that I couldn't live without him. Now, I know otherwise. I'm back to doing the things I've always loved to do: writing, camping, and photographing nature.

Best of all, I know Bernie would want me to keep doing them.

So now, I'll ask you: These questions are for other widows and widowers, especially those who cared for spouses as they battled illness or simply aged and died. Were you able to welcome independence and freedom after such difficult times? Have you managed to avoid feeling guilty for returning to life and, within reason, spending money on the things you love to do? Are you able to accept that your spouse would want you to live as well and as happily as you can for as long as you can?

Please email me at the address below. I'd love to hear your story.

REALIZATION #5: ON MOVING ON

As of this writing, I've lived at El Castillo for eleven years, which is longer than Bernie and I were able to enjoy our villa on the hill. We never stopped missing it, but hindsight confirms we were wise to leave when we did, although we lost a lot of money by having to sell it in a crisis.

During 2020, the last year of Bernie's life, he dreaded catching the Covid-19 virus but had no idea that his old nemesis—seizure disorder, aka *epilepsy*, the Big E's awful offspring—was actually the thing lurking in the background, ready to roar back and kill him.

He told me many times that, after he died, he wanted his cremains returned to some favorite place. We spent several surprisingly happy hours considering which location it should be. He finally settled on the Sonoran Desert, but it was a hard choice for him. Since his death, I've come up with a variation that I believe would please him even more.

These days, as Smokey and I roam the Southwest and the Rockies in a small camper van, I carry a stout iron trowel and biodegradable cotton pouches prefilled at home with Bernie's cremains.

I've developed a little ritual. Whenever I find an appropriate spot along a path less traveled in one of the parks we loved, or beside a favorite river, or high on some mountain trail that we hiked together, I dig a deep hole and press into it one of those filled pouches.

My new, efficient, solar powered, off-grid camper built into an 18' mid-roof Ford Transit van

Betting on Bernie   291

As I restore the earth, I tell him where we are and that I love him. I smooth the dirt and cover it with a rock.

Bernie now rests in many places that were special to him. Knowing that makes me happy, and I feel sure it would make him happy, too.

As I pass through my 70s and approach 80, life is bittersweet: a persistent awareness of loss combined with millions of happy memories.

I've lost close friends to distance, disability, and death.

I've lost my parents, whom I remember most fondly for the many boosts they gave me on my way to becoming the person I wanted to be.

I've lost the man I loved and repeatedly took chances to be with, but he will live on in my heart for as long as I live.

I know I'm moving up in the end-of-life queue, and that's okay. Quality of life has always been far more important to me than quantity of life. And Lord knows, I've had quality of life in spades.

These days, I find myself reverting to the solitary habits of my childhood. Friends, especially longtime ones, are still precious, but I'm also fine in my own company.

Santa Fe's glorious Octobers aren't quite so gladdening to me now. I welcome out-of-town visitors then, since their presence usually brightens my mood. The holiday season is more fraught, because both of Bernie's health crises hit us hardest between Thanksgiving and Christmas.

And yet, each incoming year calls to me for its promise of new things to write, new birds and critters to photograph, and new places to explore.

So now, I'll ask you: Are you in a similar "moving on" stage of your life? If so, how are you handling it? What hurdles are you finding along the way? Who or what is helping you? Who or what is *not* helping you? And if you've already moved on, the same questions (and many others like them) apply retroactively.

Please email me at the address below. I'd love to hear your story.

The process of creating this book and a website to accompany it has reminded me how truly lucky I've been to have people who loved me, resources to empower me, good health to enable me, and opportunities to pursue the hobbies and occupations that most interested me.

In recent years, I've met individuals who either taught or studied from *Destinos,* which actually has its own Wikipedia article now. From time to time, someone recognizes my name and reaches out via one of my websites to ask if I'm "the Martha Alford Marks" who co-authored the course. I modestly confess that I am. The glow lingers on.

These days, I often take myself to lunch at places where Bernie and I used to meet the Robinsons. They're all gone now, so I sit by myself, a gray-haired old lady enjoying her favorite foods with her favorite ghosts.

"Original Bernies" surround me on the walls of the last home we shared. Six large photo albums attest to our wonderful pre-E life.

Perhaps more than anything else, the six issues of "Two for Art"—those PDF newsletters that I produced from 2009–2011, during our happy-camping time, and now have uploaded to bettingonbernie.com—best capture the fun we had during those two carefree "golden years."

Not long before this book was published, a friend emailed me a photo of a framed piece that she had just seen hanging on a wall in Presbyterian Santa Fe Medical Center. Its tag reads, "'White Rock,' Watercolor Painting, Bernard Marks, Gift of the Artist." My friend's note to me said, "Beautiful painting. He continues to grace the world."

Similarly, wherever I turn, I see reminders of my husband, lover, and best friend. I am content and at peace as my own journey continues, because I'm not yet done gambling on life.

Martha Marks
martha@bettingonbernie.com

ACKNOWLEDGMENTS

I am grateful to…

Patrick J. Cronin, my half-century-long friend, brave first reader, and unexpected book coach, for helping me stay focused and offering much-needed suggestions as gently as possible. Without his encouragement, I might never have finished this emotionally difficult project.

Vanessa Mendozzi (vanessamendozzidesign.com) for the gorgeous cover she created for this book. My only difficulty in working with her was choosing between the equally wonderful alternatives that she provided.

Sandra Wendel (sandrawendel.com), a book-publishing consultant, for assembling a great group of beta readers whose names I do not know but whose insightful comments on my rough manuscript showed me ways to improve my story. I appreciate them all.

Alice Douthwaite (paper-freeediting.com), my talented, patient, and hard-working editor, who cleaned up and clarified my curiously convoluted chronologies and then, after I followed her wise guidance in straightening them out, gave the text its final polish. I learned a lot from her.

Dham Khalsa (dhamkhalsa.com), a professional photographer in Santa Fe, for fulfilling my request to make the last studio portrait of my life look as good as possible without erasing the signs of age on my face. That is, after all, the woman who wrote this book.

Murray Marks for putting the bug in my ear to write this book in the first place, and also to him and **Rozanne Marks Weinberg** for sharing family facts and stories that I might not otherwise have known.

And on the medical front...

From the start of Bernie's illness throughout the next nine years, **the Santa Fe doctor whom I've called "Dr. N"** (for neurologist) treated us professionally and kindly and did everything he could for Bernie. We both thanked him every time we spoke with him. If he should happen to read this, I want him to know that he was a hero to us. He saved Bernie's life more than once.

Thanks, too, to **all the other dedicated doctors, nurses, and support staff** at **Christus St. Vincent Regional Medical Center** in Santa Fe and the **University of New Mexico Hospital's Neuro-ICU** in Albuquerque, as well as **the many EMT crews** who, by day and by night, conveyed Bernie to, from, and between those hospitals and our home.

A PERSONAL REQUEST

Writing an intimate, painful-in-places story like this presents many challenges. Once it's finished, the relief is immense.

But the author's attention soon shifts to how to get her book before the eyes of potential readers who might appreciate it and perhaps even find it helpful as they go through their own inevitable life crises.

Betting on Bernie is (or will be) available on Amazon in standard and large-print paperback editions, as an ebook, and as an audiobook that I narrated. I hope you found the best version for yourself and that you enjoyed it.

My personal request is that you post on Amazon, Goodreads, and/or other book-review sites of your choice an honest report of your experience in reading or listening to this memoir. Thoughtful comments of any length—from just a few sentences to several paragraphs—are immensely valuable in helping others find books that they would like to read.

I humbly and respectfully ask you to review *Betting on Bernie*. Thank you in advance, if you can and will do that.

Made in the USA
Las Vegas, NV
27 November 2023